# Introduction to computer applications for non-science students (BASIC)

William Ralph Bennett, Jr.
*Charles Baldwin Sawyer Professor*
*of Engineering and Applied Science,*
*and Professor of Physics*
*Yale University*

# Introduction to computer applications for non-science students (BASIC)

*Prentice-Hall, Inc. Englewood Cliffs, New Jersey*

*Library of Congress Cataloging in Publication Data*

BENNETT, WILLIAM RALPH, JR.
  Introduction to computer applications for non-science students (BASIC).

  Includes bibliographies and index.
    1. Electronic digital computers—Programming.
  2. Basic (Computer program language)  I. Title.
QA76.6.B44      001.6′42      75-30918
ISBN  0-13-480061-3

10   9   8   7   6   5   4   3   2   1

Printed in the United States of America

PRENTICE-HALL INTERNATIONAL, INC., *London*
PRENTICE-HALL OF AUSTRALIA, PTY. LIMITED, *Sydney*
PRENTICE-HALL OF CANADA, LTD., *Toronto*
PRENTICE-HALL OF INDIA PRIVATE LIMITED, *New Delhi*
PRENTICE-HALL OF JAPAN, INC., *Tokyo*
PRENTICE-HALL OF SOUTHEAST ASIA PRIVATE LIMITED, *Singapore*

To Fran

# Contents

# Preface

Three years ago I was asked by the chairman of the Engineering and Applied Science Department at Yale University to develop an introductory computer-applications course that would have broad appeal to students in both the humanities and physical sciences. The present volume, which emphasizes material of general interest, is one result. A one-term course incorporating the present material has been given for three years under the title "The Computer as a Research Tool" and has been taken by students ranging from freshman English majors to graduate students in chemistry.† Much to the author's surprise and personal gratification, the course made the "Ten Best" list twice at Yale during this period.‡ Most students taking the course had had (or were taking concurrently) at least one term of calculus. Beyond that, there was no real common denominator. It should be emphasized, however, that a prior knowledge of calculus is not a prerequisite for the present material and that nearly everything in the present book should be fully comprehensible to students with a mathematics background consisting only of high school algebra and trigonometry. The more difficult mathematical sections occur near the ends of Chapters 2 and 3, are clearly marked, and may easily be omitted. Both programming and conceptual difficulties increase gradually within chapters and from one chapter to the next. Chapters 1 through 3 are intended as introductory background material for the main part of the course, which is contained in Chapter 4.

---

† The course at Yale also contained material on dynamics, random processes, Fourier series, and electronics that is available (together with the present chapters) in a more complete book by the author, *Scientific and Engineering Problem-Solving with the Computer*, (published by Prentice-Hall, Inc.). Of necessity, the Yale course covered the present material in highly abbreviated form. However, the present book can be the basis of a very substantial introductory one-term course for humanities students.

‡ *Yale Course Critique* (published by the *Yale Daily News*, New Haven, Conn.): 1974 edition, pp. 7. 43; 1975 edition pp. 13, 71.

Although the chapters are labeled according to subject matter, they are also organized according to programming technique:

| Chapter | Techniques Emphasized |
| --- | --- |
| 1 | Elementary programming in BASIC |
| 2 | Series summation and matrix operations |
| 3 | Teletype plotting and graphic displays |
| 4 | Character coding and printing |

The structure of the book is also based on the belief that the best way to teach students computational methods is to give them lots of interesting problems of gradually increasing difficulty. I chose BASIC as the main programming language because it is rapidly learned and "conversational." It is also efficient enough to work effectively within minicomputers. Students who have never touched a computer terminal can start right off doing meaningful problems in BASIC, and the frustrations associated with batch processing are totally avoided. Under these conditions, the students teach themselves to a large extent and one merely has to be available to give general guidance and help them out of occasional pitfalls.

The problems are given immediately after the relevant discussions in the text and where possible have been based on unusual events of general and social interest. An effort was also made to select nontrivial problems. Apart from introductory examples in each chapter, the remaining problems are of a type that would either be impossible or prohibitive to solve without a computer. For the same reason, most topics and problems discussed in the present book are rarely treated quantitatively in the normal curriculum.

An attempt has been made to try to choose material that would alternate in appeal between humanities and science students. Although it is very hard to please both groups simultaneously, one can play a game in which important methods in science are applied to problems of social importance. Also, the author has tried throughout the manuscript to provide occasional bits of comic relief. However, what sometimes seems hilariously amusing late at night does not always withstand the cold light of dawn.

Credit for the course at Yale was based entirely on the completion of assigned problems (about two or three a week) and a term research project. For the latter reason, Research Problems are occasionally suggested throughout the book with the object of stimulating further independent work on the part of the student. The standard problems are presented to illustrate what can easily be accomplished in a specific area in one afternoon through the expenditure of a few dollars in computer time (if you have to pay for it). Nearly all of them can be done on a minicomputer with a memory of only 16,000 16-bit words. However, the more meaningful ones are much too difficult for use on examinations, and the whole concept of an examination seemed pointless. I think the ability of a student to solve 30 formidable problems over a period of one term is the most important measure of his or her grasp of the subject. However, tastes vary on this point and the above approach to the grading question involves a massive investment in time spent examining program listings and problem results handed in by students. In this connection it helps to encourage the students to document their programs right from the start. One does not usually need formal flow charts, but an occasional comment in the margin of a program becomes very helpful. It is also desirable to encourage students to think through their problems carefully before going near a terminal.

There are various ways in which the material can be emphasized and presented within a one-term course, and abstracts have been included at the start of each chapter to aid in this process. Most students I have encountered had never done any real programming, and I constructed the first three chapters as an introductory technical background. Chapter 1 is for students without previous exposure to computers and could easily be skipped (or covered very rapidly) by students with prior computing experience. I have usually covered this material in one week of lectures and left most of it to be read by beginning students as needed and learned through the mechanism of problems assigned the first day. (An immediate assignment of four or five problems also serves the useful purpose of encouraging students who do not want to do any work to drop the course.) The material by Kemeny and Kurtz written on BASIC (see References to Chapter 1) is very useful at this point, if available. Also, it is assumed that a manual on BASIC provided by the individual computer service will be available for occasional reference. However, a primary objective was to make the present book self-contained. (It seems unfair to expect students to have to buy more than one book for a course.)

Chapter 2 covers a number of routine programming techniques and reviews some aspects of high school algebra and introductory calculus (particularly derivatives and Taylor series) which provide useful insight regarding the function statements built into the BASIC language. It is also desirable to have students start getting used to vectors and matrices as early as possible so that the mechanics of using them does not become a stumbling block in the later applications involving more difficult subject matter. For this reason, I have chosen to sneak up on the MAT commands in BASIC by first using them in the Ramanujan problem to store and manipulate data, and then to gradually introduce more complicated MAT operations in succeeding sections. By the time the student gets to the discussion of the input–output theory in economics, he should not only be used to using matrices but also have a genuine appreciation for the tremendous power of MAT commands.

Chapter 3 in its entirety is not essential to the rest of the book. However, most students love plotting things, and such techniques can provide helpful insight to the solution of difficult problems later. The chapter presents a survey of representative methods and devices that are currently available. The material on teletype plotting can be covered within about two weeks, and this material (or its equivalent, using high-resolution displays) is all that is really required for the rest of the book. What one specifically does beyond teletype plotting will be limited by available hardware. However, computer-controlled high-resolution display devices are becoming increasingly available, and it seemed clear that at least some discussion of the use of representative hardware should be included. The minicomputer owner, in particular, is in a position nowadays where such things may be implemented cheaply.

Many of the problems depend on substantial blocks of data being available in the BASIC DATA format. Because little educational benefit results from typing in these huge blocks of data by hand and needless amounts of terminal time get wasted in the process, it is desirable to make these DATA statements available to the students on punched tape or within disc files. To facilitate this process, the author will try to provide, at a reasonable cost, punched tape listings of such BASIC DATA statements in ASCII code. However, this offer is made subject to the condition that it may be terminated at any time should the process become impractical. Further, occasional errors made in the mechanical punching process will have to be corrected by the purchaser (for example, by checking against listings illustrated in the present book). For further information regarding this question, write directly to the author, Department of Engineering and Applied Science, Yale University, New Haven, Connecticut 06520.

WILLIAM RALPH BENNETT, JR.

# Acknowledgments

I would like to thank Professor Robert G. Wheeler of Yale University for suggesting and encouraging this project. Although the project has taken a lot more work than I initially expected, it has also been a lot of fun. I should also like to thank Professor Charles A. Walker (currently chairman of the Engineering and Applied Science Department) for his sustaining support. Obviously, the whole thing could not have been accomplished while carrying a heavy teaching load. I am particularly indebted to the Hewlett-Packard Corporation for the donation of a 2116B computer which was used in the course and to the Moore Fund at Yale for a grant to purchase additional equipment.

The following people warrant special thanks: Dr. John W. Knutson, Jr., for his assistance in presenting the course initially; William C. Campbell, Donald R. Carlin, Robert M. Fleischman, H. Thomas Hunt, and Jeffrey J. Korman for expert teaching assistance and machine-language programming help; and Marjorie G. Wynne, Edwin J. Beinecke Research Librarian at the Beinecke Rare Book and Manuscript Library for her help in tracking down several obscure references. In addition, I am indebted to all the students at Yale University who have taken the course for their patience in letting me try this material out on them, for their many suggestions, and for their permission to reproduce some of the original data quoted the text. I should also like to thank Professor Jack K. Cohen of the University of Denver (Colorado) for a careful reading of the manuscript and numerous helpful suggestions. Special thanks also go to Phyllis Springmeyer of the College Book Editorial Department at Prentice-Hall for her invaluable help.

I should also like to thank the various people and organizations specifically cited in the figure captions for their permission to reproduce figures. In addition, I would like to thank my father, William Ralph Bennett, for several helpful background discussions on communications problems. Finally, I am especially indebted to my wife, Frances Commins Bennett, for numerous helpful discussions, for editing and typing the original manuscript, and for putting up with some of the more obscure conversational topics that this manuscript has stimulated.

# 1

# Introduction

This chapter is intended for people who have never seen, used, or touched a computer terminal. Sections 1.1–1.3 discuss background concepts and define some of the basic jargon of the computer-science world. Rudimentary programming operations in BASIC are started in Section 1.4 and gradually increase in difficulty throughout the remainder of the chapter. Problems of practical importance are emphasized in these examples. The main object of the chapter is to get the beginner's feet wet as soon as possible and to work up to a few nontrivial problems by the end of the chapter. Readers with previous experience at programming should start by having a look at the problems toward the end of the chapter. If these problems are too easy, go immediately to Chapter 2. Note that the standard commands in BASIC are listed in the index at the end of the book with page references to representative examples of their use and definitions of their meanings.

Most electronic computers count, add, subtract, multiply, divide, and do logic operations in base 2. The reason is fairly obvious: The binary numbers 0 or 1 can be very naturally represented by opening or closing a switch. In practice, computers use electronic circuits that have two stable operating conditions to represent such binary numbers. The transition from one stable point to the other is induced electronically and is analogous to changing the state of a two-position switch. This type of electronic switching can be accomplished in astonishingly short time intervals ($\approx 10^{-9}$ second at the present state of the art) and is the primary technology upon which contemporary high-speed digital computing rests.

If you have a sufficiently long row of ON/OFF switches, you can use them to represent any specified binary integer. For example, the binary number 1010 corresponds to the number

$$1\times 2^3 + 0\times 2^2 + 1\times 2^1 + 0\times 2^0 = 8+2 = 10$$

in base 10 and may be represented by four ON/OFF switches. The process of handling numbers that are not integers involves utilizing negative powers of 2 (i.e., those which could be stored to the right of the *binary point*) in much the same way that decimal numbers are normally handled in base 10.

Processes in binary arithmetic can be performed by simple electronic circuits in which the output voltage is a two-valued function of two separate input voltages. For example, adding two binary integers together involves applying the following rule to the successively higher, corresponding pairs of digits:

$$0+0=0$$
$$0+1=1$$
$$1+0=1$$
$$1+1=0 \qquad \text{but carry 1 to the next-higher digit}$$

This fundamental rule in binary addition can be accomplished with a circuit that is turned ON when either input voltage (digit) is ON separately, but which is otherwise turned to the OFF position. (People who have done counting experiments will recognize this type of circuit as an *anticoincidence circuit*.) The process of carrying 1 to the next-higher digit (where $1+1=0$) can be effected with a circuit that is normally in the OFF position, unless both inputs are ON. (People used to counting experiments will recognize the latter as a *coincidence circuit*.) The other binary arithmetic operations (subtraction, multiplication, etc.) can be performed in similar fashion.

The number of operations done in one step (or how long a given binary arithmetic operation takes) is largely a function of the complexity of the circuitry in an individual computer. For example, adding $N$ to a given binary number can be accomplished directly or by adding 1 $N$ times; shifting a binary number $N$ places to the left (which is equivalent to multiplying by $2^N$) can be accomplished directly in one step or by shifting by one digit $N$ times; and so on. Hence the inherent speed of a particular computer is extremely dependent on the actual circuitry used.

The invention of binary codes and binary logic operations is very old. Francis Bacon (1561–1626) used binary codes to transmit secret diplomatic messages. Joseph Marie Jacquard (1752–1834) used binary-coded punchcards to operate looms with such success that about 11,000 of them were in use throughout France by 1812. George Boole (1815–1864) developed a mathematical theory of binary logic during the nineteenth century. Hence the mathematical background for most of the binary operations used in modern digital computing was established long before the first digital computer of any consequence had been built.

Although a mechanical desk calculator that could add, subtract, multiply, and divide had been built as early as 1623—by Wilhelm Schikard—the modern digital computer was largely a post–World War II development. Prior to that time, most of the emphasis on electronic machines had been based upon analog devices—for example, those used during World War II to permit RADAR control of antiaircraft guns.

The very first digital computers were extremely sluggish, cumbersome things in which the bistable "electronic" circuits were made up from mechanical relays. Indeed, one such machine developed at the Bell Laboratories in 1944 contained over 9000 telephone relays, covered a floor space of about 1000 square feet, and weighed about 10 tons!

One of the earliest high-speed electronic digital computers was that developed under the direction of John von Neumann at the Institute for Advanced Study in Princeton, New Jersey, during the period 1946–1952. This device contained several thousand vacuum tubes and used a memory based upon the continuous rejuvenation of arrays of binary digits which were stored electrostatically in a large bank of cathode-ray tubes (see Fig. 1-1). Because the

**Fig. 1-1.** von Neumann's computer. (John von Neumann is at the left and J. Robert Oppenheimer is at the right.) Note the bank of cathode-ray-tube storage elements across the bottom of the picture (within the cylindrical cans); these were used for the computer memory. Each tube contained a square display of $32 \times 32 = 1024$ binary storage bits that were periodically regenerated at about 1000 times per second. A section from this computer is currently on display at the Smithsonian Institution in Washington, D.C. (*Courtesy* of the Institute for Advanced Study, Princeton, New Jersey.)

lifetimes of vacuum tubes were typically about 1000 hours, the electrostatic storage technique was tricky at best, and the entire contents of the memory in the von Neumann computer had to be re-stored about 1000 times per second, it is rather amazing that the device could be made to function reliably at all over long periods of time. Nevertheless, the machine served as an effective laboratory to test many of the notions of programming and coding used in contemporary large-scale, high-speed digital computers. Prior to the design of the von Neumann machine, it was argued that decimal systems were the most appropriate for computers because of the formidable problems in decimal-to-binary conversion. One early accomplishment of the von Neumann project was the demonstration that such conversions could be accomplished with a fairly small number of machine operations (approximately 47 steps) and in time intervals of only a few milliseconds (using the circuitry of that period). The machine was also used to solve some very substantial numerical problems connected with the development of the hydrogen bomb[1]—especially problems involving the inversion of high-order matrices. [See the discussion of the von Neumann machine by Goldstine (1972). Goldstine worked on many of the fundamental mathematical and programming problems encountered with this machine, and his book contains a very interesting account of the techniques adopted, in addition to a comprehensive description of the historical background.]

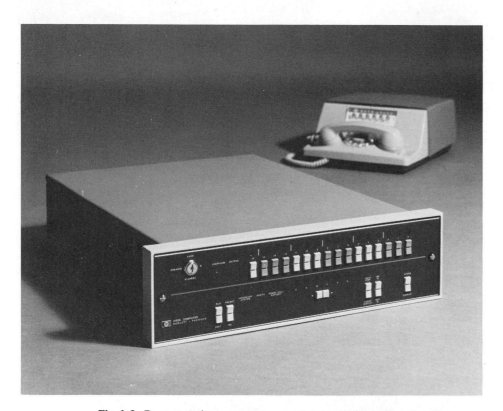

**Fig. 1-2.** Representative, contemporary minicomputer capable of storing up to 32,000 separate 16-bit numbers in its memory. (*Courtesy* of the Hewlett-Packard Co.)

[1] It is, in fact, rather ironic that J. Robert Oppenheimer, who was the Director of the Institute for Advanced Study during most of that period and a strong proponent of the von Neumann project, was crucified shortly thereafter for his initial stand against the development of the H-bomb. [See, for example, von Neumann's testimony in support of Oppenheimer reproduced by the U.S. Atomic Energy Commission (1971, p. 655), regarding the relevance of the von Neumann computer to the H-bomb project.]

The development and practical availability of transistors (with nearly infinite lifetimes) and reliable ferrite core memories (which do not require periodic rejuvenation) had a massive effect on the computer field during the next two decades. The exponential growth in this field has continued well into the present decade, as the effects of integrated circuits, circuit-chip technology, and semiconductor memories have become felt. Not only has the capability, speed, and reliability increased considerably; the physical size and cost of electronic digital computers has decreased by orders of magnitude during the past decade. The latter phenomenon is especially heartening in an age of constant inflation in the price of nearly every other type of commodity. One can now purchase for a few thousand dollars a small digital computer (or *minicomputer*) which is about the same size as a "hi-fi" set (see Fig. 1-2) and which is enormously more powerful than the early von Neumann machine (which itself cost many hundreds of thousands of dollars and occupied a small building). Hence it seems likely that we are on the threshold of an age when the "family computer" will be as realistic and useful an item as the family automobile has become in American life. At a further extreme, the use of circuit chips and small memories has permitted the development of pocket-size, battery-operated computers (which now sell for a few hundred dollars) which use full-scale digital programming techniques to calculate series solutions for the transcendental functions to high accuracy, together with the more usual arithmetic operations. Indeed, at least one of the currently available pocket computers is capable of retaining as many as 100 fully alterable program steps (see Fig. 1-3). Thus we are already well into an age where small computers can extend the mathematical ability of the human brain in much the same way that hearing aids and electronic guidance devices can extend man's other perception capabilities. Immediate access to these powerful computational aids opens up for solution a new domain of important problems in the same way that a good pair of eyeglasses can help a near-sighted individual see a larger portion of the landscape. In fact, one could make a strong argument that access to both small and large digital computers should be regarded as a fundamental individual right in our society, much like those guaranteed by the Constitution. The point here is that society is presently facing such complex problems as to warrant increased reliance on computer-simulated models for solution. Those people who do not have access to computers to investigate alternative solutions to communal problems will, in some sense, have lost their ability to participate in the democratic process. In any event, digital computers have become easily available to a large fraction of the population, and there is every indication at the present moment that this trend will continue.

**Fig. 1-3.** Pocket-sized battery-operated digital computer capable of holding 100 reprogrammable statements. (*Courtesy* of the Hewlett-Packard Co.)

## 1.2
## Machine Language

Most currently available digital computers operate in a manner that is logically similar to the method devised in the von Neumann machine. A certain set of possible binary logic operations (typically about 100) is built into the electronic circuitry of the machine. As part of man's never-ending desire to attribute human qualities to electromechanical devices, the convention by which different sequences of instructions may be fed into the computer is known as a *programming language*. (In a similar vein, one finds computer scientists referring to the rules for applying such languages as *grammar*; the storing capacity of the computer as *memory*; the various multiple-bit numbers stored in the memory as *words*; and so on.) Access to the rudimentary set of binary logic operations wired into the computer is obtained through something known as *machine language*. A *program* in machine language just consists of a sequence of large binary numbers, which are consulted in order when the computer runs. Each memory location in the computer can store a word containing a large number of binary digits, or *bits*. In the section of the computer memory used to store the machine-language program, part of each word is used to code the machine-language instruction; the other part contains the memory location upon which the instruction is to operate. In addition, the computer contains entities known as *registers* within which the various allowed binary logic operations are performed. One of these registers is set aside just to keep track of which memory location contains the next machine-language instruction to be executed.

Thus a machine-language program consists of an ordered set of instructions that is sequentially executed, starting at a specified memory (or *core*) location. Such programs tend to be exceedingly tedious affairs in which the computer is led by the hand through every single operation required. For example, the first instruction might be to take a 16-bit binary number out of one specific memory location and store it in the A register; the next instruction might be to add the contents of another memory location to the contents of the A register; the third instruction might be to store the result (now in the A register) in some other memory location (whose *address* might, in turn, have been computed in still another register); and so on. Generally, an enormous number of machine-language operations have to be performed before anything very useful is accomplished. In addition, all these machine-language instructions have to be entered by some means in the computer memory. (At the most rudimentary extreme, such sequences of binary numbers can be entered by hand using a long row of toggle switches to set up each required multiple-bit binary number.) The great virtue of the computer is that once these instructions have been entered in the memory, long sequences of them can be done over and over again with great speed (these days, anywhere from about 30 nanoseconds to 2 microseconds per machine operation, depending on the particular computer).

## 1.3 More Advanced Languages: Compilers and Interpreters (Why BASIC?)

Although the early programmers were forced to write their programs directly in machine language, most people will find that practice exceedingly tedious. This is especially true in the routine conversions that come up over and over again in going back and forth between base 10 and base 2 arithmetic.

Fortunately, some dedicated souls have spent their lives devising machine-language programs that do all these routine operations for us. Thus higher-level programming languages, such as FORTRAN, ALGOL, and BASIC, have been developed that translate standard arithmetic operations back and forth to machine-language operations in base 2. In addition, these higher-level languages generally have some standard set of options for getting data in and out of the computer and a set of *subroutines* (small, specialized programs that can be used over and over again at different points in a large program) built in for the purpose of computing common mathematical operations and functions.

As a specific illustration, the two statements

```
1  INPUT X,Y
2  PRINT X+Y
```

written in BASIC, are fairly self-evident even to someone who has never used a computer before. The statements have the meaning that when the program is run in BASIC, two general numbers ($X$ and $Y$) are entered from the keyboard of a teletype terminal and the computer then prints the sum of the two numbers back on the same terminal. In a representative computer (containing no "hard-wired" arithmetic capability), this relatively harmless-looking two-line program in base 10 arithmetic takes hundreds of separate machine-language steps involving logic operations in base 2. Because the computation would take less than 1 millisecond on even the slowest contemporary computers, the terminal operator is shielded from all the behind-the-scenes effort that went into the calculation.

Most of the early programming languages were specifically designed for something known as *batch processing*. In this mode, the user writes his program in entirety before going near the machine. (For example, one archaic method consisted of punching out the program statements on a series of cards similar to those used by Jacquard to operate looms in the eighteenth century.) The user then brings the completed program to the computer; a special machine-language program called a *compiler* converts the user's program into machine-language code; and, finally, the compiled program is executed by the computer. For some types of computing (especially situations in which the same long program is to be run over and over in precisely the same form), batch processing is obviously the most efficient approach. The program can be stored in compiled form and the time lost in interpreting the original program statements in terms of equivalent machine-language subroutines can be avoided in subsequent execution of the program. Further, a really long program can be run during off hours when the rates are cheaper and without the author of the program being present. In that type of situation, one is willing to put up with a substantial amount of agony in getting errors (*bugs*) out of the program initially. However, batch processing can be distinctly unfriendly to someone who is just starting to learn programming. The point is that the slightest error (no matter how trivial) can abort execution of the program right at the start. The user may come back after waiting 2 or 3 hours to find that the only useful information contained in the stack of printout generated when the computer was running his program was the fact that the program execution was stopped on the first line because of a "grammatical" mistake in the use of the programming language. In addition, some other features of a language such as FORTRAN (which has traditionally been used in the batch-process mode at most large computer centers in the United States) merely get in the way for the beginner—or even for the seasoned expert who just wants a quick answer to a very complicated problem. For example, the constant distinction between floating-decimal-point and integer numbers, and the use of generalized format statements in FORTRAN, make the language inherently more powerful than one such as BASIC (in which all numbers are treated as if they were floating-point numbers and in which a limited format is permitted in PRINT statements). However, this increased generality also enormously increases the opportunity to make grammatical mistakes in writing a program. It further makes it much more tedious to test small segments of a program to make sure, quite apart from grammatical errors, that the program is really computing the numbers that are wanted.

In contrast, the BASIC language was designed to be *conversational* right from the beginning.[2] By "conversational" it is meant that the user's terminal is placed in a directly interactive mode with the computer. Not only can the original program statements be entered directly in the computer memory from the user's teletype or *CRT* (for cathode-ray-tube) *terminal*, but with some BASIC interpreters, a statement that violates the grammatical rules of the language is thrown out as you try to enter it and a diagnostic error immediately displayed. Further, the language is arranged so that the user's terminal is kept in a fully interactive mode with the computer while the user's program is running. Thus one can enter different numbers from the keyboard for use within the program while the program is running; similarly, one can have the computer print various parts of a solution on the terminal as they are computed, and even stop the computer from running the program at any point

---

[2] The BASIC language was developed at Dartmouth College under National Science Foundation support by the mathematicians John Kemeny and Thomas Kurtz [see Kemeny and Kurtz, (1968)]. The acronym originally stood for Beginner's All-Purpose Symbolic Instruction Code. But do not be misled: BASIC is an extremely powerful language.

7

along the way, without having to wait for the computer to reach the normal "end" statement.

The main advantage of the conversational mode is that one can immediately run small pieces of a large program in which "print" statements can be quickly inserted and deleted to permit checking questionable sections of the program. Thus you can determine immediately if the program is actually calculating the quantities that you want. At the same time, an enormous volume of waste paper can be eliminated by merely printing the final answer you want from the program rather than the large tome of stuff (mostly needed for debugging purposes) that inevitably seems linked to batch processing in FORTRAN.

An additional advantage of BASIC is that the instruction set is so similar to normal high school algebra and arithmetic that relatively little effort is required in learning the language. Fifteen or 20 minutes spent looking over the instruction set is all that is really needed for the beginner to start doing meaningful problems. At the same time, a powerful set of matrix operations is included as part of the standard arithmetic operations in BASIC; these operations are much more convenient to use than the equivalent subroutines callable in FORTRAN. Finally, it should be noted that the BASIC language is also unusually efficient in its core requirements and can be used on relatively small computers or minicomputers. (The standard BASIC compiler takes about 7000 sixteen-bit words of computer memory.)

The speed with which programs can be run in BASIC (or any other language) varies a great deal with the particular machine and software used. Most large computers compile the entire BASIC program in machine language before running the program, and it is during the compilation period that most diagnostic error messages are sent back to the operator. Once the program is compiled and free of grammatical mistakes, the program is run in machine language until interactive instructions with the user's terminal are encountered. Some of the large time-sharing services have a provision for storing the compiled program in machine language for future use, thereby avoiding the necessity of repeating the expenditure of *cpu* (central processor unit) time (typically about 10 seconds with a large machine) to recompile the same program. For example, the GE 635 computer used in the early Mark II GE time-sharing service ran faster in BASIC than in FORTRAN. At the opposite extreme, a minicomputer such as the HP 2116B uses software that interprets each successive BASIC statement individually as the program is run. If the program goes around in a *loop* 1000 times, the statements in the loop are converted into machine language 1000 times. Because the machine takes about 1 millisecond (msec) just to interpret a command such as "LET $Y = 2$," a compiled FORTRAN program can run much faster than an equivalent BASIC program on such a minicomputer. However, even with the minicomputer, the programs have to become pretty substantial before these running-time limitations become a significant practical concern. It should be noted that the portions of a program that really eat up running time are operations such as computing $\text{SIN}(X)$ and $\text{EXP}(X)$, which are generally done in previously compiled machine-language subroutines contained in the BASIC function library. Hence those operations (which might take $\approx 10$ msec on a typical minicomputer) are done just as fast in BASIC as in a compiled FORTRAN program, and it does not make a great deal of difference that $\approx 1$ msec was lost interpreting the expression. In fairness, it should also be noted that compiling a FORTRAN program on a minicomputer can be an extremely long-winded process. Once compiled, the program can be used over and over again in exactly the same form with great facility; but to make even one change generally requires repeating the whole compilation procedure. It should also be noted that BASIC is so literally a subset of FORTRAN that it is relatively

**Fig. 1-4.** Contemporary CRT (cathode-ray-tube) terminal capable of transmitting and receiving data at approximately 600 characters per second. The particular one shown (made by the Delta Data Corporation) has an internal memory of 3000 characters (which can be used to store several hundred program statements) and an electronic editing capability for inserting and deleting characters within its own memory. A fairly substantial program may be written and edited with such a terminal in the *local mode* (not connected to the computer) and then transmitted in entirety to the computer in a few seconds.

straightforward for an experienced programmer to write a FORTRAN program that will translate a general BASIC program into FORTRAN and compile the result. Hence one method of beating the speed-limitation problem in very long programs on minicomputers is to write and debug the program in conversational BASIC and then use a routine FORTRAN program to compile the result.

Finally, there are several compensating advantages in doing computing on a minicomputer that you control entirely yourself versus operating in a time-sharing mode on a supergiant. First, the time-sharing mode in itself means that your problem is constantly being interrupted (if it is of any significant computational length) as the supergiant services its numerous other customers. Frequently, this duty-cycle effect can more than compensate for differences in running time. Second, with commercial time-sharing services one is still pretty much limited to the painfully slow data-transmission rates associated with the mechanical teletype machine ($\approx 10$ characters per second). Powerful editing programs and program storage devices (e.g., magnetic disc or tape-recorded files) at the computer center can help compensate to a large extent. However, anyone who has ever used a CRT terminal (see Fig. 1-4) working at 600 characters per second will probably give up computing altogether rather than go back to the old teletype. Further, if you have direct control over the minicomputer, it is usually practical to write (or have written for you) machine-language subroutines directly callable from BASIC which serve the purpose of transferring data back and forth between the computer and various peripheral devices at extremely high transmission rates. Thus xy plotters and oscilloscopes offer a very fast means to provide a continuous display of computational problems through the use of *digital-to-analog converters* (i.e., circuits that produce a voltage proportional to an input number). Similarly, high-speed analog-to-digital converters permit reading voltages from experimental situations and storing numbers proportional to these voltages in the computer. The increasing availability and decreasing cost of such circuitry has been a heart-warming phenomenon. For example, one can now buy a 16-bit (i.e., 1-part-in-$2^{16}$ resolution) digital-to-analog converter with a response time of $\approx 1$

9

microsecond for less than $100; for less than $10 it is now possible to get an 8-bit D-to-A (digital-to-analog) converter of comparable speed. Equivalent A-to-D (analog-to-digital) converters are typically 5 to 10 times more expensive. Consequently, with a modest investment, a little electronics shopwork, and a little programming help, one can have a powerful facility for taking and displaying data, as well as performing and displaying computations made within the BASIC language. Although the primary emphasis in the present text is on operations performable within the framework of the standard BASIC language, some of the additional facility provided to the minicomputer owner through such machine-language CALL statements will be illustrated.[3]

The remaining sections of this chapter will be devoted to a few introductory examples of programming in BASIC. We shall describe here some of the fundamental statements in the language and introduce more advanced techniques in later chapters. An index is included at the end of the book with page references to various examples of the different commands in BASIC. The instructions used in the BASIC language are also summarized in programming manuals available from most of the time-sharing computer services, many of which are based on the original work by Kemeny and Kurtz (1968).

The method of getting BASIC onto the computer will vary from one machine to the next, and there will be no useful substitute for reading up on the particular idiosyncracies of the actual machine that you intend to use. In what follows, we shall assume that the reader knows how to get to the point where the computer types

READY

on the user's terminal, meaning that the computer is ready to accept a series of program statements from the user written in the BASIC language. (In general, after completing any instruction, the BASIC compiler transmits this self-evident message.)

As with any other programming language, a program in BASIC consists of an ordered set of instructions which generally involve:

1. Putting data into the computer.
2. Calculating something based on the data.
3. Getting the answer out of the computer.
4. Telling the computer to stop running the program.

Statements and data are usually entered through a typewriter-like keyboard (see Fig. 1-4), and anyone with only a modest facility at typing will find the process reasonably efficient. Only uppercase letters are recognized in statements, and the standard character set originally introduced on the teletype keyboard is used. The most common typing errors one tends to make initially involve confusing the letter O (oh) with the number Ø (zero) and subconsciously trying to enter a lowercase L (ell) as a number 1 (one). The slash through the zero is generally used to minimize the first source of confusion. Both problems involve overcoming ingrained subconscious habits and may, in fact, be more of a difficulty with really good typists than with poor ones.

Each program statement in BASIC requires a separate line number. The statements are executed in the order that the line numbers increase. However, the line numbers do not have to increase in unit increments, and they do not have to be typed in the order that they finally appear in the program. Thus, if the original line numbers are chosen with reasonably wide spacing (e.g., in increments of 1Ø), there will usually be plenty of room for adding statements

---

[3] For a detailed discussion of the use of CALL statements in BASIC, see the Hewlett-Packard guide to 2100 series minicomputers.

throughout a program that arise as afterthoughts. (Many BASIC compilers also have specialized line-number resequencing commands which help when the spacing gets too tight.) Finally, it is important to note that the current version of the program can always be typed out on the terminal through the command LIST.

The common arithmetic statements in BASIC are so similar to those in normal arithmetic that they require little explanation. A few simple two-line programs will serve as illustration:

For example, if we enter the statements

```
10   PRINT 3+2
20   END
```

and type

```
RUN
```

(followed by the carriage-return key), the computer will respond by printing

```
5
READY
```

Similarly, the substitution

```
10   PRINT 3-2
```

would print the difference between the two numbers; whereas

```
10 PRINT 3*2
```

would give us the product and

```
10 PRINT 3/2
```

would result in the decimal equivalent of 3 divided by 2 (i.e., 1.5). Finally, the statement

```
10 PRINT 3↑2
```

is almost as obvious in meaning and results in raising 3 to the second power. (This last operation also works for fractional exponents as long as the argument is positive; i.e., the result must be real.)

Arithmetic operations of the above type may be combined in one statement, as long as they all fit within the 72-column format used in BASIC. For example,

```
10   PRINT 2*3+2/3-1+2↑3
```

would result in printing the value 13.6666 (or the first six most significant figures in the decimal equivalent of $13\frac{2}{3}$.

Note that a definite priority is assumed in executing operations of the above type: exponential operations (e.g., 2↑3) are given the highest priority; multiplication and division come next (performed in order from left to right); and finally addition and subtraction. For example,

$6/2\uparrow2 \neq 9$    but instead is equal to 1.5
$6/2*3 \neq 1$    but instead is equal to 9    etc.

Parentheses may be used in pairs to change the normal priority assumptions. In such cases, the innermost parenthetical operation is always done first. Hence

$6/(2*3) = 1$    whereas $6/2*3 = 9$

$(6/(2*3))\uparrow2 = 1$    whereas $6/(2*3\uparrow2) = 0.333333$   and   $6/(2*3)\uparrow2 = 0.166666$

When in doubt one may always add extra parentheses just to make sure that the priority assumed is that which the user wants. However, unnecessary parentheses waste space. Finally, it is important to note when using parentheses that the standard arithmetic symbols in BASIC are still required. For example, although $2(3+5)$ would be meaningful in normal algebra, the equivalent expression in BASIC has to have an asterisk between the 2 and the $(3+5)$ to denote multiplication.

11

---

**1.4
PROBLEM 1**    Write a simple two-line program to investigate the priorities of arithmetic operations in BASIC. Evaluate a few simple cases of the type illustrated in the text and make sure you understand the priorities assumed for the common arithmetic operations.

---

Machine-language programs are built into the BASIC compiler for computing the common transcendental functions (e.g., those such as the sine and cosine functions, which require summing an infinite series to some prescribed accuracy for numerical evaluation). These functions are always stated in a standard form in which the argument is contained within parentheses.

In case of the trigonometric functions, the arguments are specified in radians. Thus expressions such as

SIN(X),   COS(X),   or   TAN(X)

appearing in a BASIC program will automatically result in the evaluation of the sine, cosine, or tangent of the numerical argument assigned to the variable $X$, on the assumption that $X$ is in radians. Similarly, the BASIC arctangent function, ATN($X$), results in computing an angle in radians whose tangent occurs in the argument. ATN($X$) will be positive or negative in accordance with the sign of $X$.

The logarithm and antilogarithm functions are defined in respect to the base $e = 2.71828\ldots$ of the Naperian system. The expression

LOG(X)

results in the evaluation of the natural logarithm of the numerical value assigned to $X$; similarly, the expression

EXP(X)

computes the value of $e^x$.

Finally, the expression,

SQR(X)

results in computing the square root of the value assigned to $X$ (assuming it is positive), and

ABS(X)

results in computing the absolute value (i.e., magnitude) of $X$.

---

**1.5
PROBLEM 2**    Write a two-line program of the type

```
10  PRINT SIN(3.14159*45/180)
20  END
```

to investigate the behavior of the transcendental functions in BASIC. (Note that the example shown prints the sine of 45°.)

---

To facilitate the computing process, variables are introduced in the program. In BASIC, variables can be any single letter of the alphabet or any single letter of the alphabet followed by one of the numerals 0, 1, 2, . . . , 8, 9. Thus any of the following 286 entities could be used as variables:

A, B, C, . . . , X, Y, Z
AØ, A1, A2, . . . , A8, A9
BØ, B1 B2, . . . , B8, B9
.
.
.
YØ, Y1, Y2, . . . , Y8, Y9
ZØ, Z1, Z2, . . . , Z8, Z9

In transferring mathematical equations to programming statements, it is frequently helpful to regard the numeral following the letter in program variables in the same role as subscripts in mathematical variables. For example, $X_0$ most naturally goes over to $XØ$; $X_1$ to $X1$; and so on. In fact, it will be necessary on some later occasions in this book to write simple equations in terms of such computer variables to clarify the meaning of program segments. Hence the reader should get used to thinking of quantities such as T2 as single computer variables and *not* as the variable $T$ multiplied by 2. (The latter would be written T*2 in BASIC.) Later we shall also discuss the use of column arrays and matrices as indexed variables.

Always keep in mind that a computer computes things *numerically*. If you have not assigned a numerical value to a variable, the computer cannot do the operation. Running a program that has not had the variables properly initialized will either result in diagnostic error messages or wrong answers (assuming some other value has already been given for the variable elsewhere in the program).

There are three primary ways of getting numerical data into a program in BASIC:

1. You can define the variable in the program with a LET statement, such as

    10  LET X = 5

    The statement means that the new value of the variable $X$ on the left is set equal to the last value of the quantities on the right. Hence a statement following line 1Ø of the type

    20  LET X = X + 1

    means "define the new value of the variable $X$ to be equal to the old value plus 1." (With *some* BASIC compilers you can achieve the same result with the statement

    20  X = X + 1

    and you do not have to type LET before the command).

2. You can enter the numerical value for the variable from the teletype keyboard. For example, the statement

    10  INPUT  X

    results (when you RUN the program) in

    ? (and the computer waits for you to type in the
        number and a carriage return).

    Similarly, if you have several variables, $X$, $Y$, and $Z$, to which you wish to assign numerical values from the keyboard, the single statement

    10  INPUT X,Y,Z

    results in a question mark and pause while you enter each of the three variables (separated by commas or by carriage returns).

13

3. You can read the variables from a data table. The statement

```
10   READ X,Y,Z
```

with a data statement somewhere else in the program of the type

```
500   DATA 3,4,5,7,8,9
```

will result in assigning the variables sequentially to the numbers in the data statement. When the computer passes through line 1∅ it lets

$$X = 3, \qquad Y = 4, \qquad Z = 5$$

If we had introduced a second READ statement after line 1∅ of the type

```
20   READ U,V,W
```

the computer would let

$$U = 7, \qquad V = 8, \qquad W = 9$$

However, we would not be allowed to enter still another READ statement without either adding more DATA statements or a command of the type

```
30   RESTORE
```

(which permits re-reading the previous DATA statements from the beginning).

As we shall show later, it is possible to generate huge blocks of data from experiments of different types and read these into the computer with either a teletype terminal or high-speed input device—thus permitting data manipulation and analysis without ever having to type in the block of data tediously by hand.

For the moment we merely wish to emphasize that the following three programs in BASIC represent different ways of achieving precisely the same result:

```
10   LET X = 5        10   READ X          10   INPUT X
20   LET Y = X + 2    20   LET Y = X + 2   [? 5]
30   PRINT Y          30   PRINT Y         20   LET Y = X + 2
99   END              40   DATA 5          30   PRINT Y
                      99   END             99   END
```

In the program at the left, the variable $X$ is defined to be equal to 5 on line 1∅. In the middle program, $X$ is READ at line 1∅ from the DATA statement (line 4∅). Finally, with the program at the right, we have assumed that when the program was run, the computer typed a question mark after line 1∅ and waited while the operator typed in the number 5 and pushed the carriage-return button. After establishing the value of $X = 5$, each of these programs then assigns the value $X + 2 = 7$ to the variable $Y$ on line 2∅ and proceeds to print the numerical value of $Y$ on line 3∅. Hence each program would print the number 7 before reaching the END statement on line 99. We, of course, could equally well have entered a number other than 5 from the keyboard when using the program at the right. Similarly, we could have entered a different number in the DATA statement for the middle program or have defined $X$ differently on line 1∅ for the program at the left.

---

**1.6
PROBLEM 3**

Write a simple three-line program of the type

```
10   INPUT X
20   PRINT EXP(X)
30   END
```

to illustrate the transcendental functions in BASIC.

---

As implied so far, the simple statement

PRINT X

causes the numerical value of $X$ to be printed by the computer on the terminal in a fairly self-evident manner. However, there are other things that can be included in PRINT statements which increase the power of the command considerably.

First, some degree of column formating can be obtained through use of commas and semicolons. Specifically,

PRINT X,Y,Z

results in printing numerical values stored in the variables $X$, $Y$, and $Z$ with wide spacing (12 spaces are reserved for each number, 3 spaces are placed between each group of 12, and a maximum of 5 numbers can be printed on one line).

A tighter spacing (suitable for printing numbers that do not require specification in terms of a mantissa and exponent) is obtained through the use of semicolons. For example,

PRINT X;Y;Z

results in printing numerical values for $X$, $Y$, and $Z$ in which a minimum of 6 spaces per column is used and one can get a maximum of 12 integers printed on one line. However, if $X$ were a number requiring more spaces for specification, the wider spacing associated with the comma format would be introduced automatically between the printed values for $X$ and $Y$.

Frequently, one also wants to print alphanumeric characters themselves in addition to the numbers for which they stand. In BASIC, this objective is met by placing the alphanumeric characters within quotation marks in PRINT statements. Thus, PRINT "X" would print the character X rather than the numerical value assigned to the variable X. Here again, commas result in a wide column spacing. However, a semicolon following the second quotation mark would cause the teletype (or terminal) to stop immediately after printing the alphanumeric character and wait there for the next PRINT instruction. For example, the statements

```
10   LET X = SQR(2)
20   PRINT "X = ";X
```

would result in

X = 1.41421

when the program ran. (Note that quotation marks must be used in pairs to avoid generating error messages when you run the program.) Similarly, the statement

```
20   PRINT "X = ";X;"POUNDS"
```

would result in

X = 1.41421     POUNDS

if inserted in the same program. Almost anything other than the carriage-return and line-feed commands may be included within quotation marks in PRINT statements and controlled by the computer (bell-ringing keys, cursor movements, blinking controls on CRT terminals, etc.).

Finally, the simplest command one can write with the PRINT statement is just

PRINT

which results in executing the carriage-return and line-feed controls.

A more general format capability is provided by the TAB function. As the name implies, the function serves much the same purpose as the normal TAB button on a typewriter. For example, the statement

PRINT TAB(20);"X"

would result in moving the teletype element over 20 spaces before printing the character X. Several TAB functions may be used effectively within the same PRINT statement as long as you do not attempt to consume more than the 72-column format standard in BASIC. For example,

PRINT TAB(20);"X";TAB(30);"Y";TAB(40);"Z"

would print X on the twenty-first column, Y on the thirty-first column, and Z on the forty-first column. That is, the TAB function argument always represents the number of spaces moved from the left edge of the typing area (as long as the carriage would not have to move backward in the printing process).

"Loops" are among the most powerful programming techniques that exist. The underlying concept is based on the fact that one can use the same set of programming statements over and over again to process different numerical values. For example, the GO TO statement on line 30 of the program

## 1.8
## Loops and Conditional Statements

```
 10   READ X
 20   PRINT SQR(X)
 30   GO TO 10
 80   DATA 1,2,3,4,5,6,7,8,9...
 99   END
```

causes the computer to jump back to line 10. (The space between GO and TO could have been omitted on line 30.) Hence, as written, the program keeps reading $X$ sequentially from the data statement and printing the square root of $X$ until all the data have been exhausted. In general (especially if you are paying for computer time), it is wise to write programs so that some conditional statement gets the computer out of the loop after a prescribed number of trips around. (There is a well-known horror story in the history of computing at Yale University concerning a student who generated a bill for $25,000 by leaving a computer in a loop over Thanksgiving weekend; as it turned out, he was not even taking the course for credit!)

Conditional statements of the type

IF...THEN...

provide a simple method of getting the computer out of a loop, as well as providing a computed change in program path at other branch points throughout a program. Specifically, the following symbols may be used after the IF in conditional statements:

| Symbol | Example | Meaning (at line 35 of the program) |
|---|---|---|
| = | 35 IF A = B THEN 99 | If A equals B, then go to line 99. |
| # or <> | 35 IF A<>B THEN 99 | If A is not equal to B, then go to line 99. |
| < | 35 IF A<B THEN 99 | If A is less than B, then go to line 99. |
| <= | 35 IF A<=B THEN 99 | If A is less than or equal to B, then go to line 99. |
| > | 35 IF A>B THEN 99 | If A is greater than B, then go to line 99. |
| >= | 35 IF A>=B THEN 99 | If A is greater than or equal to B, then go to line 99. |

(The order of the symbols in the $<=$ and $>=$ statements is important.)

Armed with such conditional statements, we could reconstruct our original

16

loop along the following safer lines:

```
 5   LET I = 1
10   READ X
20   PRINT SQR(X)
30   LET I = I + 1
35   IF I > 5 THEN 99
40   GO TO 10
80   DATA 1,2,3,4,5,6,7,8,9,...
99   END
```

As written, the variable $I$ is used to count the number of trips the computer makes around the loop, and the conditional statement on line 35 stops the program after it has gone through five times.

This type of construction is of such frequent value that a simpler, equivalent programming method is also built into the BASIC language. In particular, the statements

```
 5   FOR I = 1 TO 5
10   READ X
20   PRINT SQR(X)
30   NEXT I
80   DATA 1,2,3,4,5,6,7,8,9,...
99   END
```

accomplish exactly the same result. Here the loop is set up between

```
FOR I = 1 TO 5
```

and

```
NEXT I
```

(where it is implied that $I$ increases in steps of 1)

Each time around the loop, $I$ is incremented by 1 (unless some other nonintegral, or even negative step is specifically indicated in the FOR... statement). Finally, when $I$ is incremented to 6 (and thus exceeds 5 in the FOR statement on line 5), the program advances to the line immediately following the NEXT $I$ statement. (The value stored for the variable $I$ at that point in the program is actually 6.) The computer skips over the DATA statement and ends the program at line 99.

It is worth noting immediately that nonintegral steps and computed steps may be used in a FOR statement, together with computed lower and upper limits for the index. For example,

```
FOR I = SQR(Y) TO 3*Z STEP EXP(.05*Q)
```

```
NEXT I
```

where the variables $Y$, $Z$, and $Q$ have previously been given numerical values, results in starting $I$ off equal to the square root of $Y$ and in incrementing the value of $I$ by $e^{0.05Q}$ each time the computer goes around the loop. When the incremented value of $I$ exceeds 3*Z, the program jumps to the line immediately following NEXT $I$. Although the successive values of $I$ may be used to compute other (different) quantities within the loop, the lower and upper limits, together with the step size for $I$, cannot be changed once the loop has been entered. That is, those quantities are computed and stored the first time the loop is entered.

17

It is, of course, possible to use conditional statements to get out of FOR loops prematurely and to incorporate one loop inside another. Although loops can be *highly nested* (i.e., loops within loops within loops, etc.), different loops are not allowed to cross. Thus

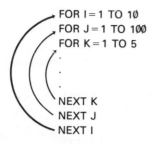

```
FOR I = 1 TO 10
FOR J = 1 TO 100
FOR K = 1 TO 5
  .
  .
  .
NEXT K
NEXT J
NEXT I
```

is allowed, whereas statements of the type

```
FOR I = 1 TO 10
FOR J = 1 TO 10
  .
  .
  .
NEXT I
NEXT J
```

in which two loops cross, are not allowed.

---

**1.8
PROBLEM 4**

Write a program consisting of a single loop that permits determining the speed of your computer for evaluating the standard arithmetic functions. For example, the program

```
10  FOR I = 1 TO 10000
20  LET Y = 2
30  NEXT I
99  END
```

will probably take an easily measurable amount of time (using a stopwatch or sweep-second hand to determine the time interval starting when you push the carriage-return button after typing RUN and ending when the computer starts to type READY), without actually computing anything. The modification,

```
20  LET Y = 2*3
```

will add an amount of time to the program which is essentially the time required to do 10,000 floating-point multiplications. Note that the time required will vary with the argument in the function. For example, it might be appropriate to sample values over the domain $0 \leqslant X \leqslant 2*3.14159$ in determining the running time for the trigonometric functions.

**1.8
PROBLEM 5**

Write a program that compares values of $N!$ with those obtained from Stirling's approximation,

$$N! \approx \sqrt{2\pi N}\, e^{-N} N^N \qquad \text{(for large } N\text{)}$$

for increasing integral values of $N$. How large a value of $N!$ can your computer handle? *Hint:* One easy way to evaluate $N!$ consists of setting up a loop for another variable $M$ which goes from 1 to $N$ in integral steps and within which we repeatedly let $F = F*M$ (where $F = 1$ initially).

In the parlance of computer scientists, in BASIC all variables are treated as floating-point numbers. This statement means that the numbers assigned to variables are handled by using a prescribed number of bits (binary digits) for the separate representation of the mantissa and exponent of the base 10 number for which the variable stands. For example, a number such as

$$0.366793 \times 10^3$$

in conventional scientific notation could be entered in BASIC by the statement

LET X = .366793E3

The mantissa (0.366793) would typically be specified within fractional errors of less than 1 part per million in normal precision. (Most large computer facilities have some provision for running in *extended precision*, using a greater number of bits to specify the mantissa.) The number in the exponent (3 in the example above) is an integer and would be specified exactly, provided that it falls within the domain allotted for exponents by the computer.

Floating-point numbers are introduced to permit treating fractions or numbers outside the domain of integers normally allotted to variables by the compiler (i.e., a fixed number of bits is set aside for each variable stored in the computer memory).

It is frequently important to be able to compute an integer from a normal floating-point variable and the INT (for integer) function has been introduced in BASIC for that purpose. In particular, the statement

LET Y = INT(X)

means that $Y$ is assigned an integer value such that $Y \leq X$; that is, $Y$ is equal to the next integer lower than or equal to $X$. (The computer still handles the variable $Y$ in the mantissa-exponent format; however, the number $Y$ is precisely equal to an integer.) As applied to the above example ($X = 0.366793E3$), $Y = INT(X)$ would mean

$$Y = 366 = \text{next integer lower than } 366.793$$

The INT function is especially useful in rounding off variables to a specified number of significant figures. For example, we can round off the number $X$ (above) to the nearest integer by the statement

LET Y = INT(X + .5)

i.e., the next integer lower than $(366.793 + 0.5)$ is 367. Similarly,

LET Y = INT(100*X + .5)/100

rounds off X to the nearest hundredth decimal place and would result in $Y = 366.79$ in the above example; and so on.

---

| **1.9** **PROBLEM 6** | Use the INT and TAB functions to print a table of sin A, cos A, and tan A, rounded off to the nearest 0.001 over the range $0 \leq A \leq 45°$ in steps of 5 degrees. |
|---|---|

---

In a typical experimental situation justifying the use of a computer, one makes lots of measurements, some routine and tedious manipulation of the numbers is required, and some properties of the numbers are computed and made available to the experimenter.

As an example, consider an experiment in which we measure the temperature in an apparatus as a function of time and express the results in degrees

Celsius (centigrade). The temperature in °C is defined in terms of a linear extrapolation of some physical property of the thermometer (e.g., length of a column of liquid, pressure of gas in an enclosed volume, voltage from a thermocouple, etc.) calibrated in such a way that the temperature of melting ice is 0°C and the temperature of boiling water at standard atmospheric pressure is 100°C (see Fig. 1-5).

Suppose that the thermometer is a *thermocouple*, i.e., a junction of two dissimilar metals across which a thermal emf (or voltage) is developed proportional to the temperature. A thermocouple is particularly appropriate in the present instance because it is easy to extract a reading of the thermal electromotive force digitally and because it will work nicely at temperatures considerably in excess of the boiling point of water. Let us suppose that we

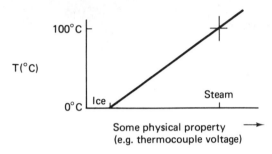

**Fig. 1-5.**

have a series of measurements of the thermocouple voltage, V (in relative units) as a function of time, which have been listed in a DATA statement format, and have taken calibration readings at the ice point ($V0$) and boiling point of water ($V1$). Then a program of the type

```
   5   PRINT "ENTER VOLTAGE AT ICE POINT AND AT BOILING POINT"
  10   INPUT V0,V1
  20   READ V
  30   LET T = 100*(V − V0)/(V1 − V0)
  40   PRINT T;
  50   GOTO 20
1000   DATA...
9999   END
```

would allow us to enter the initial calibration points from the keyboard and would then print out values of the temperature until the DATA list were exhausted. Note that the semicolon after the T in the PRINT statement on line 40 results in the numbers being closely spaced on each line. The instruction PRINT T, would result in wider spacing, whereas the statement PRINT T without either comma or semicolon would print each value on a separate line.

The instruction on line 5 is a useful reminder to the programmer to indicate just what INPUT data the computer will be waiting for on the next line. That is, the entire set of alphanumeric characters within the quotation marks after the PRINT statement will be typed out by the computer when it reaches line 5. As previously discussed, the statement

```
     PRINT"T"
```

will yield T when the program runs; whereas

```
     PRINT T
```

causes the computer to print the numerical value last assigned to the variable T. Similarly, if one left out the quotation marks on line 5, an error message would result; i.e., the string of characters ENTER VOLTAGE AT ICE POINT AND AT BOILING POINT is not acceptable as a variable.

It is helpful if often-repeated statements can be as concise and as literally correct as possible. For example, if line 5 above were in the loop, it would soon drive you to distraction. A better form might be

```
5   PRINT "V0,VI";
```

When this statement is executed, the computer prints

```
V0, V1?
```

and the meaning is self-evident. It is also helpful in avoiding needless confusion within long programs to be consistent in the choice of variables. Don't get in the habit of writing such statements as

```
 5   PRINT "ENTER V1 AND V2"
10   INPUT X,Y
```

Although the program might work properly the first time you run it, you probably will not be able to remember what you were doing a week later.

In this connection, such "remarks" as

```
29   REM T IN DEGREES CENTIGRADE NEXT FROM THERMO COUPLE VOLT.,V
```

tend to be a helpful reminder of the meaning of variables in various parts of the program. The REM statement is ignored by the computer and the next-following statement is immediately executed. Consequently, the REM statement provides a convenient mechanism for humans to remind themselves of the purpose of DATA statements, subroutines, function definitions, and entire programs. Although the value and function of this type of reminder is self-evident, there is one specific suggestion worth passing on to the reader: Apart from the purpose of a program or program segment, few things are as useful to the author of the program in the future as the date on which the program was written or last revised. The latter is especially true with complex programs that have slowly been modified over a long period of time.

## 1.11
## Taking the Temperature of a Firestorm

The apparatus shown in Fig. 1-6(a) permits generating a miniature firestorm. Air swirls in through the opening along the vertical side of the cylinder to feed a cup full of burning alcohol at the bottom. The process sets up a small tornado inside the cylinder if the overlapping edges of the cylinder are smooth. The rising combustion products in the center result in more air being pumped in at the edge; the latter swirls into the center of the cylinder, speeding up the rate of combustion. Consequently, one gets a nonlinear effect similar to that found in most firestorms. Above a critical threshold level, the process takes off exponentially and consumes the fuel more and more rapidly. Finally, the apparatus tends to be totally destroyed if one is not careful.

A thermocouple was placed at the top of the cylinder shown in Fig. 1-6(a) and was attached to a digital voltmeter. The successive (relative) voltage readings were punched out on paper tape by an apparatus that automatically starts at a preset line number and types the BASIC language DATA label and 10 successive readings per line for a previously prescribed large number of lines. The results are shown in Fig. 1-6(b).

For some of the following exercises, it will be worthwhile having a string of such DATA statements (or their equivalent) on punched paper tape (or in a disc file). For the data shown, six measurements were made per second. The particular data-acquisition device that generated the data in Fig. 1-6(b) has, in fact, been used extensively in the author's own research and has the advantage that the punched data tapes can be fed automatically into any computer that recognizes the standard BASIC DATA format. It should be noted here that generating the line numbers and DATA "flag" involves an amount of complexity in the data-acquisition device that can be avoided in many instances. For example, with large computer centers or time-sharing services that utilize the BASIC language, a long sequence of numbers can usually be written directly on a disc file using commands characteristic of the individual computer; such data files can then usually be read directly from the BASIC compiler. At the other extreme, if one is using a minicomputer to analyze data, a set of readings can generally be fed directly into the computer memory (e.g., at rates approaching the reciprocal of the machine cycle time when *direct memory access*, or *DMA*, is available) and transferred into the BASIC language with CALL statements to machine-language subroutines.

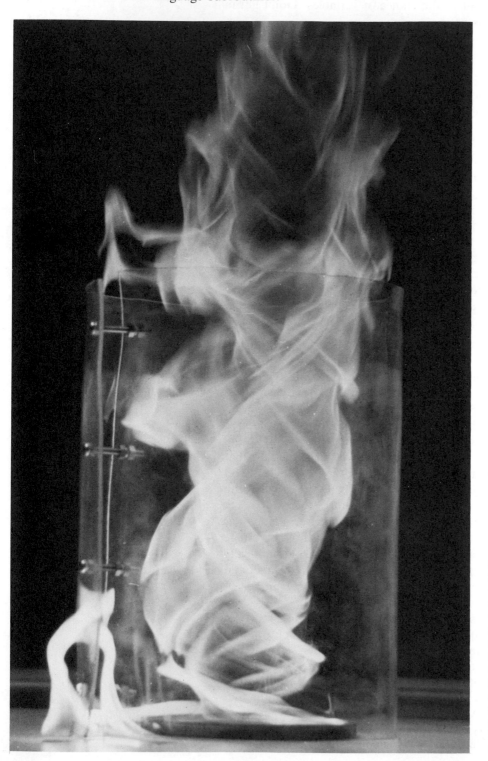

**Fig. 1-6a.** Firestorm apparatus. The apparatus shown was made from $\frac{1}{8}$-inch-thick Lucite and bent into an overlapping cylinder about 1 foot in diameter. (The overlap extended about 3 inches, leaving a 1-inch air space up the side.) By itself, the ($\approx$ 7-inch-diameter) dish of alcohol at the center produces a fairly gentle flame that would not really scare anyone. However, adding the Lucite spiral transforms the gently burning alcohol flame into a raging inferno in practically no time at all. The situation thus resembles that found in fires within large buildings: nothing much happens until some critical rate of oxygen supply is reached, when suddenly the entire building is engulfed in flames. (The author is indebted to King Walters for calling this type of demonstration apparatus to his attention.) The nonlinear properties of such firestorms might be an interesting and useful thing to study with a computer. However, the main purpose of the present discussion is to provide a large set of numbers from a real experimental situation for use in various problems, and at the same time to demonstrate how easy it is to manipulate large sets of numbers entirely with a computer.

```
1000  REM "FIRESTORM" DATA
1001  REM THERMOCOUPLE READINGS WERE -8 AT 0 DEGREES
1002  REM  AND  33  AT  100 DEGREES CENTIGRADE
1100  DATA -3,-4,-4,-3,-3,-3,-3,-4,-3,-3
1101  DATA -3,-3,-3,-3,-3,-3,-2,-3,-2,-2
1102  DATA -2,-3,-3,-3,-3,-3,-3,-3,-3,-2
1103  DATA -3,-2,-2,-2,-3,-3,-2,-2,-2,-2
1104  DATA -2,-2,-2,1,2,-2,1,2,-2,-2
1105  DATA 1,1,2,6,6,10,9,10,10,11
1106  DATA 10,13,13,13,13,12,16,15,16,17
1107  DATA 15,15,16,15,18,17,20,24,23,24
1108  DATA 29,26,29,27,25,25,28,25,28,29
1109  DATA 27,25,24,24,23,21,22,20,20,20
1110  DATA 19,19,19,24,22,23,23,21,20,21
1111  DATA 20,22,21,21,22,22,27,24,26,27
1112  DATA 26,29,28,27,28,26,25,24,22,21
1113  DATA 22,25,26,24,25,25,24,24,24,24
1114  DATA 23,24,27,24,28,31,29,28,31,32
1115  DATA 30,29,28,28,28,31,32,31,34,33
1116  DATA 35,35,37,37,35,36,35,38,38,37
1117  DATA 38,44,46,42,42,44,47,48,49,50
1118  DATA 50,50,52,59,61,60,65,64,63,62
1119  DATA 60,62,63,64,63,65,65,64,66,73
1120  DATA 76,78,82,81,79,82,84,82,88,88
1121  DATA 94,96,94,97,101,103,112,109,107,109
1122  DATA 111,112,112,112,112,116,121,122,120,117
1123  DATA 116,114,116,120,120,125,126,133,131,128
1124  DATA 134,139,137,146,143,140,139,137,132,129
1125  DATA 125,123,119,122,120,117,115,112,109,112
1126  DATA 111,111,118,119,116,114,111,113,113,113
1127  DATA 115,122,119,116,114,113,108,106,104,102
1128  DATA 99,98,97,95,98,98,102,108,112,117
1129  DATA 116,113,115,115,119,128,130,133,138,133
1130  DATA 132,132,130,127,125,127,128,135,132,137
1131  DATA 137,134,131,128,128,130,131,136,138,143
1132  DATA 142,141,138,138,136,141,140,137,135,133
1133  DATA 131,130,127,131,131,132,134,132,132,130
1134  DATA 127,125,123,122,123,121,125,123,123,123
1135  DATA 121,118,121,118,116,116,113,111,109,108
1136  DATA 108,106,107,107,108,109,108,107,106,104
1137  DATA 102,101,98,98,97,95,95,95,92,91
1138  DATA 91,92,93,93,91,90,89,86,84,84
1139  DATA 82,82,82,80,80,80,79,77,78,77
1140  DATA 78,80,0,80,81,81,80,79,77,76
1141  DATA 76,75,77,75,75,74,74,73,72,70
1142  DATA 70,69,70,68,67,69,68,67,67,65
1143  DATA 67,64,64,63,63,61,61,61,60,58
1144  DATA 59,57,57,55,54,53,53,53,53,51
1145  DATA 52,51,50,50,50,50,50,49,49,50
1146  DATA 51,55,56,56,54,54,55,52,52,54
1147  DATA 52,52,53,52,50,50,48,48,47,46
1148  DATA 46,46,44,44,44,43,43,42,42,42
1149  DATA 40,39,40,38,39,37,37,37,36,36
1150  DATA 36,35,35,34,34,33,34,34,31,-7
1151  DATA -7,-7,-6,-6,-4,-3,-6,-7,-7,-7
1152  DATA -8,-8,-8,-7,-8,-8,-8,-8,-8,-9
1153  DATA -8,-8,-8,-8,-8,-8,-8,-8,-8,-8
1154  DATA -9,-9,-8,-8,-7,-7,-8,-7,-8,-9
1155  DATA -8,-8,-8,-9,-7,-7,-7,-7,-7,-8
1156  DATA -7,-8,-7,-8,-7,-6,-6,-6,-7,-6
1157  DATA -7,-6,-6,-6,-7,-6,-7,-7,-6,-7
```

**Fig. 1-6b.** Thermocouple data. The data shown were taken from a thermocouple placed at the top of the Lucite cylinder. The fire was started at about line 1105 without the Lucite cylinder present. The cylinder was introduced at about line 1117. Finally, a recheck of the ice-point calibration was made after the fuel was exhausted at the end of line 1150.

As well as overcoming some of the inherently soporific nature of large blocks of data, the apparatus (perhaps with a stainless-steel foil) comes in handy for starting charcoal fires at picnics.

The DATA statements are used in later problem sets and should be made available on punched tape, or within disc files, for student use. (See note in Preface.)

Some large time-sharing systems have versions of BASIC with a single command (such as MAX or MIN) which directly determine the extremum values in a set of numbers stored in a column array. However, not all systems have this capability. Because one frequently needs to determine maximum or minimum values in a sequence of numbers, it is worth discussing the subject specifically.

Suppose, for example, that we wish to find the maximum value ($M$) of a set of $N$ numbers contained in a DATA statement such as that shown in Fig. 1-6(b), which were generated from the firestorm experiment. Initially, we shall define $M$ to be a large *negative* number; for example,

```
10   LET M = −1 E 10
```

which is equivalent to defining $M$ to be $-1 \times 10^{10}$ in scientific notation. We shall assume that this choice gives a number that is more negative than anything on our list. (We could, of course, have started out with the most negative number that our particular computer could handle—if we had happened to know the value offhand.) We can then construct a loop that examines each number in the data statement in turn. A conditional statement is arranged to redefine $M$ to equal each successively larger number encountered. Finally, after completing the loop, we might want to print the last value. For example,

```
20   FOR I = 1 TO N
30   READ X
40   IF M > X THEN 60
50   LET M = X
60   NEXT I
70   PRINT "MAX. = M ="; M
80   DATA      ,   ,   ,        etc.
99   END
```

It is important to emphasize that what the computer finds through repeated use of the conditional statement on line 40 is the *most positive* number on our list. The number would not necessarily have the largest absolute value [unless we modified line 40 to read: IF $M > ABS(X)$ THEN 60].

Similarly, we could construct a program to find the minimum ($M0$) number on the list through use of the opposition initialization and inequality condition. For example, adding the statements

```
15   LET M0 = +1 E 10
60   IF M0 < X THEN 65
62   LET M0 = X
65   NEXT I
75   PRINT "MIN. = M0 =";M0
```

to the previous program would permit simultaneously determining both the maximum and the minimum value in a set of $N$ data points. Here, again, it should be emphasized that the value determined for $M0$ will be the *most negative* number on the list and we would have to modify the conditional statement on line 60 [e.g., to read IF $M0 < ABS(X)$ THEN 65] if we wanted to have the computer find the minimum absolute value of $X$.

In most applications that arise in the present book (e.g., plotting, sorting, etc.) we shall be concerned with the determination of a maximum defined as the "most positive" and a minimum defined as the "most negative" in a set of numbers.

Write a program to determine the maximum and minimum temperatures (°C) in the thermocouple data shown in Fig. 1-6(b) (or in an equivalent set of data). Assuming that six measurements were made per second, make the computer determine how long after the first measurement the maximum and minimum temperatures occurred.

## 1.13 The BASIC Function Statement

In some instances, function statements provide a useful means to avoid excessive typing of programming statements. In BASIC, functions can be labeled FNA, FNB, FNC,..., FNZ and involve arguments of one or (with some versions of BASIC) more parameters. For example, one could do the thermometer calibration in Problem 7 with a function defined in the following manner:

$$\text{DEF } FNC(V) = 100*(V-V0)/(V1-V0)$$

Then, anywhere else in the program a given voltage reading, $W$, could be converted into a temperature in degrees Celsius through the statement

$$\text{LET } T = FNC(W)$$

Although too much of a luxury for the minicomputer, most large computers equipped with BASIC compilers will accept multiple-line-function definitions. The format used is of the type

```
DEF FNA(X,Y,..)
.
.
.
LET FNA = ...
FNEND
```

where the variables in the function are indicated within the parentheses on the DEF line and a large number of normal programming statements may follow on the succeeding lines prior to the FNEND statement (the end of the function definition). Multiple-line functions are particularly useful in situations where the algebraic form of the function itself depends on the variables in the function argument.

For the sake of a specific example, suppose that we wanted to create one thermometer function which would give us readings in either °C or °F from the thermocouple voltage readings in the previous experiment. We could define a function $FNT(V, S)$ in which the first variable represents the thermocouple voltage and the second determines the scale choice; for example, consider the definition

```
100   DEF FNT(V, S)
110   IF S<>0  THEN 140
120   LET FNT = 100*(V-V0)/(V1-V0)
130   GOTO 150
140   LET FNT = 32+(212-32)*(V-V0)/(V1-V0)
150   FNEND
```

in which $V0$ and $V1$ represent the ice and boiling points of water as before and must have been given numerical values elsewhere in the program before using $FNT(V, S)$. Then a statement in the main program such as

$$\text{LET } T = FNT(W, 0)$$

would give us T in degrees Celsius, whereas the statement

$$\text{LET } T = FNT(W, Q) \qquad \text{with } Q \neq 0$$

would give us T in degrees Fahrenheit.

One clearly can set up much more elaborately defined multiple-line functions and apply them to situations in which their use is more appropriate. Similarly, one might want to define a function based on summing a series, for repeated use throughout a program.

There are minor differences among BASIC compilers in the conventions used for defining multiple-line functions, and it is important to find out the specific rules that your machine follows. Finally, it is worth noting that one can always accomplish the same objectives of a multiple-line-function definition through the use of a larger number of statements in the main program or by the use of subroutines (see Section 1.14).

---

**1.13**
**PROBLEM 8**

Use the BASIC function statement to compute the temperature in °C and the temperature in °F for the data in Fig. 1-6(b) (or an equivalent string of data). Write the program so that every twentieth reading is printed out in a tabular form of the following type:

| Reading | Voltage | Temperature (°C) | Temperature (°F) |
|---------|---------|------------------|------------------|
| 2Ø | . . . | . . . | . . . |
| 4Ø | . . . | . . . | . . . |
| | | etc. | |

If your computer does not allow multiple-line functions, use two separate single-line-function definitions for the temperature in °C and in °F. (Use a FOR loop on a dummy variable to get every twentieth entry in the DATA statements.)

---

**1.14**
**Subroutines in BASIC**

A subroutine consists of a subset of program statements that may be used repeatedly at different places throughout the main program. Any line number in a BASIC program can be used as the start of a subroutine, as long as it is followed at some point by the statement RETURN. Access to the subroutine at any point within a program is gained through the statement GOSUB... (where the dots indicate the starting line number of the subroutine). The computer then jumps to the line indicated, executes all intervening program statements up until the line marked RETURN, and then jumps back to the next line after the initial GOSUB command.

A specific example will help clarify the use of this programming technique. A subroutine to compute the temperature in both degrees Celsius and degrees Fahrenheit from a thermocouple voltage and print the result could be written

```
100   REM SUB TO COMPUTE AND PRINT T IN DEG. C AND F
110   LET T1 = 100*(V − VØ)/(V1 − VØ)
120   LET T2 = 32 + (212 − 32)*(V − VØ)/(V1 − VØ)
130   PRINT T1,T2
140   RETURN
```

The REM statement on line 1ØØ is not really needed but would be helpful in reminding us of the purpose of this subroutine in a long program. We assume, as before, that $V\emptyset$ and $V1$ are the thermocouple voltages at the ice and boiling points and have been previously entered in the program (i.e., prior to saying GOSUB 1ØØ). We could then construct a main program consisting of

```
10   LET VØ = ...
20   LET V1 = ...   (whatever the values are)
30   PRINT "V"
```

```
40   INPUT V
50   GOSUB 100
60   GOTO 30
```

which perpetually goes around in a loop asking us for values of $V$ from the keyboard and jumping to subroutine 100, where the values of $T1$ (in °C) and $T2$ (in °F) are printed in wide spacing on the same line. That is, at line 50 the program jumps to the subroutine starting on line 100 and executes the statements between line 100 and line 140. When the computer reaches the RETURN statement on line 140, it jumps back to the next program statement after line 50 (from which the subroutine was originally requested).

One may also enter the subroutine at any point before the RETURN statement, provided that the variables used from then on have been defined. However, the variables used within the subroutine always have the last numerical values computed. For example, if we were to say GOSUB 130 at line 50 in our program, the subroutine would print the previous values of $T1$ and $T2$ that had been computed; whereas if we were to say GOSUB 120, the subroutine would print the previous value of $T1$, followed by the current value for $T2$.

When one realizes that nested loops and other GOSUB statements may be contained within subroutines, their enormous power becomes self-evident.

---

**1.14
PROBLEM 9**     Do the preceding problem through use of a BASIC subroutine to compute the temperatures and perform the printing operations.

---

A major economy in programming statements occurs when one starts using indexed variables, or column arrays. In BASIC, a column array may be designated by any single-letter of the alphabet followed by an integer subscript within parentheses. Thus

## 1.15
## Use of Column Arrays
## as Variables

$$A(I), B(I), C(I), \ldots, X(I), Y(I), Z(I)$$

may be used as variables in BASIC, where the indices take on integer values. If the index $I$ exceeds 10, DIM (for dimension) statements are required. One generally puts such dimension statements near the beginning of the program (usually after having figured out how many array elements are really needed in the completed program). For example,

```
10   DIM A(255), W(100)
```

tells the computer to set aside room to store 255 different variables $A(I)$ in which $1 \le I \le 255$ in integer steps and 100 different variables $W(I)$, where $I$ takes on the integer values 1 through 100. The largest number of array elements that can be set aside in this fashion depends largely on the size of the computer in use. (Representative minicomputers have array size limits of 255 elements.)

The programming power afforded by array variables rests in the fact that the array indices may be *computed*. That is, we do not have to write 255 statements of the type

```
LET A(1) = ...
LET A(2) = ...     etc.
```

to define 255 different variables. If we have a prescription for calculating these values, we can write instead a simple loop of the type

```
FOR I = 1 TO 255
LET A(I) = ...     (some function of I)
NEXT I
```

and reuse the same LET statement 255 times.

**1.15**
**PROBLEM 10†**
Write a program that lists (in close spacing) all the prime numbers up to 1000. How many are there?

[*Note:* You can tell whether a particular number, M, is prime by checking to see if $M/N(J) = \text{INT}(M/N(J))$ for all integers, $N(J)$, satisfying $2 \leqslant N(J) < M$. A clever way to do the problem is to store the successive primes in a large array, $N(J)$, starting with $N(1) = 2$, $N(2) = M = 3$, and $N = 2$. One then merely runs through the array $N(J)$ with each new M, for $J = 1$ to $N$, after which you increment M by 2. If you find a new prime, increment N by 1 and store the new prime in $N(N)$.]

† This problem and method of solution were suggested by the author's daughter, Nancy Bennett.

**1.15**
**PROBLEM 11**
The principal energy levels of the hydrogen atom are given by the Bohr relation

$$E(N) = -109678.8/N^2 \qquad \text{wavenumbers (cm}^{-1})$$

where $N = 1, 2, 3, \ldots$; the numerator is known as the Rydberg constant and has dimensions of inverse centimeters. The spontaneous transitions in the atom have wavenumbers (inverse wavelengths) given by

$$W = E(M) - E(N) \qquad \text{cm}^{-1}$$

[provided that $E(M) > E(N)$], where the values of $E(N)$ are given above. Using a column array, $W(I)$, dimensioned to hold at least 36 elements, compute and store all the allowed transition wavenumbers that can result in transitions in atomic hydrogen with principal quantum numbers $(N)$ that satisfy $2 \leqslant N \leqslant 10$. Print out the array, $W(I)$.

[*Note:* You could store the allowed transitions with statements of the type

```
FOR M = 3 TO 1Ø
FOR N = 2 TO M − 1
LET W(I) = E(M) − E(N)
LET I = I + 1
NEXT N
NEXT M
```

in which $I = 1$ initially, once the $E(N)$ have been computed.]

Write a subroutine that finds the minimum $(M1)$ and maximum $(M2)$ value of a series of $N$ numbers stored in the column array $W(I)$. Apply it to determine the minimum and maximum wavenumbers stored above.

**1.16**
**Sorting**

Suppose that we have a list of $N$ numbers which we have read into a column array, $W(I)$, and want to print them out in descending (or ascending) order. Some large computers are equipped with BASIC compilers that actually have sorting commands built into the language. For example, one system has a command of the type MAT $A = \text{DSORT}(W)$ or MAT $A = \text{ASORT}(W)$, which automatically stores the elements of array $W(I)$ in descending or ascending order in array $A(J)$. However, most small and even moderate-sized computers do not have such statements built into the BASIC language, and we might still want to accomplish the same objective.

One inefficient, but straightforward method of sorting the array elements in descending order is contained in the following steps (in which we count the ordered terms with index J, initially = 1):

1. Find the maximum number, $W(M)$, in the array.
2. Print the maximum, or store it as the Jth element in another array, $A(J)$.

3. If $W(M) = 0$, stop the process.
4. LET $W(M) = 0$ and increment $J$.
5. Go back to step 1.

This method is not too bad if you only have a few entries on the list. However, the running time increases roughly as $N^2$ and becomes prohibitive if you have a really large set of numbers ($N$) to handle (i.e., the program goes through the sorting loop $N$ times, and during each loop the program examines all $N$ elements in the original array).

---

**1.16**
**PROBLEM 12**
Use the above sorting method to print out an ordered list of allowed wavenumbers for transitions in atomic hydrogen between states for which the principal quantum numbers satisfy $2 \leqslant N \leqslant 10$. (See Problem 11.) Make a note of the running time for comparison with the next problem.

---

A much faster approach consists of storing the numbers in a second array for which the array indices are determined by the most significant digits in the numbers on the list. Here you will be limited in sorting resolution by the maximum array size that your computer can handle.

One first goes through the list to find the maximum ($M2$) and minimum ($M1$) values.[4] Then we define array integers based on the maximum number of elements ($M3$) that we can store in the array $A(J)$. Of course, $M3 \gg N$. For example, suppose that the array $A(J)$ has been dimensioned to $M3$ elements, and the elements are all initially set equal to a number $<M1$. A first-order sorting is then accomplished by statements of the type

```
100   FOR I = 1 TO N
110   LET J = INT((M3 − 1)*(W(I) − M1)/(M2 − M1) + 1 + .5)
120   LET A(J) = W(I)
130   NEXT I
```

for which the running time only increases linearly with $N$. After line 130, we have stored the values of $W(I)$ in ascending order in array $A(J)$, but the array $A(J)$ is interspersed with unaltered initial values. However, if two of the original array elements in $W(I)$ were so close in magnitude as to give the same integer $J$ on line 110, we would lose the first and only store the second value in $A(J)$. Hence, this method only works well on really large machines, or with arrays having fairly uniform differences in element size.

It is obviously desirable to accomplish the sorting within the original array itself. One particularly simple method (known as the *bubble sort*) consists of going through the array sequentially and putting adjacent pairs in ascending order. In repeated trips through the array, the largest elements "bubble up" to the top and none are lost. The process can be accomplished in $N(N + 1)/2$ trips through the array (the sum of an arithmetic series with $N$ terms) and isn't quite as slow as the straightforward method discussed initially. The method will be apparent from the following program steps.

```
99    REM BUBBLE SORT OF ARRAY W(I) WITH N ELEMENTS
100   FOR I = 1 TO N − 1
110   LET N0 = 1
```

---

[4] It should be emphasized here that $M1$ is indeed the minimum; that is, $M1$ represents either the smallest of a series of positive numbers or the "most negative" of a series of positive and negative numbers. For example, in the sequence 1, −15, 7, −2, 5, the minimum is −15.

```
120   IF W(I)<W(I+1) THEN 170
130   LET A=W(I)
140   LET W(I)=W(I+1)
150   LET W(I+1)=A
160   LET NØ=I
170   NEXT I
175   PRINT NØ;
180   IF NØ=1 THEN 210
190   LET N=NØ
200   GOTO 100
210   PRINT "ARRAY SORTED"
```

Line 175 is put in just to let the operator know where the program is in the sorting process and lines 110 and 180 identify arrays that have been previously sorted. As written, the program loses track of the original number of elements in the array $W(I)$. That number could, of course, be stored in a separate variable.

---

**1.16**
**PROBLEM 13**    Repeat Problem 12; this time use the bubble sorting method discussed above. Compare the running times.

---

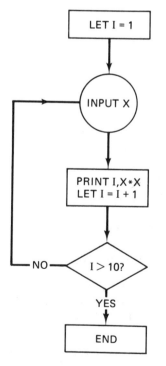

**1.17**
**Flowcharts**

Drawing flowcharts is one of those activities that most people think is a great practice—as long as someone else is doing it. The basic notion is to draw a schematic diagram of a particular program so that the reader will easily acquire an understanding of the computational method through graphic display.

Certain conventions have come into use: input quantities are usually shown within circles, computational steps within rectangles, conditional statements within triangles or diamonds, and so on. For example, the lines

```
10   LET I=1
20   INPUT X
30   PRINT I,X*X
40   LET I=I+1
50   IF I>10 THEN 90
60   GO TO 20
90   END
```

would be displayed as shown in Fig. 1-7.

Figure 1-7 illustrates one problem with flowcharts: they usually occupy more space than a *simple* listing of the program, and for simple problems they do not really give any more useful information to the reader (especially if you are not averse to drawing an occasional arrow or loop on the program listing itself). At the other extreme, for a flowchart of a really complex problem to be accurate enough to do any good, you almost have to have written the program already and have run it a few times to make sure all the bugs are out. Thus the flowchart is primarily helpful in explaining the program to others rather than to yourself.

To be sure, there is a delicately defined class of problems for which drawing a detailed flowchart ahead of time is of genuine assistance to the initial construction of the program. These problems are frequently ones that involve a large number of systematically varying program statements—so many statements that you would tend to forget where you are in the method of systematic variation without some sort of visual reminder. A good example of this type of

**Fig. 1-7.**

situation is illustrated with the binary sorting and printing sieve discussed in Chapter 4 (see Fig. 4-2). However, as noted in that chapter, a slightly more powerful version of the programming language itself does away with any necessity to draw a flowchart even in that problem. Certainly, the lower the level of power involved within the programming language, the more likely flow charts are to be of use. Thus flowcharts are extremely helpful with many machine-language problems and in programming a fairly rudimentary computer such as the HP-65 pocket calculator (see Fig. 1-3). However, with most of the fairly difficult problems in the present book, the task of drawing formal flowcharts seems a needless encumbrance. It is the sort of thing you do a lot of in programming courses when you do not have a computer available.

Please do *not* interpret these remarks to imply that *no* advance thought should be given to a problem before sitting down at a terminal. Quite the contrary. It pays to give a great deal of advance thought to difficult problems before going "on line."

It is generally desirable to sketch out most of the solution to a problem before going near a terminal—both by outlining the major steps and by writing out most of the program statements ahead of time. Then when you type in the program statements on a terminal, if you leave fairly wide line number spacings (e.g., statements every 10 line numbers), there is usually plenty of room to incorporate necessary afterthoughts without recourse to elaborate editing operations. Finally, by drawing a few loops and arrows in appropriate places, you can turn the program listing itself into an adequate flowchart for most purposes.

## 1.18
## Some BASIC String Statements (CHR$ and CHANGE)

A *string* is a specified sequence of alphanumeric characters. In larger computers, provision is generally made for both string variables and string functions.

Specific conventions on string operations differ a great deal from one compiler to the next, and there will be no substitute for reading up on the meanings assumed in the particular version of BASIC built into your computer.

The main idea is that each alphanumeric character (or, with large computers, specific sequence of alphanumeric characters) may be described by a string variable. String variables are designated by a single letter followed by a dollar sign; e.g.,

$$A\$, B\$, C\$, \ldots, Z\$$$

are string variables. These may be defined through LET statements (where the string must be enclosed within quotation marks), by READ and DATA statements, and may be input and printed by use of the computer terminal.

To perform operations on strings, an integer code is used within the programming language to designate the various alphanumeric characters. The numerical values are assigned in a manner based upon the ASCII (American Standard Code for Information Interchange) convention for identifying such characters. A list of decimal-integer values assigned to some of the standard character set is shown in Table 1.

Most BASIC compilers equipped to handle strings have some version of the CHR$(X) function (which is used in PRINT statements to print the alphanumeric character corresponding to the variable $X$) and the CHANGE statement (which permits defining numerical variables equal to the ASCII integers for alphanumeric characters in strings.)

For example, use of the CHR$ function in a program of the type

```
FOR X = 65 TO 65+25
PRINT CHR$(X);
NEXT X
```

would print the alphabet in closely-spaced sequence using the code summarized in Table 1. (Note that the ASCII integers for certain "control" keys
such as the line feed and carriage return are excluded from the normal
characters that may be used in string statements.)

The CHANGE statement is inherently more powerful and involves the use
of a column array to correspond to each string variable. Assuming the string
variable $V\$$ has been defined and the column array $V(I)$ has been dimensioned
to equal (or exceed) the number of characters in the string, the statement

### CHANGE V$ TO V

then enters the number of characters in the string $V\$$ as the zeroth ($I = \emptyset$)
element of array $V(I)$ and fills in the ASCII code for the characters in the

**1.18: Table 1** Integer Values Assigned to Some ASCII
Characters in BASIC[a]

| Alphanumeric character | Decimal-integer value |
| --- | --- |
| Sp. (space or blank) | 32 |
| ' (apostrophe) | 39 |
| – (minus sign or hyphen) | 45 |
| $\emptyset$ (zero) | 48 |
| 1 (one)[b] | 49 |
| 2 (two) | 50 |
| 3 (three) | 51 |
| 4 (four) | 52 |
| 5 (five) | 53 |
| 6 (six) | 54 |
| 7 (seven) | 55 |
| 8 (eight) | 56 |
| 9 (nine) | 57 |
| A (uppercase A) | 65 |
| B (uppercase B) | 66 |
| C (uppercase C) | 67 |
| D (uppercase D) | 68 |
| E (uppercase E) | 69 |
| F (uppercase F) | 70 |
| G (uppercase G) | 71 |
| H (uppercase H) | 72 |
| I (uppercase I) | 73 |
| J (uppercase J) | 74 |
| K (uppercase K) | 75 |
| L (uppercase L) | 76 |
| M (uppercase M) | 77 |
| N (uppercase N) | 78 |
| O (uppercase O) | 79 |
| P (uppercase P) | 80 |
| Q (uppercase Q) | 81 |
| R (uppercase R) | 82 |
| S (uppercase S) | 83 |
| T (uppercase T) | 84 |
| U (uppercase U) | 85 |
| V (uppercase V) | 86 |
| W (uppercase W) | 87 |
| X (uppercase X) | 88 |
| Y (uppercase Y) | 89 |
| Z (uppercase Z) | 90 |

[a] There are 128 in a complete list.

[b] The symbols 1–9 are helpful in using string statements to
plot topographical maps (see Chapter 3). The remaining
characters in the table are of primary concern in Chapter 4.

string in successive array elements $(I = 1, 2, 3, \ldots)$. For example, the statements

```
INPUT V$
CHANGE V$ TO V
```

permit entering up to 72 characters in a string from the teletype keyboard (the end of the string is defined when the carriage return button is pushed), providing DIM V(72) occurs earlier in the program. The ASCII code for the first letter in the string is stored in $V(1)$ and that for the last character in the string in $V(72)$. In this instance $V(\emptyset) = 72$. The string could also be read from DATA statements in a program of the type

```
READ V$
DATA ABCDEFGHIJKLMNOPQRSTUVWXYZ
```

and one could also use the CHANGE statement to convert the integers stored in a column array $V(I)$ to a string variable $V\$$ by the statement

```
CHANGE V TO V$
```

providing $V(\emptyset)$ is defined to be the total number of characters in the string. [This is the only type of situation in which we shall consider arrays having zero indices.]

From the code illustrated in Table 1, it will be apparent how conditional statements can be used with string variables. Most BASIC compilers with string capability have some version of the numerical conditional statements (e.g., IF $B\$ < D\$$ THEN ...) which apply the condition sequentially to each separate character of the two strings from left to right and in a manner such that the first difference encountered determines the relationship. The comparisons are made numerically using the ASCII integer code in Table 1. Such conditional statements can obviously be used to effect various sorting, alphabetizing, and editing procedures.

Various other powerful string statements are permitted in many of the larger computers equipped with BASIC. However, the individual statements included vary considerably from one computer to the next and it would be impractical to try to summarize their properties here.

---

| | |
|---|---|
| **1.18**<br>**PROBLEM 14** | If your computer has the CHR$ function (or equivalent statement), write a program which prints alphanumeric characters corresponding to the ASCII decimal code in Table 1. |
| **1.18**<br>**PROBLEM 15** | If your computer has the CHANGE statement and accepts string variables (or has equivalent statements), write a program which prints the ASCII decimal integers corresponding to different alphanumeric characters entered from the keyboard and compare your results with Table 1. |

---

## REFERENCES

FALK, HOWARD, ET AL. (1974). "Computer Report I . . . VIII." *IEEE Spectrum*, Vol. 11, No. 2. This issue contains a number of separate "state-of-the-art" review articles on computer technology written by Howard Falk, C. G. Bell, L. G. Roberts, Don Mennie, A. A. Hoffman, R. L. French, G. M. Lang, Henry Tropp, W. R. Beam, and the editorial staff of *Spectrum*.

FETH, G. C. (1973). "Memories Are Bigger, Faster—and Cheaper." Technology review in *IEEE Spectrum*, Vol. 10, No. 11, pp. 28–35.

GOLDSTINE, H. H., (1972). *The Computer from Pascal to von Neumann*. Princeton, N.J.: Princeton University Press.

HEATH, F. G. (1972). "Origins of the Binary Code." *Scientific American*, August, pp. 76–83.

HEWLETT-PACKARD CORPORATION (1969). *A Pocket Guide to Hewlett-Packard Computers*.

KEMENY, J. G., AND T. E. KURTZ. (1968). *BASIC Manual*. Hanover, N.H.: Dartmouth College. This manual has been reproduced within many different computer instruction manuals. Also see the discussion of CALL and WAIT statements for use within Hewlett-Packard BASIC in their manuals for the 2100 series computers and the discussion of more powerful functions within versions of BASIC given in the General Electric and Digital Data Corporation PDP10 time-sharing computer manuals.

KNUTH, D. E. (1973). *The Art of Computer Programming*. Reading, Mass.: Addison-Wesley Publishing Co., Vol. 3, *Sorting and Searching*.

MENNIE, DON (1974). "The Big Roundup of Small Calculators." *IEEE Spectrum*, Vol. 11, pp. 34–41.

U.S. ATOMIC ENERGY COMMISSION (1971). *In the Matter of J. Robert Oppenheimer*. Cambridge, Mass.: The MIT Press. This book contains a transcript of the April 12–May 6, 1954 hearings by the U.S. Atomic Energy Commission, together with a brief foreword by P. M. Stern.

VON NEUMANN, JOHN (1958). *The Computer and the Brain*. New Haven, Conn.: Yale University Press. (*The Silliman Lectures*; published posthumously.)

# 2

# More advanced programming

*This chapter assumes a knowledge of the elementary programming statements in BASIC that were discussed in Sections 1.4–1.17. The main emphasis is in summing various types of series. At the same time, concepts from introductory calculus (derivatives, Taylor series, definite integrals) and matrix algebra are reviewed. This review is always conducted from the standpoint of immediate programming application and with the object of providing greater insight regarding the more powerful statements in a language such as BASIC. Applications to fields ranging from economics to pattern recognition are discussed. However, the material should be comprehensible to readers without a formal background in calculus or college-level science. The material steadily increases in difficulty toward the end of the chapter, and students without a prior course in calculus may wish to skip the final section altogether. Relevant sections are cross-referenced as they arise in subsequent chapters on specific applications.*

In this chapter we shall introduce some slightly more advanced programming methods and review some basic mathematical techniques needed in different places throughout the remainder of the book. The main emphasis will be on the mathematical technique that is tacitly assumed in the standard operations built into the BASIC language. Our primary objective is to give the reader some insight regarding the behind-the-scenes operations that occur when you run a program containing statements such as $X \uparrow Y$, $\text{EXP}(X)$, $\text{SIN}(X)$, $\text{MAT } A = B*C$, $\text{MAT } A = \text{INV}(B)$, and so on. The object is not to avoid using these powerful commands but to emphasize their practical utility and at the same time make it apparent how similar functions of a more specialized nature might be defined.

One frequently needs to compute numerical values for a series of the type

$$S = a_1 + a_2 + a_3 + \cdots + a_n + a_{n+1} + \cdots$$

**2.1**
**Summing a Series of Numbers**

in which a known prescription exists for evaluating the $n^{\text{th}}$ term. The exact approach to the problem will vary a little, depending on whether the number of terms in the series is finite or infinite. The most straightforward way to sum the series is to initialize $S$ through a statement

```
10   LET S = 0
```

and merely compute (or read from a data statement) each term in the series sequentially. For example, if there are $M$ terms, then the program

```
20   FOR N = 1 TO M
30   LET A = ...     (some function of N)
40   LET S = S + A
50   NEXT N
60   PRINT S
90   END
```

sums the series.

It is often possible to set up the problem in a form where $a_{n+1}$ is computed from $a_n$ in a running increment to the sum. The approach can both save running time and improve computational accuracy. Here a program for a finite series with $M$ terms might take the form

```
10   LET S = 0
20   LET A = ...
30   FOR N = 1 TO M
40   LET S = S + A
50   LET A = A*(...)
60   NEXT N
70   PRINT S
80   END
```

Line 20 defines the value of the first term in the series, and line 50 computes the $(N+1)^{\text{th}}$ term from the Nth term. If, for example, the Nth term were of the form

$$A_N = \frac{X^N}{N!}$$

a separate computation of

$$X^N \quad \text{and} \quad N!$$

could easily exhaust the domain of variables in any real computer for suitably large values of $X$ and $N$. On the other hand, computing the statement

```
LET A = A*(X/N)
```

is enormously less demanding.

**2.1**
**PROBLEM 1**

The BASIC function RND($X$) provides a sequence of numbers intended to simulate a random distribution over the interval 0 to 1. (The argument in the function is a dummy variable but nevertheless must be assigned a definite numerical value.) Write a program that computes 1000 successive values from the RND($X$) function and see how close the average value is to 0.5.

**2.1**
**PROBLEM 2**

Find the sum of the arithmetic series

$$S = 1 + 2 + 3 + \cdots + (M-1) + M$$

for variable $M$, and compare the result with the closed-form expression,

$$S = \frac{M(M+1)}{2}$$

(The latter result can be obtained by writing the series backward and noting that the terms 1, $(M-1)$, etc., combine in pairs, each having the value $M$.)

**2.1**
**PROBLEM 3**

Write a program that sums the geometric series

$$S = 1 + a + a^2 + a^3 + \cdots + a^M$$

for different values of $a$ and $M$ (input from the keyboard), and compare the result with the closed-form expression

$$S = \frac{1 - a^{M+1}}{1 - a}$$

(The latter result is obtained by subtracting $aS$ from $S$ and canceling like powers of $a$ in pairs.)

---

In many instances, one wants to sum an infinite series,

$$S = a_1 + a_2 + \cdots$$

**2.2**
**Infinite Series and Convergence**

to a prescribed accuracy. Here we have to construct the program in a form that starts the series off at the first term and keeps it going until a specified conditional statement on the increment $a_N$ is satisfied. For example,

```
10  LET S = 0
20  LET N = 1
30  LET A = ...     (some function of N)
40  LET S = S + A
50  IF ABS(A) < ... THEN 80
60  LET N = N + 1
70  GO TO 30
80  PRINT N,S
90  END
```

The variable $N$ (lines 20, 60 and 80) is not always necessary but is frequently helpful in the definition of the running term and in keeping track of the total number of terms computed. Note that for $A < 0$, a conditional statement on the absolute value of the increment is useful (line 50).

If ABS($A_{N+1}/A_N$) < 1 for all $N$, the above type of *computed* series will generally terminate at a finite limit for sufficiently large $N$. This fact is assured by the conditional statement on ABS($A$) in line 50, where the dots must be replaced by a specific numerical criterion. However, the computed limit may not always be the right one. The reader should be especially wary of two pitfalls:

1. The conditional statement on line 50 in the sample program above could

be satisfied in cases where a finite limit does *not* exist (e.g., $\lim_{N \to \infty}(A_{N+1}/A_N) \nrightarrow 0$].

2. Rounding errors can result in large discrepancies between actual and computed limits in convergent series for which the terms alternate in sign.

---

**2.2**
**PROBLEM 4**

Write a program to evaluate the infinite series $S = 1 + x + x^2 + \cdots$, within the rounding errors of your computer where $-1 < x < 1$ and compare the result with the closed-form expression

$$S = \frac{1}{1-x}$$

(obtained from the finite geometric series expression in the limit $N \to \infty$).

---

**2.3**
**Infinite Series Derived from the Binomial Theorem (Pth Roots)**

It is easy to write a program that accomplishes the same result as the BASIC statement, $I \uparrow P$, provided that $P$ is an integer. For example, one could write a simple loop of the type

```
10  LET A = I
20  FOR N = 1 TO P−1
30  LET A = A*I
40  NEXT N
```

where $I$ has been defined before line 10. Clearly, $A = I^P$ after the loop has been completed.

However, the problem becomes more involved if you should want to duplicate the results of the BASIC statement $Y \uparrow (1/P)$, where $P$ is still an integer. One way to accomplish this more difficult objective consists of first finding the smallest integer $I$ such that

$$I^P > Y$$

(To avoid imaginary quantities, we shall assume that $Y > 0$.) This first part of the problem can, of course, be accomplished through judicious use of statements 10–40. After determining the smallest integer $I$ that satisfies the above requirement, we next note that if we define $X$ so that

$$Y^{1/P} = I(1+X)^{1/P}$$

then

$$X = \frac{Y}{I^P} - 1 \quad \text{and} \quad \text{ABS}(X) < 1$$

Hence, if we can write a program to expand $(1+X)^{1/P}$ as an infinite series in $X$ and sum that series to a prescribed accuracy, we will have achieved our goal. This objective can be accomplished by use of the *Binomial Theorem*.

In particular, the usual form of the binomial expansion,

$$(A+B)^N = A^N + N\frac{A^{N-1}B^1}{1!} + N(N-1)\frac{A^{N-2}B^2}{2!} + \cdots + B^N$$

results in a convergent infinite series,

$$(1+X)^{1/P} = 1 + \frac{1/P}{1!}X^1 + \frac{(1/P)[(1/P)-1]}{2!}X^2 + \cdots$$

for fractional powers $(1/P)$, provided that $\text{ABS}(X) < 1$.

Hence, in order to compute $Y^{1/P}$, all we have to do is find the smallest integer $I$ such that $I^P > Y$, compute $X = Y/I^P - 1$, and then sum the series for

$(1+X)^{1/P}$. (Note that although we have used positive signs in the binomial expansion to minimize confusing the nature of that expansion, the quantity $X$ is inherently negative in the definition above.)

---

**2.3
PROBLEM 5**

Write a program that uses the Binomial Theorem† to compute $Y^{1/P}$ to the accuracy of your computer without using the BASIC exponentiation function and then compares the result with the BASIC statement $Y\uparrow(1/P)$. Enter values of $Y$ and $P$ from the keyboard and restrict the values so that $P$ is a positive integer and $Y>0$.

† The serious student will want to investigate the treatise on the Binomial Theorem by Professor James Moriarty (see A. Conan-Doyle, "The Final Problem").

---

Consider a continuous function $y=f(x)$, as shown in Fig. 2-1. The derivative of $y$ in respect to $x$ (written as $dy/dx$) is defined as the limit of the quantity

**2.4
Derivatives**

$$\left[\frac{f(x+\Delta x)-f(x)}{\Delta x}\right]$$

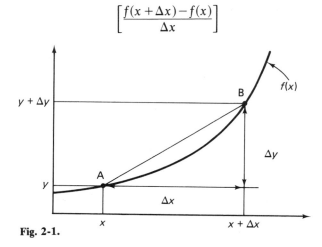

**Fig. 2-1.**

as $\Delta x$ shrinks to zero. This definition is frequently written

$$\frac{dy}{dx}\equiv\lim_{\Delta x\to 0}\left[\frac{f(x+\Delta x)-f(x)}{\Delta x}\right] \tag{1}$$

As may be seen from Fig. 2-1, the derivative of the function is just the slope of the curve (or tangent to the curve) at the point $x$ where the derivative is evaluated (i.e., the point $B$ moves toward the point $A$ along the curve).

Although one could always write a computer program to provide a numerical evaluation of the derivative of a specified function directly from this fundamental definition, it is important to recognize that the derivatives of many functions can be written explicitly in closed form. In such cases, it is usually desirable to evaluate the functional form of the derivative rather than to compute the derivative numerically from the limiting process.

The derivative of the functional form

$$y=f(x)=x^N$$

is of very great importance to Taylor-series expansions (discussed in Section 2.5) and can be evaluated easily by application of the Binomial Theorem. In this case,

$$f(x+\Delta x)=(x+\Delta x)^N=x^N+\frac{Nx^{N-1}(\Delta x)^1}{1!}+\frac{N(N-1)x^{N-2}(\Delta x)^2}{2!}+\cdots$$

Therefore, applying the definition of the derivative,

$$\frac{d}{dx}(x^N)=\lim_{\Delta x\to 0}\left[\frac{x^N+Nx^{N-1}(\Delta x)^1+N(N-1)x^{N-2}(\Delta x)^2/2!+\cdots-x^N}{\Delta x}\right]$$

39

(in which the terms involving $x^N$ cancel), yields

$$\frac{d}{dx}(x^N)= \lim_{\Delta x \to 0} \left[ Nx^{N-1}+\frac{N(N-1)x^{N-2}(\Delta x)^1}{2!}+\text{terms of order }(\Delta x)^2 \cdots \right]$$

The terms involving $\Delta x$ vanish in the limiting process. Hence we obtain the extremely important general result,

$$\frac{d}{dx}(x^N)=Nx^{N-1} \tag{2}$$

---

**2.4**
**PROBLEM 6**

Write a program to compute the derivative of $\chi^N$ numerically. Check the program by comparing its results with those based on an analytic form for the derivative.

Using the BASIC function definitions

```
DEF FNY(X) = X↑N
DEF FND(X) = (FNY(X + D) − FNY(X))/D
```

write a program that takes the limit of the second function as $D \to 0$ and compares the result with $N*X\uparrow(N-1)$ for values of $X$ and $N$ entered from the keyboard. For example, LET $D = \emptyset.\emptyset1*X$ initially and reiteratively multiply the values of $D$ by $\emptyset.1$ until the successive values of $\text{FND}(X)$ differ by less than the rounding error on your machine. (Although it would be foolish to evaluate the derivative of $x^N$ in this manner in a serious program, one could advantageously use the same technique to evaluate the derivatives of numerically determined functions.)

---

There are many important functions [e.g., SIN($X$), COS($X$), EXP($X$), etc.] which can only be computed by the use of power-series expansions in the independent variable. Before the general availability of computers, tables of such functions were tediously evaluated by hand (using desk calculators) and published in book form. Indeed, one such project sponsored by the WPA during the 1930s was probably conceived just to provide work for unemployed mathematicians.

**2.5**
**Taylor Series**
**(Alias MacLaurin Series)**

Although ready access to digital computers has largely done away with the need for printed tables of this sort, one still needs to use series expansions to evaluate the functions. Very efficient forms of these expansions for the common transcendental functions have been stored in machine language within the BASIC compiler. However, it is still useful to consider a general method for determining the expansion coefficients in such series. The method, which goes under the name *Taylor series* (or sometimes *MacLaurin series*) is probably one of the most useful tools in computational analysis, apart from the concept of the derivative itself.

We shall start by assuming that the function $y = f(x)$ can be written in the infinite series

$$y = C_0 + C_1 x^1 + C_2 x^2 + C_3 x^3 + \cdots + C_N x^N + \cdots \tag{3}$$

As will become evident, the assumption implies that the function and its derivatives must be continuous and finite over the domain of $x$ in which we want to compute the function. The series also had better converge to a finite limit.

To evaluate the coefficients $C_0, C_1, \ldots, C_N, \ldots$, we adopt a procedure in which we repeatedly determine the derivatives of Eq. (3) and set $x = 0$ in the result.

To get the leading coefficient in the expansion, we merely set $x = 0$ in the original equation. Clearly,

$$C_0 = (y)_{x=0}$$

Next we take the derivative of both sides of Eq. (3), yielding

$$\frac{dy}{dx} = C_1 + 2C_2 x^1 + 3C_3 x^2 + \cdots + NC_N x^{N-1} + \cdots \tag{4}$$

in which use has been made of our general expression for $d(x^N)/dx$ in Eq. (2). Letting $x = 0$ in Eq. (4) gives us

$$C_1 = \left(\frac{dy}{dx}\right)_{x=0}$$

Similarly, taking the derivative of Eq. (4) yields

$$\frac{d}{dx}\left(\frac{dy}{dx}\right) \equiv \frac{d^2 y}{dx^2} = 2C_2 + 3 \cdot 2C_3 x^1 + \cdots + N(N-1)C_N x^{N-2} + \cdots \tag{5}$$

and therefore that

$$C_2 = \frac{1}{2}\left(\frac{d^2 y}{dx^2}\right)_{x=0}$$

Doing the same process over and over demonstrates that

$$C_N = \frac{1}{N!}\left(\frac{d^N y}{dx^N}\right)_{x=0}$$

Hence the original function may be expressed as[1]

$$y = (y)_{x=0} + \frac{1}{1!}\left(\frac{d^1 y}{dx^1}\right)_{x=0} x^1 + \frac{1}{2!}\left(\frac{d^2 y}{dx^2}\right)_{x=0} x^2 + \cdots \tag{6}$$

which may be rewritten

$$y = \sum_{N=0}^{\infty} \frac{1}{N!}\left(\frac{d^N y}{dx^N}\right)_{x=0} x^N \tag{7}$$

where we have used the convention that $0! \equiv 1$, that $(d^N y/dx^N)_{x=0}$ is the Nth derivative of the original function evaluated at $x = 0$ and that the zeroth derivative is the function itself. Hence, if we can evaluate the required set of derivatives, we have a straightforward method of computing the values of $y$ as a function of $x$. In practice, such series solutions will frequently converge fairly rapidly and one does not, of course, have to take an infinite number of terms to compute the function to a prescribed accuracy.

As discussed in introductory courses in calculus, the function $e^x$ has the remarkable property that

## 2.6
## Taylor Series for $e^x$ [or EXP(X)]

$$\frac{d}{dx}(e^x) = e^x \tag{8}$$

where $e = 2.71828\ldots$ is the base of the *natural* or *Naperian, logarithms*. That is, the function is equal to its derivative. For that reason, it is especially easy to write a Taylor series for $e^x$. Because

$$\left[\frac{d^N}{dx^N} e^x\right]_{x=0} = (e^x)_{x=0} = 1 \tag{9}$$

---

[1] Shifting the origin by $a$ in Eq. (6) gives the more general form of the expansion credited to a student of Newton's named Taylor:

$$y(x) = y(a) + \left(\frac{dy}{dx}\right)_{x=a}(x-a)^1 + \frac{1}{2!}\left(\frac{d^2 y}{dx^2}\right)_{x=a}(x-a)^2 + \cdots$$

Whittaker and Watson note that this formal expansion was originally published by Brook Taylor in his *Methodus Incrementorum* in 1715. The result obtained by putting $a = 0$ in Taylor's theorem is usually called *MacLaurin's theorem*; it was first discovered by Stirling in 1717 and published by MacLaurin in 1742 in his *Fluxions*.

the series for $e^x$ is just

$$S = e^x = 1 + x + \frac{x^2}{2!} + \frac{x^3}{3!} + \cdots + \frac{x^N}{N!} + \cdots \tag{10}$$

[i.e., substitute Eq. (9) into Eq. (7)].

Note that the Nth term in this series is simply $(x/N)$ times the $(N-1)$th term; i.e.,

$$A_N = A_{N-1} \cdot \frac{x}{N} \tag{11}$$

where

$$S = A_0 + A_1 + A_2 + \cdots + A_N + \cdots \quad \text{and} \quad A_0 = 1$$

Hence no matter how large a value of $x$ is chosen initially, there will eventually be some term $A_N$ in the series which is negligible compared to the preceding term. Not only does this result mean that the series will converge to a finite limit for arbitrary $x$; Eq. (11) also provides an efficient rule for computing the series. In particular, note that the values for $A_{N-1}$ and $(x/N)$ can be quite manageable even when $x^N$ and $N!$ separately involve numbers that are too large for your computer to handle. Hence it is much better to use Eq. (11) to evaluate the successive terms in the series than to try to compute

$$A_N = \frac{x^N}{N!}$$

separately for each term in the series.[2]

---

**2.6**
**PROBLEM 7**

Write a program that sums the infinite series for $e^x$ and compares the computed result with the value obtained from the BASIC function EXP(X). Enter the value of $X$ from the keyboard and print the running values of the sum and the increment to the sum for each term using the rule summarized in Eq. (11). Put in a conditional statement which terminates the program at a fractional error compatible with the accuracy of your computer. For example,

IF ABS(A)<1E−6 THEN ...   (print results)

would get your program out of the summation loop when the increment $(A)$ to the series had an absolute value of less than $10^{-6}$. See how large a positive value of $X$ your computer can handle in this program. Also note that for sufficiently large negative values of $X$, the computed series limit will be more seriously in error than for positive values of $X$ having the same magnitude. This effect results from finite rounding errors in the computer and the fact that the terms in the series for negative $X$ alternate in sign. Here the series limit can be very much smaller than terms occurring early in the series, and the rounding errors prevent these terms of alternate sign from canceling out to the extent that they actually should. Note that one can minimize this difficulty for $X < 0$ by computing the series for $-X$ (which now has only positive terms) and by taking the reciprocal of the final sum; i.e., $e^{-X} = 1/e^X$.

---

[2] Most compilers use machine-language subroutines to compute the transcendental functions that truncate the infinite series at a fixed number of terms and evaluate the resultant polynomials using a technique known in high school textbooks as *synthetic substitution*. The method depends on storing a set of coefficients for the polynomial and using the properties of the specific function to limit the domain of the argument entered in the algorithm used to evaluate the polynomial. For example, it is always possible to find a value $N(=Y-X)$ such that

$$e^Y = e^N \cdot e^X$$

where $N$ is an integer and $X \leq 1$. Hence, if we store $e = 2.7182818 \ldots$ to the requisite number of decimal places as a constant in the program, we can evaluate $e^Y$ for general $Y$ by computing a

To perform a Taylor expansion for the sine and cosine functions, we first need analytic expressions for the derivatives of these functions. Using a well-known identity from trigonometry,

$$\sin(x + \Delta x) = \sin x \cos \Delta x + \cos x \sin \Delta x$$

and the basic definition of the derivative given in Eq. (1), it is seen that

$$\frac{d}{dx}\sin x = \lim_{\Delta x \to 0}\left[\frac{\sin(x + \Delta x) - \sin x}{\Delta x}\right]$$
$$= \lim_{\Delta x \to 0}\left[\frac{\sin x \cos \Delta x + \cos x \sin \Delta x - \sin x}{\Delta x}\right] \quad (12)$$

The limiting values of $\sin \Delta x$ and $\cos \Delta x$ can be deduced using *Pythagoras' theorem* and the definition of radian angular measure. Consider a right triangle

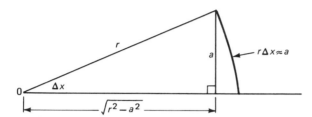

with hypotenuse $r$ and side $a$ opposite to the angle $\Delta x$. The circular arc centered at point 0 has length $r\,\Delta x$ by definition.

Therefore

$$\lim_{\Delta x \to 0}(\cos \Delta x) = \lim_{a \to 0}\left(\frac{\sqrt{r^2 - a^2}}{r}\right) = 1$$

and for small $\Delta x$, $\qquad\qquad\qquad\qquad\qquad\qquad\qquad\qquad\qquad (13)$

$$\sin \Delta x = \frac{a}{r} \approx \frac{r\,\Delta x}{r} = \Delta x$$

Hence Eq. (12) reduces to

$$\frac{d}{dx}\sin x = \lim_{\Delta x \to 0}\left(\cos x\,\frac{\sin \Delta x}{\Delta x}\right) = \cos x \quad (14)$$

---

polynomial of the type

$$P = 1 + X + \frac{X^2}{2!} + \frac{X^3}{3!} + \frac{X^4}{4!}$$

and noting that $e^Y \approx e^N \cdot P$. For example, a seventh-degree polynomial gives $e^X$ to better than 1 ppm for $X < 1$. One may then write a very efficient algorithm for computing $P$. If we write the polynomial in the form

$$P = C_0 X^4 + C_1 X^3 + C_2 X^2 + C_3 X^1 + C_4$$

it is seen that

$$P = (((C_0 X + C_1)X + C_2)X + C_3)X + C_4$$

Hence the same multiplicative and additive statements may be built into a very simple loop for evaluating a high-order polynomial, $P$. For example, if the coefficients $C_1$–$C_4$ above were stored in an array C(I), the fourth-degree polynomial could be evaluated through a BASIC program of the type

```
LET P = C0     (= C₀ above)
FOR I = 1 TO 4
LET P = P*X + C(I)
NEXT I
```

The same procedure may be applied to polynomials of any degree, provided that we can store enough constants to requisite accuracy.

Similarly, by using the trigonometric identity,

$$\cos(x + \Delta x) = \cos x \cos \Delta x - \sin x \sin \Delta x$$

and the limits in Eq. (13), one can show that

$$\frac{d}{dx} \cos x = -\sin x \tag{15}$$

where the angles are again specified in radians.

Having established expressions for the derivatives of $\sin x$ and $\cos x$, we can go on to determine the Taylor series for these functions. For example, assume that $\sin x$ may be written

$$\sin x = C_0 + C_1 x + C_2 x^2 + C_3 x^3 + C_4 x^4 + \cdots \tag{16}$$

Letting $x = 0$ yields

$$C_0 = \sin 0 = 0$$

Taking the derivative of Eq. (16) yields

$$\cos x = C_1 + 2C_2 x^1 + 3C_3 x^2 + 4C_4 x^3 + \cdots \tag{17}$$

and we see that

$$C_1 = \cos 0 = 1$$

Taking the derivative of Eq. (17) yields

$$-\sin x = 2C_2 + 3 \cdot 2C_3 x^1 + 4 \cdot 3C_4 x^2 + \cdots \tag{18}$$

and

$$C_2 = 0$$

Similarly, taking the derivative of Eq. (18) yields

$$-\cos x = 3 \cdot 2 \cdot 1 C_3 + 4 \cdot 3 \cdot 2 C_4 x^1 + \cdots \tag{19}$$

and results in

$$C_3 = -\frac{1}{3!}$$

etc.

Combining results, we obtain an infinite series for the $\sin x$ given by

$$\sin x = x - \frac{x^3}{3!} + \frac{x^5}{5!} - \frac{x^7}{7!} + \cdots \tag{20}$$

where it should be emphasized that $x$ is in radians ($\pi$ radians $= 180°$).

One could similarly evaluate the coefficients in an infinite series for the cosine function. However, it is much quicker just to take the derivative of Eq. (20) and note that

$$\frac{d}{dx} \sin x = \cos x = 1 - \frac{x^2}{2!} + \frac{x^4}{4!} - \frac{x^6}{6!} + \cdots \tag{21}$$

---

**2.7
PROBLEM 8**

Write programs to evaluate the series expansions for the sine and cosine and compare your computed results with the BASIC functions SIN($X$) and COS($X$). Enter values of $X$ (in radians) from the keyboard and use a conditional statement to terminate the loop at a point compatible with the rounding errors in your computer. Compute each term in the series from the value of the preceding one. Note that it is quite easy to compute both functions simultaneously within the same program. The series are subject to the same difficulties with large values of $X$ as those discussed in the evaluation of $e^{-x}$ in the previous problem. In the case of the sine and cosine functions, one can use the periodicity to advantage in minimizing errors for $|X| > 1$ (i.e., you never really have to get out of the domain $-\pi/2 \leqslant x \leqslant \pi/2$).

Some higher-level programming languages (e.g., "super" BASIC and FORTRAN IV) have explicit provision built in to handle complex numbers. However, not all machines are equipped with these languages, and one might still want to do an occasional problem involving complex numbers on a computer that has only been programmed to handle real numbers (i.e., numbers with no imaginary component).

We shall define a complex number to be one that has the form

$$z = A + iB \tag{22}$$

in which both $A$ and $B$ are real and in which the entity $i$ is defined by

$$i \equiv \sqrt{-1}$$

Hence

$$i^2 = -1, \quad i^3 = -i, \quad i^4 = +1, \quad i^5 = i, \quad \text{etc.} \tag{23}$$

An extremely useful result can be obtained from the Taylor series for $e^x$, $\cos x$ and $\sin x$. In particular, if we substitute $x = i\theta$ in the expansion for $e^x$, Eq. (10) becomes

$$e^{i\theta} = 1 + i\theta - \frac{\theta^2}{2!} - i\frac{\theta^3}{3!} + \frac{\theta^4}{4!} + i\frac{\theta^5}{5!} + \cdots \tag{24}$$

through use of Eq. (23). Separating the real and imaginary parts in Eq. (24) then yields

$$e^{i\theta} = 1 - \frac{\theta^2}{2!} + \frac{\theta^4}{4!} + \cdots + i\left(\theta - \frac{\theta^3}{3!} + \frac{\theta^5}{5!} - \cdots\right)$$

or

$$e^{i\theta} = \cos\theta + i\sin\theta \tag{25}$$

by comparison with Eqs. (20) and (21).

We may rewrite our general complex number in Eq. (22) through use of Eq. (25). Specifically, if we define $M$ and $\theta$ by

$$z = A + iB \equiv Me^{i\theta} = M\cos\theta + iM\sin\theta \tag{26}$$

it is seen that

$$A = M\cos\theta \quad \text{and} \quad B = M\sin\theta \tag{27}$$

for the real and imaginary parts of Eq. (26) to be equal. Squaring and adding the two requirements in Eq. (27) yields

$$M = \sqrt{A^2 + B^2} \tag{28}$$

where we have used the fact that $\cos^2\theta + \sin^2\theta = 1$. Taking the ratio of the two requirements in Eq. (27), it is seen that

$$\theta = \tan^{-1}(B/A) \tag{29}$$

where we have used the identity, $\tan\theta = \sin\theta/\cos\theta$. Equations (28) and (29) thus permit writing our general complex number $z = A + iB$ in the *polar form*, $z = Me^{i\theta}$. Here the quantity $M$ is known as the *modulus* and $\theta$ is a *phase angle*.

It is important to note that, whereas the addition and subtraction of two complex numbers are most appropriately done by expressing the numbers in terms of their separate real and imaginary parts, multiplication and division are best done in polar form. That is, in addition and subtraction, one merely adds or subtracts the real and imaginary parts separately. However, to multiply two complex numbers, $z_1 = M_1 e^{i\theta_1}$ and $z_2 = M_2 e^{i\theta_2}$, it is simpler to evaluate

$$z_1 z_2 = (M_1 M_2)e^{i(\theta_1 + \theta_2)} \tag{30}$$

than to work out

$$z_1 z_2 = (A_1 + iB_1)(A_2 + iB_2) = (A_1 A_2 - B_1 B_2) + i(B_1 A_2 + A_1 B_2) \tag{31}$$

Equation (30) only requires one multiplication and one addition, whereas Eq. (31) requires four multiplications, one addition, and one subtraction. Similar conclusions hold for the division of two complex numbers and for raising a complex number to a power.

---

**2.8**
**PROBLEM 9**

Write a program that evaluates the *p*th root (i.e., $z^{1/p}$) for a general complex number

$$z = A + iB$$

where $A$ and $B$ are entered from the keyboard and $A$, $B$, and $p$ are real. Use Eqs. (28) and (29) to express the complex number in polar form and note that, if $z = Me^{i\theta}$,

$$z^{1/p} = (M^{1/p})e^{i\theta/p}$$

Print out the real and imaginary parts of the final answer. Use the BASIC function $M\uparrow(1/P)$ to compute the modulus of the result and make sure that you get the angle in the right quadrant (determined by the separate signs for $A$ and $B$). Print out the real and imaginary parts of the result.

---

The roots of the quadratic equation

$$Y = ax^2 + bx + c$$

occur at

$$X_\pm = \frac{-b \pm \sqrt{b^2 - 4ac}}{2a} \tag{32}$$

and are *real* if

$$b^2 > 4ac$$

*degenerate* if

$$b^2 = 4ac$$

and *imaginary* if

$$b^2 < 4ac$$

These results (developed initially by the Hindus) are easiest to visualize graphically in terms of the family of parabolas illustrated in Fig. 2-2.

**2.9**
**Finding Real Roots or Zero Crossings of Polynomials**

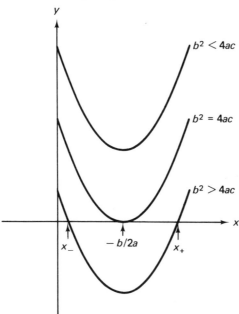

**Fig. 2-2.** Dependence of the roots of the quadratic equation $y = ax^2 + bx + c$ on the parameters $a$, $b$, and $c$.

Write a program that computes roots for a general quadratic equation and tells whether they are real, degenerate, or imaginary.

Although analogous formulas for higher-order equations exist in specific cases (e.g., Cardan's formula for the cubic), they are too complicated to be worth the effort in most problems. Generally, it is much easier to find the roots numerically than to set up the complicated closed-form expressions. The numerical method has the virtue of working for polynomials of any degree.

In general, there will be $N$ roots for an Nth-order equation. The complex roots will occur in complex-conjugate pairs (if there are any). The real roots will all represent zero crossings. One can also deduce some aspects of the problem from the limiting behavior at $X \to \pm\infty$, etc.

The most rudimentary kind of program for determining zero crossings merely uses the operator as part of the loop. For example, consider the following program:

```
10   DEF FNY(X) = ...
20   PRINT "X";
30   INPUT X
40   PRINT FNY(X)
50   GO TO 20
100  END
```

Here the specific polynomial is defined with the BASIC function FNY($X$) on line 10 and the program depends on the operator's insight. One just keeps feeding in values of $X$ from the keyboard and printing $Y = f(x)$. The (only) advantage of this approach is that it couples all one's previous knowledge and experience into the program with minimum programming effort. With a little practice, zero crossings can be ground out with remarkable speed.

Use an interactive program of the type discussed in the text to find the real roots to $y = 5x^5 + 4x^4 + 3x^3 + 2x^2 + x + 1$.

A more automatic method is, of course, desirable. Consider an approach in which we sweep through some domain of the independent variable in steps of reasonable size and record approximate values of the zero crossings as they occur. We can then develop a reiterative technique based on a Taylor expansion to narrow in on the zero crossings. For this purpose, values of the derivative of the function are needed. One could, of course, compute approximate numerical values of the derivative from two successive values of the function. However, it is generally much faster and more precise to evaluate the derivative in closed form. We shall therefore incorporate two BASIC function statements,

```
10   DEF FNY(X) = ...      [ = y(x)]
20   DEF FND(X) = ...      ( = dy/dx)
```

defined as the original function and its derivative. We shall then introduce a column array large enough to store all the zero crossings for an Nth-order polynomial,

```
30   DIM Z( ... )
```

and use the index $J$ to count the zero crossings as we find them.

```
35   LET J = 1
```

Next we will search a range $X1 < X < X2$ in coarse steps, $S$, and examine the function at $X$ and $X + S$ to see if it underwent a sign change (therefore zero crossing).

47

```
37   INPUT X1, X2, S
40   FOR X = X1 TO X2 STEP S
50   LET Y1 = FNY(X)
60   LET Y2 = FNY(X + S)
70   IF SGN(Y1) = SGN(T2) THEN 200
100  ...
200  NEXT X
```

Recalling that the BASIC function SGN($X$) takes the values

$$\text{SGN}(X) = \begin{cases} +1 & \text{for } X > 0 \\ 0 & \text{for } X = 0 \\ -1 & \text{for } X < 0 \end{cases}$$

it is clear that line 7Ø will throw out values FN$Y(X)$ and FN$Y(X+S)$ which fall on the same side of the $x$ axis. Therefore, the program only gets to line 1ØØ if the function has hit a zero crossing in the interval between $X$ and $X+S$.

Starting on line 1ØØ, we will narrow in on the zero crossing reiteratively: first we let $XØ = X$ and compute the derivative in the linear term of a Taylor expansion for the function about the point $X = XØ$. Then we compute a required displacement $D$ so that we would land on the zero crossing in one step, $D$, if the higher terms in the Taylor series were all negligible. We shall probably miss the zero crossing on the first step. However, the process will get more and more accurate as we make more and more interations. Thus we want to find a step $D$ so that

$$0 \equiv f(XØ + D) = f(XØ) + (df/dx)_{xØ}D$$

Hence

$$D = -f(XØ)/(df/dx)_{xØ} \tag{33}$$

We then let $XØ = X + D$ and reiterate until $f(XØ) = 0$ within a specified limit of error. At that point we will have found the zero crossing and will store it in the array element, $Z(J)$, increment $J$, and go back to the original search procedure within the domain $X1 < X < X2$. These steps can be incorporated through a series of statements of the type

```
100  LET X0 = X
110  LET Y1 = FNY(X0)
120  IF ABS(Y1) < ... THEN 180
130  LET X1 = FND(X0)
140  IF X1 = 0 THEN 200
150  LET D = -Y1/X1
160  LET X0 = X0 + D
170  GOTO 110
180  LET Z(J) = X0
190  LET J = J + 1
200  NEXT X
```

Line 14Ø checks to make sure the derivative is not 0. If the slope is zero, we will not get anywhere with the above method, and it is best to choose the point $XØ = X + S$ and start over. Once the criterion is met on accuracy, we store the zero crossing (line 18Ø) and increment $J$ (line 19Ø).

We then go back to the next value of $X$ in the search procedure (line 2ØØ). After completing the loop on $X$, statements of the type

```
FOR I = 1 TO J - 1
PRINT Z(I);
NEXT I
```

list all the zero crossings found.

The method above can be extended to find the maxima and minima as well. We merely need to replace FNY(X) with FND(X) and FND(X) with the second derivative of the function. There will be a tendency to miss points of inflection in this approach unless one rounds off the values of FND(X) using the integer function before comparing the signs. Hence a better conditional check on line 7Ø for determining extrema might be

70   IF SGN (INT(FND(X) + .5)) = SGN(INT(FND(X + S) + .5)) THEN 20Ø

Then if the step size, S, is suitably chosen, one could land close enough to the point of inflection so that the SGN function = 0 (rather than ±1). Without the rounding, one will most probably step right through the point of inflection, in which case the SGN function will not change its value.

---

**2.9**
**PROBLEM 12**

The probability of finding the electron in the 4s excited state of hydrogen a distance $r$ from the nucleus is proportional to

$$f(r) = \left(1 - \frac{3r}{4} + \frac{r^2}{8} - \frac{r^3}{192}\right)^2 e^{-r/2}$$

where $r$ is in units of the *Bohr radius* $(= 0.529173 \times 10^{-8}$ cm). Find the points where the probability goes to zero.

---

## 2.10 Vectors

A vector is a quantity that has both magnitude and direction. Many entities in the three-dimensional world (e.g., force, velocity, and acceleration) possess both magnitude and direction and may be conveniently regarded as vectors. However, the mathematical concepts involved may easily be extended to problems with any number of dimensions.

The primary usefulness of vectors arises from the law for vector addition. Stated in the most elementary way, one does the vector sum

$$\vec{C} = \vec{A} + \vec{B}$$

by drawing the tail of the arrow representing vector $\vec{B}$ at the head of the arrow standing for vector $\vec{A}$:

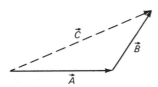

The magnitudes are proportional to the lengths of the arrows and the directions are indicated by the heads of the arrows in the drawing. Because both vectors $\vec{A}$ and $\vec{B}$ have been represented by straight lines, it follows from Euclidean geometry that the two vectors and their resultant, $\vec{C}$, all fall in one plane. One also sees on this simple geometrical level that vector addition obeys the commutative law. that is,

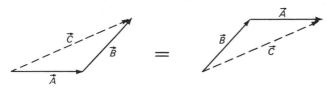

or

$$\vec{C} = \vec{A} + \vec{B} = \vec{B} + \vec{A} \tag{34}$$

For example, no matter in what order you add them, the simultaneous application of two forces $\vec{A}$ and $\vec{B}$ to one point on an object is fully equivalent to applying a single force with new direction and magnitude given by $\vec{C}$ in Eq. (34) at the same point.

One can apply the same geometrical argument to the addition of any number of vectors by breaking the sum up into pairs of coplanar vectors. One thus sees that the final sum is independent of the order in which the individual vectors are added.

The inverse process—that of breaking up a vector into components along a set of prescribed directions—is probably the most useful single technique in vector analysis. Once this decomposition has been effected, the addition (or subtraction)[3] of two or more vectors is accomplished merely by the scalar addition (or subtraction) of their components along the prescribed directions. This process is particularly efficient when the basic directions for the decomposition are mutually orthogonal. For example, breaking up general vectors into components along the orthogonal coordinates of a rectangular (or *Cartesian*) reference frame is especially useful. If we write

$$\vec{A} = A_x \hat{i} + A_y \hat{j} + A_z \hat{k} \quad \text{and} \quad \vec{B} = B_x \hat{i} + B_y \hat{j} + B_z \hat{k} \tag{35}$$

where $\hat{i}$, $\hat{j}$, and $\hat{k}$ are unit vectors along the $x$, $y$, and $z$ directions, and where $A_x$, $A_y$, and $A_z$ are the components of $\vec{A}$ and $B_x$, $B_y$, and $B_z$ are the components of $\vec{B}$ along these dirctions, the addition of $\vec{A}$ and $\vec{B}$ becomes

$$\vec{C} = \vec{A} + \vec{B} = (A_x + B_x)\hat{i} + (A_y + B_y)\hat{j} + (A_z + B_z)\hat{k}$$
$$= C_x \hat{i} + C_y \hat{j} + C_z \hat{k} \tag{36}$$

The resultant vector is then automatically specified in terms of components along the original set of base vectors, $\hat{i}$, $\hat{j}$, and $\hat{k}$.

It is natural to use different rows of the same column array to specify the different components of a vector within a computer program. Specifically, a convention in which the vector $\vec{R}$ is represented by the column array R(I) with

$$R(1) = R_x = \text{component of } \vec{R} \text{ in the } x \text{ direction}$$
$$R(2) = R_y = \text{component of } \vec{R} \text{ in the } y \text{ direction}$$
$$R(3) = R_z = \text{component of } \vec{R} \text{ in the } z \text{ direction}$$

leads to considerable economy in programming statements. One frequently can write a general statement defining the Ith component within a loop in which the index, I, runs over the number of components required.

The *scalar* or *dot product* of the vectors $\vec{A}$ and $\vec{B}$ is defined by

**2.11
Scalar or Dot Product**

$$\vec{A} \cdot \vec{B} = AB \cos \theta \tag{37}$$

where $\theta$ is the angle between the two vectors and $A$ and $B$ are the magnitudes of the two vectors. (Note the "dot" between $\vec{A}$ and $\vec{B}$ on the left side of the equation.) The resultant has magnitude and no direction—hence the name *scalar product*. This product is especially useful in the decomposition of vectors into components along orthogonal axes.

In the case where the vectors $\vec{A}$ and $\vec{B}$ are orthogonal, $\theta = 90°$ and $\vec{A} \cdot \vec{B} = 0$. Similarly, if the two vectors are collinear, $\theta = 0$ and $\vec{A} \cdot \vec{B} = AB$.

---

[3] As with subtraction in ordinary arithmetic, vector subtraction is accomplished by adding a vector of opposite sign (hence direction). thus

$$C = \vec{A} - \vec{B} = \vec{A} + (-\vec{B}) \quad \text{or} \quad \vec{A} - \vec{B} \diagup \vec{B} \quad = \quad \vec{A} + (-\vec{B}) \diagup (-\vec{B})$$

Clearly, the dot product between any two orthogonal, base vectors is zero; i.e.,

$$\hat{i} \cdot \hat{j} = \hat{j} \cdot \hat{k} = \hat{k} \cdot \hat{i} = 0 \tag{38}$$

where $\hat{i}$, $\hat{j}$, and $\hat{k}$ are the unit vectors along the x, y, and z axes.

Noting that the components of the vector $\vec{A}$ along these axes will be of the form $A \cos \theta_i$ (where $\theta_i$ is the angle between $\vec{A}$ and the ith coordinate axis), it is apparent that

$$\vec{A} = (\vec{A} \cdot \hat{i})\hat{i} + (\vec{A} \cdot \hat{j})\hat{j} + (\vec{A} \cdot \hat{k})\hat{k} = A_x\hat{i} + A_y\hat{j} + A_z\hat{k} \tag{39}$$

Finally, note that

$$\vec{A} \cdot \vec{B} = (A_x\hat{i} + A_y\hat{j} + A_z\hat{k}) \cdot (B_x\hat{i} + B_y\hat{j} + B_z\hat{k})$$
$$= A_xB_x + A_yB_y + A_zB_z \tag{40}$$

for any two vectors $\vec{A}$ and $\vec{B}$, because of the orthogonality of the unit base vectors.

Thus if we store the separate components of $\vec{A}$ and $\vec{B}$ (along orthogonal base vectors) as elements in three-rowed column arrays, $A(I)$ and $B(I)$, the dot product $\vec{A} \cdot \vec{B}$ is obtained in a BASIC program of the type

```
10  LET S = 0
20  FOR I = 1 TO 3
30  LET S = A(I)*B(I) + S
40  NEXT I
50  PRINT S
```

(We shall consider a more compact way of evaluating the dot product based on matrix operations in a later section.)

It will be appreciated that the same notions could be applied mathematically to problems having any number of dimensions. That is, as long as the base vectors are all mutually orthogonal, we could compute a generalized dot product for an N-dimensional problem by letting I run from 1 to N on line 20 above. This concept is particularly useful in problems involving expansions in sets of functions which are orthogonal in a purely mathematical sense. Such problems arise in fields ranging in diversity from pattern recognition to literary style analysis.

The *vector or cross product* of two vectors $\vec{A}$, $\vec{B}$ is defined by

## 2.12
## Vector or Cross Product

$$\vec{A} \times \vec{B} = AB \sin \theta \hat{n} = -\vec{B} \times \vec{A} \tag{41}$$

and is a vector in the direction that a right-handed screw would advance when $\vec{A}$ is rotated into $\vec{B}$. ($\hat{n}$ is a unit normal in that direction and is perpendicular to both $\vec{A}$ and $\vec{B}$.) The cross product is particularly useful in setting up orthogonal sets of base vectors.

It is convenient to choose *right-handed coordinate systems*. For example, unit vectors $\hat{i}$, $\hat{j}$, and $\hat{k}$ used to describe the rectangular coordinates x, y, and z are usually chosen so that

$$\hat{i} \times \hat{j} = \hat{k}, \quad \hat{j} \times \hat{k} = \hat{i}, \quad \text{and} \quad \hat{k} \times \hat{i} = \hat{j} \tag{42}$$

In such a rectangular coordinate system, the cross product of two vectors $\vec{A}$

and $\vec{B}$ may be shown from the above definition to be equal to a determinant:

$$\vec{A} \times \vec{B} = \begin{vmatrix} \hat{i} & \hat{j} & \hat{k} \\ A_x & A_y & A_z \\ B_x & B_y & B_z \end{vmatrix} = \hat{i}(A_yB_z - B_yA_z) - \hat{j}(A_xB_z - B_xA_z) + \hat{k}(A_xB_y - B_xA_y)$$

$$(43)$$

One of the most powerful aspects of the BASIC language is the ease with which large matrices may be handled. The MAT commands range from purely manipulative operations to ones that perform formidable numerical computations. We shall approach these commands in a gradual manner, starting with the more pedestrian ones first.

A matrix is a rectangular array of numbers denoted by row and column indices. By convention, the first subscript in a general element in an array of the type

$$\begin{pmatrix} M_{11} & M_{12} & M_{13} & M_{14} \\ M_{21} & M_{22} & M_{23} & M_{24} \\ M_{31} & M_{32} & M_{33} & M_{34} \end{pmatrix}$$

represents the number of the row in which it is found and the second subscript represents the column number. As shown, one starts counting rows and columns from the upper left-hand corner. These subscripts are represented by separate indices in BASIC. Thus the general element $M_{IJ}$ in the above matrix would be denoted by $M(I, J)$ in BASIC and the element would occur in the $I$th row and the $J$th column.

The names for matrices are restricted to single letters of the alphabet in BASIC. Thus one can have 26 separate matrices at most within a given program. However, each matrix can have an enormous number of elements. Unless specifically instructed, the BASIC compiler will set aside room for a $10 \times 10$ array when it first encounters a particular matrix in a given program. Dimension statements can be introduced (preferably at the start of a program) to specify the maximum number of array elements in particular matrices. For example, the statement

```
10   DIM M(3,4), N(255,40)
```

would set aside space for a matrix $M$ having 3 rows and 4 columns, together with a matrix $N$ having 255 rows and 40 columns.

The individual elements may be defined in BASIC through statements of the type

```
LET M(I,J) = . . .
```

where I and J are integers varying from 1 to the maximum number consistent with the dimension statements. Matrices may also be read row-wise from the successive numbers in DATA statements through the instruction

```
MAT READ M
```

if the number of rows and columns in $M(I, J)$ is specified in the program. Similarly, the elements stored in a matrix may be printed on the user's terminal with MAT PRINT commands. For example,

```
MAT PRINT M;
```

results in closely spaced row-wise printing of the elements. (Note that if there are more columns in the matrix than the number required to fill the 72-column teletype format, the above instruction results in a carriage return and line advance while each row of the original matrix is printed out.) MAT READ and MAT PRINT commands also may be used on column arrays.

Matrices may be initialized by use of statements of the type

```
MAT M = ZER     (all elements = 0)
MAT M = CON     (all elements = 1)
MAT M = IDN     (all diagonal elements = 1, off diagonal = 0)
```

The above three statements also permit redimensioning the matrix during a program when written in the form

    MAT M = ZER (1Ø,15)

provided that the initial dimension statement contains at least as many rows (1Ø) and columns (15). The mnemonics involved in the above three commands are reasonably self-evident: ZER stands for "zero," CON stands for "constant" ( = 1), and IDN stands for "identity" (as in "identity matrix").

---

**2.13
PROBLEM 13**
Write a simple program in which you initialize a matrix $M$ with $4 \times 4$ elements using the ZER, CON, and IDN commands. Display the result in each case using the MAT PRINT command.

---

In many instances, matrices are primarily useful as a systematic means for storing computed quantities. In these cases, the symmetry properties and other aspects of the matrix elements may be of more interest than the normal manipulations possible with matrix algebra. One case in point involves the incident of the taxi cab number, 1729, and the young Indian mathematics genius, Srinivasa Ramanujan, who was then dying from tuberculosis and the English climate.

**2.14
Ramanujan Problem**

According to C. P. Snow (see the Foreword to Hardy, 1967, p. 37):

> "Hardy used to visit him, as he lay dying in hospital at Putney. It was on one of those visits that there happened the incident of the taxi-cab number. Hardy had gone out to Putney by taxi, as usual his chosen method of conveyance. He went into the room where Ramanujan was lying. Hardy, always inept about introducing a conversation, said, probably without a greeting, and certainly as his first remark: 'I thought the number of my taxi-cab was 1729. It seemed to me rather a dull number.' To which Ramanujan replied: 'No, Hardy! No, Hardy! It is a very interesting number. It is the smallest number expressible as the sum of two cubes in two different ways.'"

The object of the problem is to determine the first few members of the set of numbers "expressible as the sum of two cubes in two different ways," that is, integers for which

$$I^3 + J^3 = K^3 + L^3 \qquad (44)$$

where $I$, $J \neq K$, $L$. The problem has two equally important parts: (1) find a method that works in principle, and (2) make it efficient enough to do the problem in a realistically short time. The reader should be warned that it is not too hard to set this problem up in a way that could take several days of computing time on a high-speed machine. On the other hand, by using various tricks to limit the search, the first two solutions can be found within about 15 seconds using BASIC on a relatively slow computer such as the HP 2116B.

One clearly wants to avoid computing values of $I^3$ needlessly for different integers. It therefore makes sense to store a number, $N$, of integers—cubed in an array at the beginning of the program. For example, to check the first solution, 1729, we shall clearly need

$$N \geqslant (1729)^{1/3} \geqslant 12$$

The reader will be able to verify that the successive solutions occur at

$$N = 12, 16, 24, 27, 32, 34 \,(2), 36, 39, 40, 48 \,(2), \text{etc.}$$

where the parentheses mean that there are two solutions at $N = 34$ and 48.

Hence as a start on the problem, statements of the type

```
30  FOR I = 1 TO N
40  LET A(I) = I↑3
50  NEXT I
```

will store the necessary array. It is next helpful to define a matrix whose elements are made up by sums of the various possible array elements. For example, the statements

```
60   FOR I = 1 TO N
70   FOR J = 1 TO N
80   LET M(I,J) = A(I) + A(J)
90   NEXT J
100  NEXT I
```

define more of these matrix elements than we actually need but will help in discussing the problem.

To solve the problem we merely need to find different elements $M(I, J)$ and $M(K, L)$ such that

$$M(I, J) = M(K, L) \qquad (45)$$

when the indices $I, J$ and $K, L$ are not trivially related. One could merely start with $M(1, 1)$ and compare that element with every other element; then go on to $M(1, 2)$, and so on. However, the machine running time would increase roughly as $N^4$ in that approach, and it pays to use some of the properties of the matrix to advantage.

For specific illustration, consider printing out the matrix defined above in a manageable case, for example, with $N = 8$. Incorporation of a

MAT PRINT M;

statement after the above program results in printing the upper left-hand corner of the general matrix shown in Fig. 2-3.

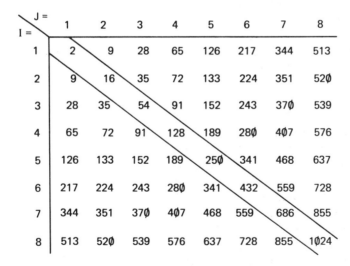

**Fig. 2-3.**

---

**2.14**
**PROBLEM 14**

Write a program that computes and prints the matrix defined on line 80 above for $N = 10$. Note the format that results from the

MAT PRINT $M$,   and   MAT PRINT $M$; statements.

---

Next note that the matrix is symmetric about the diagonal. For any solution we find on one side of the diagonal, there must be a trivially related solution on the other and we do not have to compute, store, or examine more than half the matrix.

Also note that the numbers increase along any row. Hence, if you pick an element on one row, you do not have to compare it with any other element on that same row.

Further, the numbers always increase down the columns. Therefore, if we start a systematic comparison in the upper left-hand corner with the element $M(I, J)$, the comparison only has to be made with elements $M(K, L)$, where $K$ starts on the $(I+1)$th row and runs to the $(J-1)$th row and $L$ starts with the $K$th column. The column index $L$ for the $K$th row in $M(K, L)$ only has to be advanced to

$$L_{max} \approx (M(I, J) - A(K))^{1/3} + 0.5 \qquad (46)$$

because $L^3 + K^3 = M(I, J)$ for the equality to occur ($I$ runs from 1 to $N$ and $J$ from $I$ to $N$). The additional 0.5 in Eq. (46) is to avoid rounding-error difficulties.

---

**2.14 PROBLEM 15**  Write a program to check Ramanujan. Use the limits discussed in connection with Eq. (46) and be cautious about running time. (This one can "break the bank" if you are careless.) Set up the problem for a general, large matrix $M$ and use the

**MAT M = ZER(N,N)**

command to initialize $M$. Print $M(I, J)$ and $I$; $J$, $L$; $K$ for each solution. After you are confident that the program works efficiently, calculate the first several solutions.

---

## 2.15 Matrix Algebra

Next we shall consider some of the more powerful matrix commands—ones that actually do some computing rather than just manipulating arrays of numbers.

Matrix operations in BASIC are performed by MAT instructions analogous to the LET command used with single variables. The instruction

**MAT C = . . .**

applies to every element in the array. The new value of matrix $C$ is set equal, element by element, to the last value of whatever matrix quantity appears on the right side of the equality. In contrast to the LET statement, one cannot use the same matrix on both sides of the = sign in most cases or do more than one MAT operation in the same statement. The reasons for this restriction arise from the economy of storage locations inside the computer. For example, in an operation such as

**MAT C = TRN(A)**

in which the matrix $C$ becomes the transpose of matrix $A$, or

$$C(I, J) = A(J, I)$$

the computer would lose half of the elements in the original matrix if it were instructed to let $A(I, J) = A(J, I)$ for all $I$ and $J$ without use of an intermediate storage matrix.

One of the few exceptions to the above restriction occurs in the command

**MAT C = (K)*C**

in which the new matrix $C$ on the left is determined from the original one on the right by multiplying each element with the same scalar quantity, $K$.

Two matrices are added by summing all corresponding elements. Thus the command

$$\text{MAT } C = A + B$$

results in

$$C(I, J) = A(I, J) + B(I, J) \tag{47}$$

for every value of $I$ and $J$. Obviously all three matrices must have the same dimensions.

Similarly, two matrices are subtracted by subtracting corresponding elements. Hence the statement

$$\text{MAT } C = A - B$$

results in

$$C(I, J) = A(I, J) - B(I, J) \tag{48}$$

for all values of $I$ and $J$. Again, the three matrices obviously have to have the same dimensions.

Although we cannot use the same matrix on both sides of the equality for the more-complicated MAT commands, it is a simple matter to redefine matrices by adding more statements to the program. For example, redefining the matrix $A$ to be the sum of the previous matrices $A$ and $B$ is accomplished through the statements

$$\text{MAT } C = A + B$$
$$\text{MAT } A = C$$

Although any of the MAT commands could be duplicated by use of a sufficient number of loops and LET statements, it is useful to recognize that the MAT commands have been previously compiled in machine-language subroutines within the BASIC language. Consequently, they not only require fewer program statements in BASIC, they usually run much faster than equivalent sets of LET statements written out in long form.

---

**2.15**
**PROBLEM 16**

Write a program that permits comparing the running time for the addition of two large matrices using one

$$\text{MAT } C = A + B$$

command and equivalent LET $C(I, J) = A(I, J) + B(I, J)$ statements within nested loops for $I$ and $J$.

---

**2.16**
**Matrix Multiplication**

The command for matrix multiplication can be one of the most useful ones in BASIC. Multiplication of the matrices $A$ and $B$ is accomplished by the instruction

$$\text{MAT } C = A * B$$

and follows the standard rule,

$$C(I, J) = \sum_{K=1}^{N} A(I, K) B(K, J) \tag{49}$$

where $N$ is the number of columns in matrix $A$ *and* the number of rows in matrix $B$. (There are no restrictions on the number of rows in matrix $A$ or the number of columns in matrix $B$, except those imposed by the dimension statements.) The MAT $C = A * B$ command works out the appropriate summation for *each* element in matrix $C$.

It is worth emphasizing the power of this simple MAT command by specifying the equivalent statements in normal BASIC required to achieve the same result. For example, suppose that we wanted to read in 1000 values from DATA statements to fill in a $20 \times 50$ matrix A (row-wise), 1500 values from subsequent DATA statements to fill in a $50 \times 30$ matrix $B$, and print out the 600 elements in a matrix $(C) = (A)*(B)$. Apart from the DATA statements themselves, the objective is accomplished through the program

```
10    DIM A(20,50),B(50,30),C(20,30)
20    MAT READ A
30    MAT READ B
40    MAT C = A*B
100   MAT PRINT C;
```

in which the semicolon after the MAT PRINT command results in closely spaced printing of the matrix elements. Line 40 in the above program accomplishes the equivalent of the following eight BASIC statements:

```
40    FOR I = 1 TO 20
45    FOR J = 1 TO 30
50    LET C(I,J) = 0
55    FOR K = 1 TO 50
60    LET C(I,J) = C(I,J) + A(I,K)*B(K,J)
65    NEXT K
70    NEXT J
75    NEXT I
```

Because the statement MAT $C = A*B$ makes use of previously compiled machine-language statements, that command is generally executed much more rapidly than would be statements 40 through 75 above. Also note that the upper limits on the FOR statements (lines 40, 45, and 55 above) would automatically be filled in from the dimension statements in the command MAT $C = A*B$. Conversely, if the computer has not been given appropriate dimension statements, it will not know what to do with the command MAT $C = A*B$.

As is apparent from the definition of matrix multiplication, the process is definitely not commutative. One has to be careful about the order of multiplication and there can be substantial differences between the statements

```
40    MAT C = A*B
```

and

```
40    MAT C = B*A
```

In fact, for the specific program given above, MAT $C = B*A$ would not even have been allowed. (The dimensions do not permit multiplication.)

However, the associative and distributive laws are still obeyed. As may be shown from the definitions of matrix multiplication and addition, both

$$A(BC) = (AB)C \quad \text{and} \quad A(B + C) = (AB) + (AC)$$

## 2.17
## Some Useful Tricks with Matrix Multiplication

The fact that the primary definition of matrix multiplication involves a summation immediately suggests some useful shortcuts in a wide variety of problems. Frequently, many programming statements can be avoided and running time can be greatly reduced by setting up summations as matrix products. A few examples will clarify the advantage.

Consider the extreme situation where we merely want to add up all the numbers in a long DATA statement. For specific example, suppose that there are 250 numbers in the series of DATA entries. We can accomplish the summation with MAT commands if we introduce a few specially dimensioned matrices:

```
10    DIM S(1,1),A(250,1),B(1,250)
```

Matrix $S$ will consist of one element in which we shall compute the desired sum. We can initially read the DATA statements into matrix $A$ (which is literally equivalent to a column array with 250 rows)[4] with the statement

    20   MAT READ A

and prepare a row matrix $B$ (having 250 columns) by the statement

    30   MAT B − CON

which defines every element equal to unity. The sum is then obtained through the statements

    40   MAT S = B*A
    50   MAT PRINT S

[i.e., apply the definition of matrix multiplication summarized in Eq. (49)]. Here we have merely multiplied each element in $A$ by unity and have only used the rule for matrix multiplication to do the summation. The economy in programming statements is debatable in this particular case; however, considerable saving in running time over straightforward summation can be obtained on long sums (especially with minicomputers in which each line in the BASIC program is interpreted sequentially while the program is running).

A fuller utilization of the power of matrix multiplication is obtained in the evaluation of scalar products of row and column matrices (especially in cases where there is a large number of elements in the arrays). For example, suppose that we wanted to compute the generalized dot (or scalar) product of two vectors having 100 projections (or components) on orthogonal axes. Assuming that the values for the components of these two vectors have been entered sequentially in DATA statements elsewhere in the program, we can get the data into the program by statements of the type

    10   DIM A(100,1),B(1,100),S(1,1)
    20   MAT READ A
    30   MAT READ B

We again dimension $S$ to represent a matrix with one element and compute the desired scalar product [Eq. (40)] through the command

    50   MAT S = B*A

That is, $S(1, 1) = \sum B(1, J)A(J, 1)$ by definition (49).

As a variant on the above approach, one could enter both sets of data in column matrix format and then transpose one matrix prior to the multiplication command. For example,

    10   DIM A(100,1),B(100,1),C(1,100),S(1,1)
    20   MAT READ A
    30   MAT READ B
    40   MAT C = TRN(A)
    50   MAT S = C*B

accomplishes the same result as the previous program.

---

**2.17
PROBLEM 17**    Write a program that permits the operator to enter a large $N$-bit binary integer one digit at a time and which then prints the base 10 equivalent of the number. Do the problem by a MAT multiplication command; e.g., store the binary digits in a row matrix and the values of $2^M$ (for $0 \le M \le N$) in a column matrix. The decimal equivalent is then given by the product of the two matrices.

---

[4] BASIC tacitly treats column arrays as column matrices in all MAT commands. One could have written DIM $A(250)$ instead of DIM $A(250, 1)$.

One very frequent application of matrix algebra occurs in the solution of simultaneous linear equations. Consider the set of equations

$$y_1 = a_{11}x_1 + a_{12}x_2 + \cdots + a_{1N}x_N$$
$$y_2 = a_{21}x_1 + a_{22}x_2 + \cdots + a_{2N}x_N$$
$$\cdot$$
$$\cdot \qquad\qquad\qquad\qquad\qquad\qquad (50)$$
$$\cdot$$
$$y_N = a_{N1}x_1 + a_{N2}x_2 + \cdots + a_{NN}x_N$$

involving $N$ unknown quantities $(x_1, x_2, \ldots, x_N)$, $N$ known quantities $(y_1, y_2, \ldots, y_N)$, and a set of $N \times N$ known coefficients $(a_{11}, a_{12}, \ldots, a_{NN})$.

Such equations may be solved by hand through a well-known and extremely tedious method based on the evaluation of determinants: one first computes the determinant of the coefficients

$$\det A = \begin{vmatrix} a_{11} & a_{12} & \cdots & a_{1N} \\ a_{21} & a_{22} & \cdots & a_{2N} \\ \cdot & & & \\ \cdot & & & \\ \cdot & & & \\ a_{N1} & a_{N2} & \cdots & a_{NN} \end{vmatrix} \qquad (51)$$

and (assuming the above determinant is not equal to zero, or "singular"), the unknown quantities are given by

$$x_1 = \frac{\begin{vmatrix} y_1 & a_{12} & \cdots & a_{1N} \\ y_2 & a_{22} & \cdots & a_{2N} \\ \cdot & & & \\ \cdot & & & \\ \cdot & & & \\ y_N & a_{N2} & \cdots & a_{NN} \end{vmatrix}}{\det A}, \qquad x_2 = \frac{\begin{vmatrix} a_{11} & y_1 & \cdots & a_{1N} \\ a_{21} & y_2 & \cdots & a_{2N} \\ \cdot & & & \\ \cdot & & & \\ \cdot & & & \\ a_{N1} & y_N & \cdots & a_{NN} \end{vmatrix}}{\det A}, \quad \text{etc.} \quad (52)$$

Although the approach is not too bad for evaluating two or three simultaneous equations, hand analysis is distinctly painful for $N$ much greater than 3. One very great virtue of a programming language such as BASIC is that an equivalent analysis can be very concisely handled by MAT operations. First, note that the original set of linear equations (50) can be expressed as one matrix equation,

$$(Y) = (A)(X) \qquad\qquad\qquad (53)$$

provided both $Y$ and $X$ are column matrices with $N$ rows and $A$ is a square matrix with $N$ rows and columns. That is, we define the matrix elements so that

$$Y(I, 1) = y_I, \quad X(I, 1) = x_I, \quad \text{and} \quad A(I, J) = a_{IJ} \qquad (54)$$

in the initial set of linear equations. Then from the definition of matrix multiplication in Eq. (49),

$$Y(I, 1) = \sum_{J=1}^{N} A(I, J)X(J, 1) \qquad \text{for } I = 1 \text{ to } N$$

and the original set of equations (50) is contained within successive rows of the matrix equation (53). We, of course, have to dimension these matrices appropriately in a computer program and somehow get the numerical values in for the known elements. Once these preliminary operations have been performed, the set of equations is solved "merely" by inverting the matrix $A(I, J)$.

The inverse $(A^{-1})$ of the matrix $(A)$ satisfies the requirement that

$$(A^{-1})*(A) = (\mathbf{1}) = (A)*(A^{-1}) \qquad\qquad (55)$$

Here (**1**) is the identity matrix

$$(\mathbf{1}) = \begin{pmatrix} 1 & 0 & 0 & 0 & 0 & \cdots \\ 0 & 1 & 0 & 0 & 0 & \cdots \\ 0 & 0 & 1 & 0 & 0 & \cdots \\ 0 & 0 & 0 & 1 & 0 & \cdots \\ 0 & 0 & 0 & 0 & 1 & \cdots \\ \cdot & \cdot & \cdot & \cdot & \cdot & \cdots \end{pmatrix} \tag{56}$$

and has the property that

$$(A)*(\mathbf{1}) = (A) = (\mathbf{1})*(A) \tag{57}$$

where enough rows and columns on the identity matrix are used to satisfy the requirements of the summation in the definition of matrix multiplication.

If we multiply our original matrix equation (53) through from the left by $A^{-1}$, it is seen that

$$(A^{-1})(Y) = (A^{-1}A)(X) = (\mathbf{1})(X) = (X)$$

where we have used Eqs. (55) and (57). Hence the solution to the original set of equations is contained in the statement

$$(X) = (A^{-1})(Y) \tag{58}$$

In order to get the inverse matrix, one has to do something which is formally equivalent to the determinant solution (52) of the original linear equations (50). One of the great virtues of the BASIC language is that a machine-language program is built into the compiler which does all this dull tedium for us. The command

MAT B = INV(A)

(assuming that $B$ is appropriately dimensioned) causes the computer to go off into machine language and return a small fraction of a second later with the inverted matrix. One must keep in mind, however, that the computer will run into the same restrictions that a human would encounter in solving the same set of equations by hand. Namely, if the determinant of $A = 0$ (or is made equal to zero due to rounding errors), the computer will not be able to invert the matrix and will return with an error-diagnostic message instead (e.g., "MAT SINGU-LAR IN LINE...").

Suppose, for instance, that we want to solve four simultaneous equations for which the numerical values of $Y(I, 1)$ and $A(I, J)$ have been entered row-wise in DATA statements. The following program accomplishes the objective:

```
10   DIM X(4,1),Y(4,1),A(4,4),B(4,4)
20   MAT READ Y
30   MAT READ A
40   MAT B = INV(A)
50   MAT X = B*Y
60   MAT PRINT X;
```

Assuming that MAT $B$ is not singular, the solution is printed on line 6∅.

If we have no more than 10 simultaneous equations to solve, specific DIM statements (such as those on line 1∅ above) are not required. However, we still must use some command [e.g., MAT $X = $ZER$(N, 1)$] to indicate the required number of rows and columns in each matrix in the program.

The celebrated input–output theory of economics developed by Wassily Leontief and others consists largely of an exercise in matrix inversion. One assumes that one can apply a set of linear equations to relate the output production and input requirements in an isolated economic system. Once

**2.19
Economics and Matrix Inversion**

adequate numerical coefficients have been determined for the system, the method provides quantitative answers for production input necessary to achieve specified net output objectives in a controlled economy. In any real system, a tremendous number of interrelated production activities would have to be included, and the success of the approach would depend both on the accuracy of the measured numerical coefficients and the ability to invert high-order matrices. Further, the validity of the assumption of linearity in such a system is not obvious, and the long-term reliability of the approach is somewhat tenuous. (For example, it would be very hard to allow quantitatively for the nonlinear effects that will inevitably result from the depletion of fossil fuels.) However, on a short-term basis involving small changes in a closed economic system with a relatively small number of variables, the method appears to have useful potential.

For the sake of a specific example, consider an economic system composed of the following four industries: a dairy farm, a high-protein-feed producer, an electric power company, and an oil refinery. These industries are mutually dependent and in some cases consume a significant fraction of their own output. For example, an efficient dairy farm requires high-protein cattle feed as well as electricity and tractor fuel for operation. It also consumes milk. (Newborn calves are required both to replace older cows and to stimulate the flow of milk in adult cows.) Similarly, the work force in all four of these industries consumes milk at a rate that should be proportional to the number of man-hours expended, and in two of the remaining industries some of the output has to be fed back into the input to "prime the pump."

The easiest way to specify the interdependence of the four industries quantitatively is to ask what inputs are required from the four industries for unit gross output in each case. Suppose, for example, that a gross output of 1 gallon of milk from the dairy industry requires the following input on the average:

0.035 gallon of milk

2.34 pounds of high-protein feed

0.58 kilowatt-hour of electrical power

0.0083 gallon of tractor fuel

and that equivalent data are available for the other industries.[5] If we assume that the equations describing the economic system are linear (i.e., depend only on the first powers of the variables), we can add all such data sets in one matrix equation.

Specifically, we might relate the required input quantities ($I$) to the gross output quantities ($G$) through a square matrix ($M$) containing the coefficients characteristic of the industries:

$$
\begin{pmatrix} I_1 \\ (\text{gal}) \\ I_2 \\ (\text{lb}) \\ I_3 \\ (\text{kWh}) \\ I_4 \\ (\text{gal}) \end{pmatrix}
=
\begin{pmatrix}
0.035\,\frac{\text{gal}}{\text{gal}} & 0.00006\,\frac{\text{gal}}{\text{lb}} & 0.000015\,\frac{\text{gal}}{\text{kWh}} & 0.00007\,\frac{\text{gal}}{\text{gal}} \\
2.34\,\frac{\text{lb}}{\text{gal}} & 0\,\frac{\text{lb}}{\text{lb}} & 0\,\frac{\text{lb}}{\text{kWh}} & 0\,\frac{\text{lb}}{\text{gal}} \\
0.58\,\frac{\text{kWh}}{\text{gal}} & 0.01\,\frac{\text{kWh}}{\text{lb}} & 0.12\,\frac{\text{kWh}}{\text{kWh}} & 0.01\,\frac{\text{kWh}}{\text{gal}} \\
0.0083\,\frac{\text{gal}}{\text{gal}} & 0.0018\,\frac{\text{gal}}{\text{lb}} & 0.075\,\frac{\text{gal}}{\text{kWh}} & 0.1\,\frac{\text{gal}}{\text{gal}}
\end{pmatrix}
\begin{pmatrix} G_1 & \text{milk} \\ & (\text{gal}) \\ G_2 & \text{feed} \\ & (\text{lb}) \\ G_3 & \text{power} \\ & (\text{kWh}) \\ G_4 & \text{fuel} \\ & (\text{gal}) \end{pmatrix}
$$

[5] The dairy data used here are based on a New York State farm operated by John Bruise (see *The New York Times*, Nov. 23, 1974, p. 64, cols. 3–8). The author is indebted to Mrs. Bruise for a helpful discussion of the economics of dairy farming and to Mr. Klebanow of Maxim Mills for information regarding the economics of high-protein-feed production. The data on electric power and fuel industries are estimates from miscellaneous reports during the fall of 1974.

$$(I) = (M)(G) \tag{59}$$

in which $(I)$ and $(G)$ are four-rowed column matrices and $(M)$ is the large $4 \times 4$ square matrix. Because there are a lot of different units involved in this equation, the units have been written explicitly. The diagonal elements in $M$ are all dimensionless. However, the off-diagonal elements involve quantities such as gallons of milk per gallon of fuel, pounds of feed per kilowatt-hour, etc. Note that the columns in the matrix $M$ represent the required inputs for unit gross output of the different gross products in array $G$. Specifically, if we let $G_1 = 1$ gallon of milk and let $G_2 = G_3 = G_4 = 0$, we get the set of required input quantities for the dairy industry (0.035 gallon of milk, 2.34 pounds of feed, 0.58 kilowatt-hour, and 0.0083 gallon of tractor fuel). Similarly, if we let $G_2 = 1$ pound of high-protein feed and $G_1 = G_3 = G_4 = 0$, we get the required input quantities for the feed industry for unit gross output; i.e., 0.00006 gallon of milk (from the man-hour equivalent), 0.01 kilowatt-hour and 0.0018 gallon of fuel (assumed for the present discussion to be the same as tractor fuel) are required to produce 1 pound of feed.

The *net* output $(O)$ is then given by the matrix equation

$$O = G - I \tag{60}$$

where all quantities are four-rowed column matrices and our basic relation becomes (after substituting $O + I$ for $G$)

$$I = M*(O + I) \tag{61}$$

We may solve the latter equation by computing the inverse matrix for $M$ (i.e., by computing $M^{-1}$) and by multiplying through from the left by $M^{-1}$. That is,

$$M^{-1}*I = M^{-1}*M*(O + I) = (\mathbf{1})*(O + I) = O + I \tag{62}$$

where $(\mathbf{1})$ is the identity matrix. Hence the matrix containing the net output quantities $(O)$ for the input quantities $(I)$ is given by

$$O = M^{-1}*I - I = (M^{-1} - \mathbf{1})*I \tag{63}$$

Finally, by inverting the matrix $(M^{-1} - \mathbf{1})$, we can determine the required input quantities $(I)$ necessary to result in a specified net output $(O)$. That is,

$$I = (M^{-1} - \mathbf{1})^{-1}*O \tag{64}$$

where $\mathbf{1}$ again stands for the identity matrix (a square matrix containing ones on the diagonal and zeros everywhere else). In the last equation, two matrix inversions are to be performed: first we invert the matrix $M$; then we subtract the identity matrix; and then we invert the resultant matrix. The last equation tells what amounts must be plugged back into the industry to give the specified net output.

---

**2.19
PROBLEM 18**   Using the numerical values for the matrix $M$ given in Eq. (59) for the four-industry economic system, compute the necessary input quantities to result in a net output of 10,000 gallons of milk, 100,000 pounds of protein-enriched feed, 1,000,000 kilowatt-hours, and 200,000 gallons of fuel [i.e., solve Eq. (64)].

---

One of the major accomplishments with the early von Neumann computer was the development of efficient algorithms for the inversion of high-order matrices (see von Neumann and Goldstine, 1947). Unfortunately, there is

**2.20
Practical Limitations
on Matrix Inversion**

considerable variation from one BASIC compiler to the next in the accuracy with which matrix inversion is carried out, and few systems have been set up with the sort of capability that was programmed into the von Neumann machine.

The point at which "singularities" in the matrix-inversion process occur is strongly dependent on the nature of the original matrix, the number of bits used by the computer in evaluating the mantissa of floating-point numbers, and the particular inversion algorithm. About all the remote-access time-sharing user can do is to treat the particular computer available as a "black box" and see what it will do. In this process it is useful to have a standard test to perform and a feeling for what representative computers are capable of doing. Generally, one is not too concerned with the time required to accomplish the inversion; usually, one is more concerned with whether or not the inversion can be accomplished at all.

One particularly useful test consists of seeing how large an $N \times N$ matrix of the type

$$M = \begin{pmatrix} 1 & \frac{1}{2} & \frac{1}{3} & \cdots & 1/N \\ \frac{1}{2} & \frac{1}{3} & \frac{1}{4} & \cdots & 1/(N+1) \\ \frac{1}{3} & \frac{1}{4} & \frac{1}{5} & \cdots & 1/(N+2) \\ \cdot & & & & \\ \cdot & & & & \\ \cdot & & & & \\ 1/N & 1/(N+1) & \cdots & \cdots & 1/(2N-1) \end{pmatrix} \quad (65)$$

in which

$$M(I, J) = \frac{1}{(I+J-1)} \quad (66)$$

can be inverted with the particular computer. This matrix (known as a *Hilbert matrix*) provides a good challenge to an inversion subroutine simply because the elements get closer and closer together as $N$ becomes large.

The results obtained by the author in inverting this matrix on different machines in BASIC have been somewhat surprising. There is a natural tendency to assume that the bigger the machine, the bigger the matrix one should be able to invert. It is usually true that one can invert a larger Hilbert matrix by running the same machine in *extended precision* (i.e., using more bits per number). However, the way in which the bits used for each number are split up between mantissa and exponent is left to the whim of the person who originally designed the compiler. For example, it was somewhat astonishing to learn that the version of BASIC available on the Yale University IBM 370 supergiant could not invert more than a $4 \times 4$ Hilbert matrix in normal precision, whereas a little Hewlett-Packard 2100 series minicomputer could invert at least a $5 \times 5$ Hilbert matrix running in BASIC (using a 24-bit mantissa). Running the IBM 370 in extended precision would still only invert a $7 \times 7$ Hilbert matrix, whereas a test on a relatively modest Hewlett-Packard 3000 time-sharing BASIC system indicated that as large as a $12 \times 12$ Hilbert matrix could be inverted in *long precision*. (The H.-P. 3000 BASIC would actually return numerical values for the inverse of a $50 \times 50$ Hilbert matrix. However, occasional off-diagonal elements of $(M^{-1}M)$ were much greater than unity in that instance.) This aspect of life, of course, has relatively little to do with the inherent power of the machine; it is more a question of how the computing power has been applied in the design of individual compilers. However, it can have a very strong bearing on the suitability of a particular time-sharing system for handling the sort of problem that you want to analyze.

Using the definition of the Hilbert matrix in Eq. (66), see how large a Hilbert matrix your particular computer will invert. As a check, multiply the inverse times the original matrix and print out the result. (Ideally, the result should have 1s on the diagonal and zeros everywhere else. The departure from zero of the off-diagonal terms is a measure of the error in the computation.)

Because integration is defined formally as the inverse of differentiation, closed-form expressions for integrals are usually obtained through hindsight. For example, because we already know from Eq. (2) that

**2.21**
**Integration**

$$\frac{d}{dx}(x^m) = mx^{m-1}$$

if we were told that

$$\frac{dy}{dx} = mx^{m-1} \tag{67}$$

we would expect that the function $y(x)$ was originally given by

$$y = x^m + \text{constant} \tag{68}$$

We would not be able to determine the constant in Eq. (68) without additional information. Whatever the constant might have been, its derivative would be zero. Hence, we cannot deduce its value merely from the information in Eq. (67).

The process of determining the result in Eq. (68) from Eq. (67) is known as *integration* and frequently would be written

$$y = \int^y dy = \int^x mx^{m-1}\, dx = x^m + \text{constant}$$

Here we have rewritten the derivative

$$dy = mx^{m-1}\, dx$$

and then *integrated*.

If one can pick out a closed-form expression for the integral of a function (as done in the example), there is usually little point in doing a numerical integration with a computer. However, there are many functions that simply cannot be integrated in closed form. For example, the function itself might only be available through numerical evaluation on a point-by-point basis. In such cases, the computer becomes an indispensible tool for determining integrals.

It is easiest to construct programs to do integrals if the area interpretation of integrals is kept in mind. In particular, consider a function $y = f(x)$ which we would like to integrate in respect to $x$ (see Fig. 2-4).

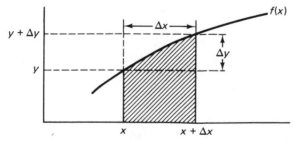

**Fig. 2-4.**

Let us assume that the function $A = A(x)$ exists such that $\Delta A$ represents the area between $x$ and $x + \Delta x$ and between $y = 0$ and $y = f(x)$ (i.e., the shaded area in Fig. 2-4). Obviously,

$$y \, \Delta x < \Delta A < (y + \Delta y) \, \Delta x$$

or

$$y < \frac{\Delta A}{\Delta x} < y + \Delta y$$

Therefore, in the limit that $\Delta x \to 0$, $y = dA/dx$. Hence

$$dA = y \, dx \quad \text{and} \quad A = \int dA = \int^x y \, dx$$

represents the area under the curve $y = f(x)$ up to the point $x$. The constant of integration clearly involves the point from which we start measuring the area. Also note that the area can be positive or negative depending on the extent to which the curve for $y = f(x)$ falls above or below the $x$ axis. The fact that the rate of change of area under the curve is equal to the integrand evaluated at the point $x$ is frequently called the *Fundamental Theorem of Calculus*.

## 2.22 Definite Integrals

Because digital computers work problems numerically, they can only evaluate "definite" integrals. As an example, suppose that we want to specify the area under the curve $y = f(x)$ between the points $x = a$ and $x = b$. We would write this quantity as the difference between two integrals,

$$\int^{x=b} y \, dx - \int^{x=a} y \, dx \equiv \int_a^b y \, dx \tag{69}$$

in which the (same) constant of integration would cancel out. (The final notation used at the right to describe the definite integral was originally introduced by Joseph von Fourier in his early-nineteenth-century paper on the theory of heat flow.)

We can do such definite integrals with a computer by breaking up the interval into a large number of increments and by adding up approximate values for each of the small area elements. The accuracy of such a computation will generally increase with both the number of area elements used and the accuracy with which they are determined.

For example, to do the definite integral $\int_a^b f(x) \, dx$, we could lay out $n$ equally spaced points along the $x$-axis with a constant separation

$$\Delta x = \frac{x_n - x_1}{n - 1}$$

Then $x_1 = a$ and $x_n = b$ and we want to do the integral

$$I = \int_{x_1}^{x_n} f(x) \, dx \tag{70}$$

by means of a summation over the $(n-1)$ intervals of width $\Delta x$.

At the simplest extreme, one might assume the value of $y$ to be constant over each interval. For example, if we merely assumed that $y = y_1 = f(x_1)$ for $x_1 \leqslant x \leqslant x_2$, $y = y_2 = f(x_2)$ for $x_2 \leqslant x \leqslant x_3$, and so on, we would obtain a sort of zeroth-order approximation to the integral which is particularly easy to evaluate:

$$I_0 \approx (y_1 + y_2 + y_3 + \cdots + y_{n-1}) \, \Delta x \tag{71}$$

The approximation turns the curve into a "staircase" and clearly underestimates the area elements when the curve goes up and overestimates the area elements when the curve goes down (see Fig. 2-5). Corrections through at least one more order of sophistication are easy to make and there usually is little excuse for leaving the problem at the zeroth approximation represented by Eq. (71). (Note that the zeroth approximation can easily be accomplished using MAT multiplication commands.)

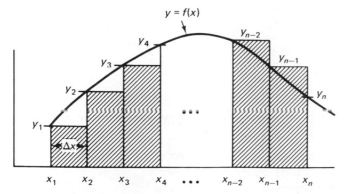

**Fig. 2-5.**

The next level of approximation is that known as the *Trapezoidal Rule.* Here we just draw straight-line segments between the successive points and add up the areas of all the trapezoids so produced (see Fig. 2-6). This method

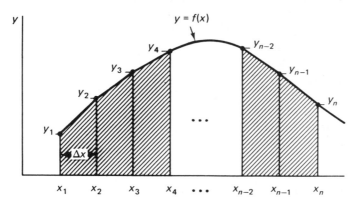

**Fig. 2-6.**

is equivalent to taking the average value, $\bar{y}$, of the function over each successive interval and calculating the sum of the terms $\bar{y} \, \Delta x$. The result for the integral in this case is

$$I_1 = 0.5(y_1 + y_2) \Delta x + 0.5(y_2 + y_3) \Delta x + \cdots + 0.5(y_{n-1} + y_n) \Delta x$$
$$= (y_1 + y_2 + y_3 + \cdots + y_{n-1}) \Delta x + 0.5(y_n - y_1) \Delta x$$
$$= I_0 + 0.5(y_n - y_1) \Delta x \tag{72}$$

where

$$\Delta x = \frac{x_n - x_1}{n - 1}$$

Note that the result for the Trapezoidal Rule differs only by the term $0.5(y_n - y_1) \Delta x$ from the zeroth-order approximation in Eq. (71) and that this additional correction adds a negligible amount of computing time to the problem when $n$ is large. Also note that the additional correction vanishes identically when $y_n = y_1$ (as occurs, for example, when the function is periodic in the distance, $x_n - x_1$).

In progressively higher-order approximations to the problem, one fits still-higher-order curves through progressively larger numbers of points. Thus the next level of approximation, known as *Simpson's rule*, consists of fitting parabolas through successive groups of three points and of doing an integration of the three-point parabolas in closed form. Current ramifications of this technique go under the heading *spline interpolation* (see for example, Schultz, 1972).

It is useful to note that the increasing orders of approximation outlined above amount formally to expanding the initial function in a Taylor series in $\Delta x$, over each interval $\Delta x$. Thus the zeroth approximation uses the leading term [dependence on $(\Delta x)^0$], the Trapezoidal Rule involves a first-order correction [dependence on $(\Delta x)^1$], Simpson's rule involves a second-order correction [dependence on $(\Delta x)^2$], and so on. Consequently, the error neglected in each approximation involves the next-higher power of $\Delta x$. For example, we are neglecting errors of order $(\Delta x)^2$ in the expansion for the integrand when we apply the Trapezoidal Rule. One can generally reduce this error to a prescribed level by taking sufficiently small intervals. Consequently, the higher-order approximations are only valuable for the computer analysis of integrals when they result in a shorter running time for the same accuracy. In most cases, it is both cheaper and more convenient merely to increase the number of points using the Trapezoidal Rule than to invoke the next-higher-order approximation with the original number of points. For that reason, we shall not bother here with anything more complicated than the Trapezoidal Rule.

---

**2.22**
**PROBLEM 20**

The Trapezoidal Rule will be least reliable in regions where the first derivative of the integrand is negligible compared to higher derivatives. Investigate this effect by writing programs to evaluate

$$\int_0^1 x^m \, dx = \frac{1}{m+1} \quad \text{and} \quad \int_1^2 x^m \, dx = \frac{2^{m+1}-1}{m+1}$$

For example, how many numerical integration intervals do you need for $m=2$ in each case to get the answer within 0.1 percent? Note the oscillatory nature of error with decreasing interval size (which arises from rounding errors).

---

## 2.23
## Pattern Recognition and Integration

Pattern recognition represents a potentially important area of computer application in problems ranging in diversity from the identification of letters on a printed page to the analysis of microscope slides for the presence of precancerous cell nuclei.

One approach to the problem consists of expanding the unknown "function" (which might be computed from the intensity distribution in scanning a photograph) in a set of *orthogonal functions* and then categorizing the sequence of expansion coefficients so obtained. Two functions, $f_n(x)$ and $f_m(x)$, are said to be orthogonal over the interval $0 \le x \le 1$ if

$$\int_0^1 f_n(x) f_m(x) \, dx = 0 \quad \text{for} \quad n \ne m \tag{73}$$

and are normalizzed over this interval if

$$\int_0^1 [f_m(x)]^2 \, dx = 1 \qquad \text{for all } m \tag{74}$$

A set of functions satisfying the combined properties (73) and (74) is said to be *orthonormal*. (We shall limit the discussion to real functions.) Suppose, for example, that $V(x)$ represents the reflected light intensity from a printed page as seen through a vertical slit one line high as the slit scans the horizontal space occupied by one letter. For convenience, we shall assume that the space occupied by one letter is normalized to the interval $0 \le x \le 1$. We could then define a set of coefficients $C_n$ by the requirement that

$$V(x) \equiv \sum_n C_n f_n(x) \qquad \text{for } 0 \le x \le 1 \tag{75}$$

The specific values of $C_n$ may be computed as follows. We first multiply Eq. (75) by $f_m(x)$ and then integrate both sides of the equation over the region from $x = 0$ to 1. Because of the orthogonality of the functions, $f_n(x)$, all terms in the sum vanish except that involving $C_m$. Therefore,

$$\int_0^1 V(x)f_m(x)\,dx = C_m \int_0^1 [f_m(x)]^2\,dx = C_m \qquad (76)$$

where the last simplification is permitted by the normalization of the functions. That is, the conditions of orthonormality summarized in Eqs. (73) and (74) were used to obtain Eq. (76) from Eq. (75).

The expansion used in Eq. (75) is analogous to finding the components of a vector along different orthogonal axes. In principle, one can only make the statement in Eq. (75) for a general function $V(x)$ if the set of orthogonal functions, $f_n(x)$, is *complete*. In other words, there is no guarantee that just because a particular set of functions is orthogonal, a sum such as that in Eq. (75) will add up precisely to a general function, $V(x)$, defined over the same interval. Analogously, one cannot expect to reconstruct a general three-dimensional vector just by use of an orthogonal pair of base vectors contained in a plane. However, Eq. (76) for the general expansion coefficients is perfectly well defined even if we do not choose to invoke it for all the members of a complete set. The usefulness of the method as applied to the pattern-recognition problem, in fact, depends on our ability to choose a convenient set of orthogonal functions which can be used to identify a large number of different intensity distributions with a *small* number of expansion coefficients. For example, we could indeed use the projection coefficients of a three-dimensional vector within a two-dimensional plane to classify the orientation of the vector if the length of the vector were constant. In that instance, two expansion coefficients could be used to categorize an infinite number of orientations in three dimensions. Similarly, if two expansion coefficients permit distinguishing unambiguously among 100 different printed characters, they provide a useful basis for character identification even if they could not be used alone to reconstruct the shape of the characters. On the other hand, if it were to take 100 expansion coefficients to identify 100 characters, we might as well forget the expansion-coefficient method and merely match up the character intensity distributions themselves. Two orthogonal functions of opposite symmetry provide the best bet for the most concise identification.

It is desirable to choose the different pattern functions $V(x)$ so that they all satisfy a common normalization condition of the type

$$\int_0^1 [V(x)]^2\,dx = 1 \qquad (77)$$

In this case, it follows from Eqs. (73)–(75) that

$$\int_0^1 [V(x)]^2\,dx = \sum_m \sum_n C_m C_n \int_0^1 f_m(x)f_n(x)\,dx = \sum_m C_m^2 = 1 \qquad (78)$$

when the final sum goes over a complete set. The exact value of the normalization constant in Eq. (77) is not of real consequence. The important thing is that the generalized vectors corresponding to the different pattern functions all be of the same length. In that case we have the best chance of categorizing different patterns on the basis of a few projection coefficients $C_m$ out of those for the complete set. Identification of a particular unknown pattern distribution $V'(x)$ amounts to finding a particular known subset of expansion coefficients $C_m$ such that

$$C'_m = C_m$$

within some arbitrarily chosen degree of accuracy for each member $m$ of the subset, where

$$C'_m = \int_0^1 V'(x)f_m(x)\,dx$$

and $V'(x)$ also satisfies Eq. (77). The only remaining problem consists of choosing a suitable set of orthogonal functions to use in our equations.

Walsh (1923) developed a complete set of orthonormal functions which are especially useful in the pattern identification problem. These functions are defined over the interval $0 \leqslant x \leqslant 1$ and take on the values $+1$ or $-1$. They may

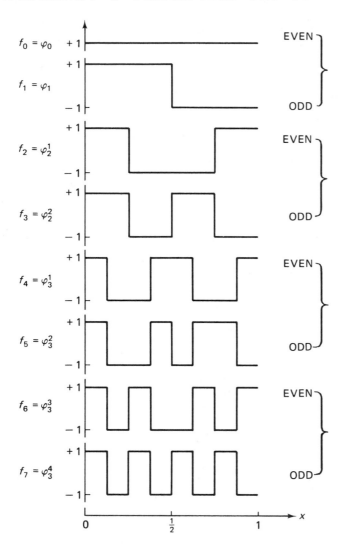

**Fig. 2-7.** The first few Walsh functions, arranged in even and odd symmetric pairs and increasing numbers of sign changes within the interval $0 \leqslant x \leqslant 1$.

be arranged in pairs of functions having even- and odd-symmetry about the point $x = \frac{1}{2}$ and increasing numbers of sign changes (see Fig. 2-7). We have used a simplified notation $f_n(x)$ to describe these functions in which the subscript $n$ denotes the number of sign changes over the domain of the function. Walsh originally specified these functions in the notation $\phi_n^k(x)$, where the two indices $n$ and $k$ were used in a systematic method to generate the functions.

Because the basic prescription given by Walsh to evaluate these functions is awkward to implement on a computer, we give the following algorithm for computing the functions $f_n(x)$ over the interval $0 \leqslant x \leqslant 1$:

1. Do a binary expansion of the variable $x$ in the form

$$x = \frac{a_1}{2^1} + \frac{a_2}{2^2} + \frac{a_3}{2^3} + \cdots + \frac{a_m}{2^m} \tag{80}$$

where $a_i = 0$ or 1 and we terminate at $i = m$, where $m$ is the next integer larger than $1 + \log_2 n$.

2. Note that

$$f_0 \equiv 1 \qquad \text{and} \qquad f_i = (-1)^{a_i} \tag{81}$$

3. The even order functions may be determined through the binary sequence,

$$
\begin{aligned}
f_2 &= (-1)^{a_1 + a_2} \\
f_4 &= (-1)^{a_2 + a_3} & f_6 &= f_4 \cdot f_2 \\
f_8 &= (-1)^{a_3 + a_4} & f_{10} &= f_8 \cdot f_2 \\
& & f_{12} &= f_8 \cdot f_4 \\
& & f_{14} &= f_8 \cdot f_6 \\
f_{16} &= (-1)^{a_4 + a_5} & f_{18} &= f_{16} \cdot f_2 \\
& & f_{20} &= f_{16} \cdot f_4 \\
& & \cdots \\
& & f_{30} &= f_{16} \cdot f_{14}
\end{aligned}
\tag{82}
$$

and so on. Note that the values in the right hand column are computed from previously determined values in the left-hand column.

4. Finally, the odd-symmetric functions from the relation

$$f_{2i+1} = f_{2i} \cdot f_1 \quad \text{for } i > 1 \tag{83}$$

This type of algorithm can be very efficient in machine language (where the binary expansion coefficients are frequently already available from standard base 10 to base 2 conversion subroutines) and is easy to implement in BASIC subroutines.[6] In this process it is easiest to compute $f_n(x)$ by storing the successively higher order functions in an array $F(K)$, where $K$ goes from 1 to $N$. However, in a language such as BASIC, it is not actually necessary to compute the binary expansion coefficients explicitly. It is much faster to note instead that the Walsh functions of order $K = 2^I$ may be evaluated directly by use of the INT function in statements of the type

```
LET   K = 2 ↑ I
LET   F(K) = (-1) ↑ INT(K*X + .5)
```
(84)

where $I = 0, 1, 2, \ldots$.

Thus, for a given value of $x$, the Walsh functions

$$f_1, f_2, f_4, f_8, f_{16}, \ldots$$

may be immediately evaluated from Eq. (84) and stored in an array $F(K)$. The remaining even-order functions of order less than $2^{m+1}$ (where $m$ is defined in Eq. (80)) can then be filled in through the multiplicative process outlined in the right-hand column of Eq. (82) by use of the previously stored functions of lower order. Finally, we use Eq. (83) to determine the odd-symmetric functions from the previously stored even-symmetric ones.

---

[6] The author is indebted to Henry Stark and Larry Rissman for checking the algorithm and for helpful discussions regarding the presentation of this material.

Thus, the Walsh functions of order $1 - N$ may be computed in one subroutine of the type

```
600    REM SUB COMPUTES WALSH FCNS F(1)...F(N) AT X
610    LET M = 1 + INT(1.5 + LOG(N)/LOG(2))
620    LET F(1) = (−1) ↑ INT(X + .5)
630    FOR I = 1 TO M
640    LET K = 2 ↑ I
650    LET F(K) = (−1) ↑ INT(K*X + .5)
660    LET F(K + 1) = F(K)*F(1)
670    FOR J = 2 TO K − 2 STEP 2
680    LET F(K + J) = F(K)*F(J)
690    LET F(K + J + 1) = F(K + J)*F(1)
700    NEXT J
710    NEXT I
720    RETURN
```

without having to evaluate the binary expansion coefficients at all. Line 650 makes use of Eq. (84) to compute the successive functions in the left-hand column of Eq. (82). For each value of $K$, the loop between lines 670 and 700 fills in the remaining even-order functions to be computed in line 680 using the relations summarized in the right-hand column of Eq. (82). Finally, the various odd-order functions are computed on lines 660 and 690 using Eq. (83). $F(1)$ was obtained on line 620 using Eq. (84) in the case $I = 0$.

In a real application of Walsh functions to a pattern identification problem, it would be desirable to store the various order functions needed over the required increments in $x$. However, the subroutine outlined above provides a useful systematic method for tabulating the functions in the first instance and for investigating their orthogonal properties.

---

**2.23
PROBLEM 21**

Write a program that computes and tabulates $f_1(x)$ through $f_{12}(x)$ over the interval $0 \le x \le 1$ in steps of $\frac{1}{16}$. Use the results of this program to investigate the orthogonality of any two of these functions over that domain.

**2.23
PROBLEM 22**

Consider the set of functions defined by the BASIC statement

```
DEF FNF(N) = (−1)↑INT(N*X + .5)
```

where $N = 0, 1, 2, 3, 4$. Write a program to investigate the orthonormality of this set of functions over the domain $0 \le X \le 1$. Evaluate the integral in Eq. (73) for different values of $N$ and print the results as a $5 \times 5$ matrix.

**2.23
PROBLEM 23**

Assume the width occupied by letters on a printed line is normalized in each case to the interval $0 \le x \le 1$ and that ten average intensity measurements have been made for each character as we scan a vertical slit along the interval. Assume the intensity distributions for the symbols $T$, $H$, $E$, $F$, $O$, and $Q$ are given by

```
1000   REM DISTRIBUTION FOR T
1001   DATA 1,1,1,1,10,10,1,1,1,1
1002   REM DISTRIBUTION FOR H
1003   DATA 10,10,1,1,1,1,1,1,10,10
1004   REM DISTRIBUTION FOR E
1005   DATA 10,10,3,3,3,3,2,2,2,2
1006   REM DISTRIBUTION FOR F
1007   DATA 10,10,2,2,2,2,1,1,1,1
1008   REM DISTRIBUTION FOR 0
1009   DATA 3,3,2.5,2,2,2,2,2.5,3,3
1010   REM DISTRIBUTION FOR Q
1011   DATA 3,3,2.5,2,2,2.5,3.5,4,4.5,4.5
```

Write a program which reads each intensity distribution, computes a normalized distribution function $V(x)$ using Eq. (77), and then computes and prints a table of expansion coefficients $C_1$ and $C_2$ for $V(x)$ using Eq. (76) and the Walsh functions $f_1(x)$ and $f_2(x)$. Note that these two Walsh functions may simply be obtained from the BASIC function defined in Problem 22 for $N=1$ and 2. Do the integrals in Eq. (76) by matrix multiplication. For example, store average values of the Walsh functions over each integration interval in two $1 \times 10$ row matrices and store the successive pattern matrices in $10 \times 1$ column matrices. Note that although $C_1^2 + C_2^2 \ll 1$ in each case, we may easily distinguish between all six characters.

**2.23**
**PROBLEM 24**

Consider expanding

$$\sin 2\pi x = \sum_n C_n f_n(x) \qquad \text{for} \quad 0 \leq x \leq 1$$

where the $f_n(x)$ are Walsh functions described by Eqs. (80)–(83). Write a program to compute the first 16 expansion coefficients using Eq. (76). Note that only odd-symmetric functions about $x = 0.5$ will be important. (Use an integration interval $\Delta x = \frac{1}{32}$ and the trapezoidal rule.) Check your results by printing a tabular comparison of $\sin x$ and Eq. (75) using the computed expansion coefficients over $0 \leq x \leq 1$ in steps of $2\Delta x$.

**2.23**
**RESEARCH**
**PROBLEM**

Investigate the feasibility of identifying the standard character set found on a typewriter with the type of pattern identification program discussed in the text.

## REFERENCES

BELL, E. T. (1951). *Mathematics–Queen and Servant of Science.* New York: McGraw-Hill Book Company.

COURANT, R. (1949). *Differential and Integral Calculus*, translated by E. J. McShane. New York: John Wiley & Sons, Inc. (Interscience Division).

HARDY, G. H. (1967). *A Mathematician's Apology.* New York: Cambridge University Press. Reprinted in 1967, with a foreword by C. P. Snow.

SCHULTZ, M. H. (1972). *Spline Analysis.* Englewood Cliffs, N.J.: Prentice-Hall, Inc.

VON NEUMANN, JOHN AND H. H. GOLDSTINE (1947). "Numerical Inverting of Matrices of High Order." *Bull. Amer. Math. Soc.*, Vol. 53, pp. 1021-1099.

WALSH, J. L. (1923). "A Closed Set of Normal Orthogonal Functions" *Amer. J. Math.*, Vol. 45, pp. 5–24.

WEATHERBURN, C. E. (1950). *Elementary Vector Analysis.* London: G. Bell & Sons, Ltd.

WHITTAKER, E. T., AND G. N. WATSON (1902). *A Course of Modern Analysis.* Cambridge: Cambridge University Press. Reprinted in 1965.

# Plotting and graphic display

3

*A wide variety of plotting techniques is discussed and illustrated in problems of practical application. The main emphasis is on teletype display. However, the material is arranged so that it may easily be applied to high resolution, random access plotting devices when available. Section 3.1 treats single-point graphs and histograms. Sections 3.2 and 3.3 discuss plotting multiple functions of the same independent variable. Section 3.4 treats the parametric representation of curves and the use of random-access display devices. Sections 3.5 and 3.6 deal with the random-access problem on teletype displays. Section 3.7 discusses surface plotting and the hidden line problem. Sections 3.8 through 3.10 deal with stereoscopic projections.*

73

It is extremely helpful in many instances to be able to display a set of data or the results of a calculation graphically. What method you use to accomplish this objective is largely dependent on the equipment available and the nature of the data to be plotted. In each instance, some method of digital-to-analog conversion will be required. At one extreme, the teletype terminal itself can be used as the digital-to-analog converter and thus generate a relatively low resolution and slowly executed plot of the data. At the opposite extreme, a high-speed electronic digital-to-analog converter can be used to plot results on $xy$ recorders, oscilloscopes, or other high-resolution devices. Using devices other than the teletype (or CRT terminal) also depends on the availability of some extra software instructions outside the normal BASIC language. For example, many computer centers have facilities that permit writing data from a BASIC program onto a disc file. Additional specialized programs are frequently available for reading the contents of a file and transmitting it to a high-speed line printer or graphic display device. Similarly, provisions can be incorporated within the BASIC compilers used in minicomputers to CALL machine-language subroutines which directly transfer digital data points to an analog display. We shall illustrate some of these methods; however, the precise instructions required will vary somewhat from one computer facility to the next.

In general, the problems associated with plotting data points on a high-resolution analog display (such as a digital pen recorder) are far simpler than those involved in the generation of a teletype or line-printer display. Although equivalent things can be accomplished in most instances with a teletype display, it requires more complex programming statements to achieve any very general plot in multiple-function or random-access problems.

Consequently our main emphasis will be on teletype plotting techniques throughout the present chapter. These methods may, of course, be easily modified for graphic display on high-resolution, random access devices. In some instances one can in fact use these more powerful analog devices with greater effectiveness after having worked through the equivalent teletype plotting problem.

With any plotting device, one is faced with a previously defined scale. There is generally a finite number of equal intervals available in both the X and Y directions on the plotting device in respect to an absolute origin. To fit the function on the plot it is necessary to normalize the function and to shift the origin adequately so that the range of the variables and domain of the function fall within the bounds of the plotting device. That, of course, is just what you always do when you plot something on a sheet of graph paper by hand. When the resolution with the particular plotting device is severely limited, it also pays to normalize the individual function so that it just fits within the maximum range available and to round off the function to the nearest integer on the absolute scale. The most desirable procedures vary with the particular device and function under consideration.

The most commonly available graphic display device is the teletype terminal itself. Here, one coordinate becomes the direction of the roller advance. The other coordinate is simply the lateral position at which an alphanumeric character is printed. Both coordinates may be controlled by judicious use of the PRINT statement in BASIC.

There are two main problems quite apart from plotting speed: (1) the resolution is limited to 72 columns across the page; and (2) the computer can only advance the roller in one direction. For these reasons, it is important to normalize the function so that you get the maximum available resolution out of the plot and to round off the result to the nearest integer (column). The direction of the roller advance also becomes the most natural choice for the independent variable, and problems that involve rectangular symmetry are easiest to handle.

One frequently wants to plot values ($Y$) of a function in BASIC that may include zero, or even negative numbers, and display these with the maximum resolution available—hence over column numbers ranging from 1 to 72. If we know that

$$M\emptyset \leqslant Y \leqslant M1$$

we can define a new variable $Y1$ such that

$$1 \leqslant Y1 \leqslant 72$$

by use of the BASIC statement

LET Y1 = 71*(Y − M∅)/(M1 − M∅) + 1

where $M\emptyset$ and $M1$ are the minimum and maximum values of $Y$. Use of the integer function through a statement of the type

LET Y1 = INT(Y1 + .5)

ensures that the column number is rounded off to the nearest integer.

If one wants to plot a *bar graph* (or *histogram*), it is then merely necessary to print a character on the keyboard (e.g., *) $Y1$ times for each successive value of the independent variable $X$. As an example, consider plotting a histogram of the function $Y = SIN(X)$ over one period:

```
10  FOR X = ∅ TO 2*3.14159 STEP 2*3.14159/50
20  LET  Y = SIN(X)
30  LET Y1 = INT(71*(Y + 1)/2 + 1.5)
40  FOR J = 1 TO Y1
50  PRINT "*";
60  NEXT J
70  PRINT
80  NEXT X
90  END
```

Line 1∅ provides 51 successive values of $X$ uniformly spaced over the interval $0 \leqslant X \leqslant 2\pi$. The normalization and rounding procedure is contained in line 3∅, where we have simply inserted the minimum ($M\emptyset = -1$) and maximum ($M1 = +1$) values of the sine function; the additional factor 0.5 has also been included in the argument of the INT function on line 3∅ for rounding purposes. The loop on $J$ in lines 4∅ through 6∅ prints $Y1$ successive asterisks on the same line because of the semi-colon after the PRINT statement on line 5∅. The carriage return and line feed are activated by the PRINT statement on line 7∅, after which the program is ready to plot the function for the next value of $X$. The results of running the program are shown in Fig. 3-1.

Alternatively, a *single-point graph* of the sine function could have been plotted in the above program by printing a blank space $Y1$-1 times on lines 4∅ through 6∅, followed by an asterisk on the $Y1$th column. For example,

```
40  FOR J = 1 TO Y1 − 1
50  PRINT " ";
60  NEXT J
70  PRINT "*"
```

would accomplish the objective. Here, the absence of the semi-colon after the PRINT statement on line 7∅ results in activating the carriage return and line feed after printing the single asterisk on the $Y1$th column.

It is useful to note that the TAB function (which is always used within PRINT statements in BASIC) provides an efficient way to move the typing head a specified number of spaces. The argument of the TAB function is

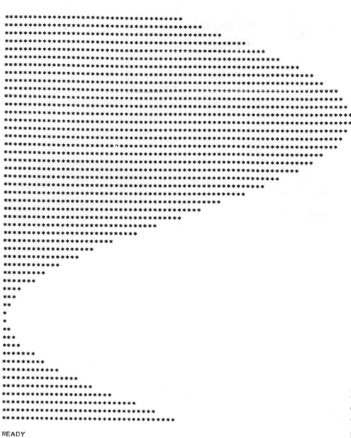

READY

**Fig. 3-1.** Results of running the program discussed in the text for plotting a histogram of the sine function on a teletype machine.

interpreted on an absolute basis (in respect to the left margin) and can be based on a computed expression. For example, the statement

PRINT TAB(Y1 − 1);

results in moving the typing head *Y1*-1 spaces without activating the carriage return and line feed. Consequently, that simple statement is equivalent to the loop within lines 4Ø through 6Ø above. Further, lines 4Ø through 7Ø in the single-point plotting routine may be completely replaced by the single statement

40   PRINT TAB(Y1 − 1);"*"

Further economy in programming statements is possible in the above plotting routines, but with some decrease in the conceptual clarity provided by program listings. For example, the use of the integer function on line 3Ø is actually redundant: Exactly the same results would have been obtained in each of the above programs if we had merely deleted line 3Ø and replaced *Y1* in line 4Ø by the argument of the original integer function. This simplification is permitted simply because the INT function is effectively consulted by the BASIC compiler in executing the FOR loop on *J* and in executing the TAB function. One could further compute the values of the function within the upper limit of the FOR loop on *J*, or within the argument of the TAB function. Thus, for example, the same single-point plot of the sinewave would be provided by the program

```
10   FOR X = Ø TO 2*3.14159 STEP 2*3.14159/5Ø
40   PRINT TAB(71*(SIN(X) + 1)/2 + .5);"*"
80   NEXT X
90   END
```

However, here we have reached a point of diminishing return: the program is now so concise that its functioning tends to be obscure in a quick glance at the program.

---

**3.1**
**PROBLEM 1**

Plot a single-point graph of the function $\sin A + \sin 3A$ for $0 \le A \le 2\pi$.

**3.1**
**PROBLEM 2**

The unemployed working force in the United States varied from 5.9 to 8.2 percent over the interval January 1972 through January 1975 in accordance with the numbers in the following DATA statements (representing 1-month intervals):†

```
 999  REM % UNEMPLOYED JAN. '72 → JAN. '75 IN 1 MONTH STEPS
1000  DATA 5.9,5.8,5.9,5.8,5.7,5.6,5.6,5.5,5.6,5.5,5.3,5.1
1001  DATA 5,5.1,5,5,4.9,4.9,4.8,4.8,4.7,4.7,4.6,4.8
1002  DATA 5.1,5.2,5.1,5,5.2,5.2,5.3,5.4,5.8,6,6.5,7.3
1003  DATA 8.2
```

Plot a histogram of the above data using the full teletype scale.

**3.1**
**PROBLEM 3**

Plot a histogram of the letter frequency distribution for one of the languages for which data is summarized in Table 4 of Chapter 4. If you have the CHR$ function, write your program to print the different specific letters within the bar graph. e.g.,

AAAAAAAAAAAAAAAAAAAAAAAAAAAAAAAAA
BBBBBBBBBBBB
CCCCCCCCCCCCCCCCCC

, etc. (See Section 1.18 of Chapter 1 for a discussion of the ASCII Code.)

† From *The New York Times*, Feb. 8, 1975, p. 1, cols. 6 and 7.

---

**3.2**
**Plotting Two Simultaneous Functions on the Teletype Terminal**

Suppose that we compute two functions, $Y1$ and $Y2$, simultaneously for the same values of the independent variable $X$ and wish to plot the results. At first glance the program

```
10  FOR X = 0 TO ...
20  LET Y1 = ...⎫
                  ⎬ (defines the two functions)
30  LET Y2 = ...⎭
40  PRINT TAB(Y1 − .5);"*"; TAB(Y2 − .5);"*"
50  NEXT X
60  END
```

would seem to accomplish the objective (assuming that $Y1$ and $Y2$ are properly normalized for the 72-column format). The program will be fine as long as $Y2 > Y1$, since both TAB functions are evaluated on an absolute basis. However, if $Y1 \geqq Y2$, erroneous points will result. In that case, the second * will be printed just after the first one. Consequently, some conditional statements will be needed if the two functions cross. For example, the program

```
 10  FOR X = 0 TO ... STEP ...
 20  LET Y1 = ...⎫
                  ⎬ (two functions of X)
 30  LET Y2 = ...⎭
 40  IF INT(Y1 + .5)#INT(Y2 + .5) THEN 70
 50  PRINT TAB(Y1 − .5);"X"
 60  GO TO 110
 70  IF Y1 > Y2 THEN 100
 80  PRINT TAB(Y1 − .5);"A";TAB(Y2 − .5);"B"
 90  GO TO 110
100  PRINT TAB(Y2 − .5); "B";TAB(Y1 − .5);"A"
110  NEXT X
```

77

would plot only one point (X) where the functions were the same and would plot *Y1* using the letter A, *Y2* using the letter B, and would handle the two inequality limits appropriately. In some versions of BASIC, programming statements of the above type could be pruned substantially by using computed GO TO or more elaborate conditional statements. For example, some time-sharing services incorporate a type of super BASIC in which one is allowed to make such statements as

```
70  IF Y1 > Y2 THEN PRINT TAB(Y2 − .5);"B";TAB(Y1 − .5);"A"
```

However, most BASIC compilers do not have that option.

---

**3.2**
**PROBLEM 4**

Write a program that will simultaneously plot the sine function over one period (0 through $2\pi$) and the axis representing the angle variable. For example, use the * symbol for the function and the + symbol for the axis. Make the program print a * symbol where the function intersects the axis.

**3.2**
**PROBLEM 5**

Write a program that will simultaneously plot the sine and cosine functions over the range from zero to $2\pi$ and use different characters for the two functions. Where the two functions coincide, have the computer print X.

**3.2**
**PROBLEM 6**

Write a program that plots a circle on the teletype. Note that the circle can be represented by the two functions

$$Y1 = Y0 + SQR(R*R − (X − X0)*(X − X0))$$

and

$$Y2 = Y0 − SQR(R*R − (X − X0)*(X − X0))$$

Also note that the teletype characters are more closely spaced on a line than the lines are separated, by a ratio $\approx \frac{3}{5}$. Hence, to avoid producing ellipses rather than circles, it is helpful to multiply the SQR terms in the above two cases by a number $\approx \frac{5}{3}$.

---

The technique of Section 3.2 could be extended to any number of simultaneous functions by use of more conditional statements. The process would be terribly cumbersome for more than a few functions and it is much more efficient to adopt some kind of procedure that automatically sorts and stores the points as they are computed and plots points using the same character. For example, suppose we wanted to plot a function of the type

**3.3**
**Plotting *N* Simultaneous Functions of the Same Variable with the Teletype**

$$y = x^n$$

over the range $0 \le x \le 1$.

Here we could use a 72-column array to advantage for the teletype plotting problem, and our program might start out

```
10  DIM Y(72)
20  FOR X = 0 TO 1 STEP .02
30  FOR I = 1 TO 72
40  LET Y(I) = −1
50  NEXT I
```

The STEP size indicated on line 20 will provide a 51-point plot in a later portion of the program. The array initialization on lines 30 through 50 is to permit telling at the plotting stage of the program whether or not a point has been computed corresponding to a particular array index, *I*. We shall next compute values of $Y = X^N$ normalized to the 72-column width for $0 \le X \le 1$ and store those values in proportionate elements of the array, $Y(I)$.

```
60   FOR N = 1 TO 9
70   LET Y = 71*X↑N
80   LET I = INT(Y + 1.5)
90   LET Y(I) = Y
100  NEXT N
```

Line 8∅ defines an integer proportional to $Y$ which is rounded off to nearest integer in the domain $1 \leqslant I \leqslant 72$ when $0 \leqslant X \leqslant 1$. Note that after line 1∅∅, every value of each function has been stored for a given value of the independent variable, $X$.

We are therefore ready to plot the points corresponding to each function by use of a series of statements of the type

```
110   LET A=−1
120   FOR I=1 TO 72
130   IF Y(I)<=A THEN 170
140   PRINT TAB(Y(I)−∅.5);"*";
150   LET A=INT(Y(I)+.5)
160   IF Y(I)>=72 THEN 190
170   NEXT I
180   PRINT
190   NEXT X
```

The utility of the variable $A$ arises from its definition in line 15∅. The initial choice, $A=-1$, corresponds to no points having been plotted for the current value of the independent variable $X$. The program then plots the computed values for $Y(I)$, noting that they have been previously stored in an order that increases with the array index, $I$. If no point has been computed for a particular array element, $Y(I)=-1$ from the initialization statement on line 4∅. Points that have not been computed, or are equal in value to one previously computed, are therefore rejected by line 13∅. Lines 17∅ and 18∅ permit advancing the roller at the end of the $I$ loop unless a character has just been printed in column 72 (in which case the roller advances automatically).

Note that the sorting techniques discussed in Section 1.16 could be used in place of lines 6∅ through 1∅∅ to store a more general set of computed points in the array $Y(I)$ for each value of $X$.

---

**3.3
PROBLEM 7**
Plot $Y=X^N$ on the teletype for integral steps of $N$ over the range $1 \leqslant N \leqslant 9$ and 50 points covering the range $0 \leqslant X \leqslant 1$.

---

Some functions are most naturally computed in terms of parameters, other than the rectangular coordinates x, y. For example, one common parametric representation involves the use of the polar coordinates $R$ and $A$ in two-dimensional plotting (see Fig. 3-2). Here $R$ is the radius from an origin $X∅$, $Y∅$ to the point $(X, Y)$ on the curve, and $A$ is the angle (in radians) between $R$ and a reference line (e.g., the $x$ axis).

**3.4
Parametric Representation
of Curves; Polar Coordinates
and Probability Clouds**

One needs rectangular coordinates to feed most computer-driven plotting devices. These coordinates are related to the parameters $R$ and $A$ by means of the equations

$$X = X∅ + R \cos A$$
$$Y = Y∅ + R \sin A$$

by definition of the sine and cosine functions.

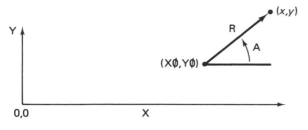

**Fig. 3-2.**

For example, one can compute the points on a circle by holding $R$ constant and by varying the angle $A$ from 0 to $2\pi$ radians in suitably chosen steps. Similarly, varying $R$ with the angle $A$ in a program of the type

```
10   FOR A = 0 TO 10*3.14159 STEP .06
20   LET R = A
30   LET X = X0 + R*COS(A)
40   LET Y = Y0 + R*SIN(A)
60   NEXT A
```

will result in the successive computation of $\approx 100$ points on a spiral. It is helpful to imagine how simple life would be *if* we could merely insert a statement in line 50 that would simply plot a point with the coordinates $X$ and $Y$ on an analog device by means of a simple command such as

```
50   PLOT(X,Y)
```

Although this statement is *not* a standard part of BASIC, one can devise machine-language programs that produce the same effect with oscilloscope and *xy* pen recorder displays.[1] In that case, one may easily display a wide variety of spiral functions merely by changing the dependence of $R$ on $A$ in line 20 (see Fig. 3-3.)

Another technique that is readily implemented with random-access plotting devices consists of the display of probability clouds. Suppose, for example, that we were able to write a probability function $P$ in terms of the polar coordinates $R$ and $A$ above, such that $P(R, A)$ represents the probability of an event occurring between $R$ and $R + dR$ and between $A$ and $A + dA$. One could then

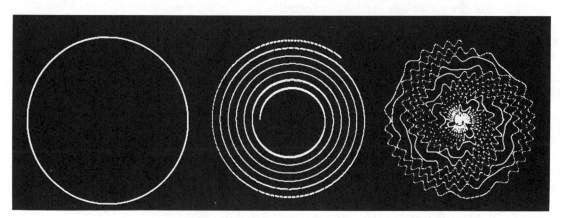

**Fig. 3-3.** Representative variety of functions that may easily be displayed on a random-access plotting device by minor modification of the dependence of radius on angle in line 20. Note that a modulated phonograph record is just as easy to draw as a circle.

simulate a probability cloud by plotting a number of points proportional to $P(R, A)$ at coordinates which are given different random displacements about $R$ and $A$. The technique will become clearer by reference to the following representative program:

```
99    REM PROGRAM PLOTS CLOUD FOR PROBABILITY FCN P = P(R,A)
100   FOR R = .5*R0 TO R2 STEP R0
110      FOR A = .5*A0 TO 2*3.14159 STEP A0
```

[1] For example, statements of the type

```
CALL(1,X,Y)
```

that result in plotting one point with coordinates $X$, $Y$ on device number 1 during normal running of a program can be added to the BASIC language. (See the Hewlett-Packard manual on 2100 series computers).

```
120      LET P=... (some function of R and A)
130      FOR I=PØ TO P STEP PØ
140          LET A1=A+AØ*(RND(1)−.5)
150          LET R1=R+RØ*(RND(2)−.5)
160          LET X1=XØ+R1*COS(A1)
170          LET Y1=YØ+R1*SIN(A1)
180      REM PLOT A POINT WITH COORDINATES X1 AND Y1
. . . . . . . . . . . .
190          NEXT I
200      NEXT A
210      NEXT R
```

(The indentation in program statements is introduced merely to clarify the steps involved within the three nested loops.) The exact form for $P$ would have to be inserted in line 12Ø, together with appropriate upper limits and step sizes on the three FOR loops. However, such plots tend to be most efficient when the initial values, step sizes and random displacements are as shown in the above program segment. For example, the random fluctuation on $R1$ in line 15Ø is spread evenly over the domain $R \pm 0.5*RØ$; hence the final plot will show randomly located points having an average density which is uniformly spread over the range $0 \le R \le R2$ when $P$ is constant as a result of the lower limit and step size in line 1ØØ. In some instances, symmetry properties of the probability function can be used effectively to speed up the running time. An illustration of the method is shown in Fig. 3-4.

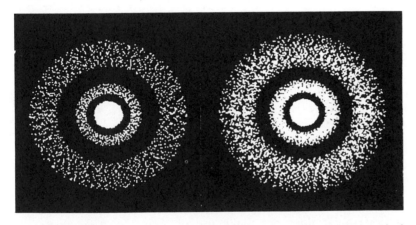

**Fig. 3-4.** Simulation of the electron cloud in the median plane of an excited hydrogen atom (in the 4s state). The value of $PØ$ on the line 13Ø of the program in the text was reduced by 50 percent in going from the left- to the right-hand figure.

## 3.5
## Infinite-Core Method: Contour Plots with the Teletype

A serious limitation of the teletype terminal (and line printer) is that the computer cannot move the roller backward. Consequently, the teletype fits most naturally into problems that involve rectangular coordinates in which one calculates the various values of $Y$ (the column position) for each sequential increment in $X$ (the row typed). If one wants to plot something in parametric form (e.g., a spiral), one has to compute and store all the required points in the computer memory and then plot all these points at the end of the computation period. As sometimes is the case, the most straightforward approach to the problem squanders the most computer core.

The most straightforward approach here consists of defining a large matrix, $M$, with enough rows and columns to achieve the desired resolution. For example, 45 rows and 72 columns would correspond roughly to a square display on the teletype with the maximum available resolution. (The 45:72 ratio roughly corresponds to the 3:5 ratio of type width to height.) Hence we would have to start off with a dimension statement

1    DIM M(45, 72)

which implies storage for 3240 floating-point numbers; or, for example, in a typical minicomputer using two 16-bit words for each floating-point number, the dimension statement calls for 6480 core locations before we have gotten to the program. The approach is quite realistic with most moderate sized computers. However, one should keep in mind that the BASIC compiler itself takes up $\approx 7000$ words, so one needs at least $\approx 16,000$ words of memory available before the approach is realistic with a minicomputer.

Pursuing this method, we next might initialize the matrix by setting all 3240 elements to zero:

2    MAT M = ZER(45, 72)

and proceed to compute our function. Assuming that our function has been normalized to fit on a $45 \times 72$ grid, we could do the equivalent of plotting points on paper by incrementing the matrix element $M(X, Y)$ whose row and column correspond to the $X$ and $Y$ coordinates of the point. (This means that the $X$ coordinate will be in the direction of the teletype line advance and $Y$ will correspond to the teletype column position.) For example, plotting a point with coordinates that are rounded off to the integers $X$ and $Y$ would correspond to the statement

LET M(X,Y) = M(X,Y) + 1

After completing the computation of all elements $M(X, Y)$ we could then run through a plotting routine that would plot a point at each coordinate $X$ and $Y$ for which $M(X, Y) \neq 0$. For example, the plotting could be accomplished by a program such as

```
100    FOR X = 1 TO 45
110    FOR Y = 1 TO 72
120    IF M(X,Y) = 0 THEN 150
130    PRINT TAB(Y - 1);"*";
140    IF Y = 72 THEN 170
150    NEXT Y
160    PRINT
170    NEXT X
```

Although the method preserves the $45 \times 72$ resolution for a series of points that could be computed in random order, it so far does not make use of the "dynamic range" of the method. That is, so far we have only plotted one point whenever $M(X, Y) \neq 0$. We could, of course, try to make use of the magnitude of $M(X, Y)$. For example, one could raise the cutoff point on line 120, "enhance" the contrast in some way, only plot a point when $M(X, Y)$ equaled a specified value [thereby obtaining a set of surfaces whose altitude corresponded to $M(X, Y)$], and so on.

One method of utilizing the range in values of the matrix elements consists of using the teletype (or line printer) to print different ASCII characters in a manner proportional to the magnitude of these elements. However, if we print more than one teletype column for each matrix element, we lose spatial resolution. One approach is to compress the range of the matrix elements to a scale from 0 through 9 and print the corresponding numerical characters (having ASCII decimal-code designations running from 48 through 57). For example, consider producing a contour map of a surface of the type

$$z \propto (e^{-r} \sin 2\pi r)^2$$

where

$$r^2 = x^2 + y^2$$

```
                  111111111111111111111
               11111122222222222222222211111
            1111222222333333333333332222221111
           111112222233333333333333333333332222111
          11112223333333333333333333333333333332222111
         111222333333333333333333333333333333333222111
        11122233333333332222222222222222233333333333222111
       1122233333333332222111111111111122223333333322211
      112223333333322221111             11111122233333333322111
     112233333333222111111             111112223333333322111
     11223333333332221111        11122222111     1122223333333221 1
     11223333333322111      1112333333333322211     11122233333332211
    111122333333322211     1222344466666664433211     1112233333322111
    11223333333322211     1233466777788887766443321     1112233333332211
   112233333333221 1     1123466788899999998877664322 1     11223333333332211
   11223333333221 1     112346778999999999999987764322     1122333333332211
   11223333333221 1     1234677899988666888999987764321     11223333333332111
   11223333333221 1     123366789998665555568899987663321     1122333333332211
   11223333333221 1     12346789998663322233588999876432 1     1122333333332211
   11223333333221 1     123467899986532     235689998764321     11223333333322 11
   11223333333221 1     1234678999866532223355689998764321     1122333333332211
   11223333333221 1     12334778999866555556889998663311     1122333333332211
   11222333333221 1     1234678999888666888999988764321     11223333333332211
    11223333333221 1     1123467789999999999998876432 1     1122333333332211
   112233333333221 1     112346678899999999998876643211     11223333333332211
    11223333332221 1     1123344667778887777664332 1     111223333333322 11
    112223333333221 11     12233444666666644432211     1111223333333322111
    112233333333222 11     11222333333333221     11122223333333322111
     11223333333332211     1111222221111     11112223333333322111
      1122233333332221111             1111122223333333222111
       11222333333333332222211111111111111112222333333333322211
        11122233333333333322222222222222222223333333333222111
         11112223333333333333333333333333333333333322111
          11112222333333333333333333333333333333332222111
           111122223333333333333333333333333222111
            1111222222333333333333333222221111
              111111122222222222222222221111111
                  111111111111111111111
```

**Fig. 3-5.** Contour map of the function

$$Z = (9/.621843)*(EXP(-R/35)*SIN(2*3.14159*R/35))\uparrow 2$$

plotted with a teletype terminal using a 5/3 ratio to correct for the difference between character width and height.

First we store the surface (normalized to a maximum value of 9) on a point–by–point basis in the $45 \times 72$ element matrix. In this process it is useful to introduce the polar coordinates, $R$ and $A$, as generating parameters:

```
10   DIM M(45,72)
20   MAT M = ZER(45,72)
25   REM PICK ORIGIN NEXT
30   LET X0 = 1+INT(3*36/5+.5)
35   LET Y0 = 1+INT(36+.5)
40   FOR R = 1 TO 35
41   PRINT R;
45   FOR A = 0 TO 2*3.14159 STEP 1/R
50   LET X = X0+INT((3/5)*R*COS(A)+.5)
60   LET Y = Y0+INT(R*SIN(A)+.5)
70   LET M = EXP(-R/35)*SIN(R*2*3.14159/35)
75   LET M(X,Y) = INT(9*M*M/.621843+.5)
80   NEXT A
90   NEXT R
```

Note that the $\frac{3}{5}$ normalizing factor occurs in lines 30 and 50 for the quantities that involve $X$, but not in lines 35 and 60, which involve the $Y$ coordinate. Line 75 normalizes the maximum value of the particular function (0.621843) to 9. The print statement on line 41 is merely to let us know where we are in the computation of $M(X, Y)$. The only tricky point is the variation of angular step size in line 45. Here we wish to decrease the angular step with increasing radius so that we avoid ending up with noncomputed matrix elements where the function is nonzero. At the same time, we wish to avoid wasting excessive computing at the center of the plot (where relatively coarse angular increments are permissible). Therefore we want the angular step to decrease as $1/R$.

Finally, we want to be able to print the right ASCII characters in the right place after all matrix elements have been computed. For example, it is useful to print a space when $M(X, Y) = \emptyset$, the character 1 when $M(X, Y) = 1$, and so on.

One method of accomplishing this printing task is to run the matrix elements through a binary printing sieve analogous to that discussed in Chapter 4 for letter printing (see Section 4.2). On the other hand, the CHR$ function (or equivalent CALL statement) can be used to considerable advantage when available (see Section 1.18). For example, the statements

```
210   FOR X = 1 TO 45
220   FOR Y = 1 TO 72
230   IF M(X,Y)#∅  THEN 26∅
240   PRINT " ";
250   GOTO 270
260   PRINT CHR$(M(X,Y)+48);
270   NEXT Y
280   PRINT
290   NEXT X
```

solve the problem with reasonable economy and efficiency. However, there is the mild disadvantage that when $M(X, Y)$ exceeds 9 in line $26\emptyset$ you start getting the assortment of nonnumeric ASCII characters on your contour plot which were listed earlier in Table 1 of Chapter 1 in the ASCII character set. The result of running the program is shown in Fig. 3-5.

---

**3.5**
**PROBLEM 8**

The probability of finding the electron in the median plane of a particular excited state of the hydrogen atom (the $4f_{m=0}$ state) is proportional to $P$ given by the following BASIC statements:†

```
DEF   FNA(A) = 2*COS(A)↑3 − 3*COS(A)*SIN(A)↑2
DEF   FNR(R) = EXP(−R/4)*R↑3
LET   P = R*(FNR(R)*FNA(A))↑2
```

where $A$ represents the angular position of the electron and $R$ is the radial location in units of the Bohr radius ($0.529173 \times 10^{-8}$ cm.) Use the technique of the present section to plot a contour map of this probability function over the range $1 \leq R \leq 30$.

† Ref. Condon and Shortley (1963).

---

**3.6**
**Random-Point Problem on Small Machines: Plotting a Spiral on the Teletype**

The preceding method is extravagant unless one really makes use of the dynamic range for each point (i.e., somehow utilize the number of points stored within each individual matrix element).

With the specific example given and machine used, a $45 \times 72$ point resolution was obtained in the $xy$ plane, but the information stored in the $z$ coordinate would typically be computed to better than 1 ppm and could probably range up to $\approx 10^{38}$.

In cases where one merely wants to plot one point at most for a given pair of coordinates and also will be content with a maximum initially prescribed number of plotted points ($\ll 72$) for the same value of the variable along the roller-advance direction, it takes less computer memory to store the successive $Y$

coordinates in the matrix elements $M(I, J)$ and use the column index $(J)$ to keep track of the number of plotted points stored for each value of $I$.

Let us assume that we might want to plot as many as 10 separate points on each of 40 separate rows and that we will store the $Y$ coordinates in the matrix $M$. In this case, we only need a dimension statement involving 400 floating-point variables,

```
1   DIM M(40,10)
```

to get a resolution of 1 part in 72 on each point. Here it is useful to initialize all the matrix elements to the value $-1$. This can be accomplished through the statements

```
5   MAT M = CON        (fill out M with 1s)
6   MAT M = (-1)*M     (multiply each component by -1.
                       Note: This is one of the few MAT
                       commands where it is legal to
                       have the same matrix on both sides
                       of the equal sign.)
```

As an illustration we shall compute a spiral in parametric form and then plot it with the teletype machine. First we shall determine the $X$ and $Y$ coordinates of successive points using a parameter $K$:

```
10   FOR K = 1 TO 10 STEP .01
12   LET A = K*3.14159
15   LET R = A
20   LET X = 32 + R*COS(A)
30   LET Y = 32 + R*SIN(A)
```

We next determine the row index for the storage matrix rounded off to the nearest integer by the statement

```
60   LET I = INT(3*X/5 + .5)
```

where the $\approx \frac{3}{5}$ factor correcting for the character- and line-spacing dimensions has been included. Then we want to store the $Y$ coordinate of the $J$th point ($1 \leq J \leq 10$ here) corresponding to the particular value of $I$ computed on line 60:

```
65   FOR J = 1 TO 10
67   IF M(I,J)<0 THEN 70
68   NEXT J
69   GO TO 80
70   LET M(I,J) = INT(Y + .5)
```

The conditional statement in line 67 lets the $Y$ coordinate be stored in line 70, provided that no previous point was stored in $M(I, J)$. Line 69 prevents attempting to store more than 10 points (and hence generating an error message). The value of the $Y$ coordinate is rounded off to the nearest integer in line 70 as it is stored in the matrix for use in the specific plotting program given below. After storing the computed point, the loop on the parameter $K$ is closed on line 80.

```
80   NEXT K
```

The points can then be plotted in the following straightforward manner:

```
100   FOR I = 1 TO 40
110   FOR K = I TO 72
120   FOR J = 1 TO 10
130   IF M(I,J)#K-1 THEN 160
140   PRINT "*";
150   GO TO 180
160   NEXT J
170   PRINT " ";
180   NEXT K
190   NEXT I
```

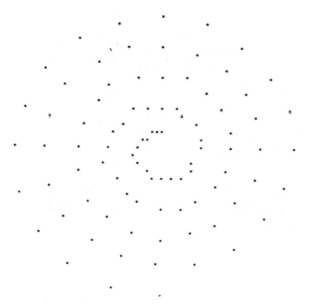

**Fig. 3-6.** Spiral plotted on a teletype terminal.

For each of the 40 rows provided in the original matrix, the teletype scans through the 72 columns (FOR loop on $K$). For each value of $K$ and each possible stored point, $J$, the conditional statement on line 13Ø checks to see if a point should be plotted; i.e., unless $M(I, J) = K - 1$, a point should not be plotted. If no points have been stored over the range from $J = 1$ to 10, a blank space is entered on line 17Ø and the teletype advances to the next column ($K$).

The plotting program, as it stands, depends on the fact that the line feed will automatically be advanced after $K = 72$. One could speed up the program somewhat when plotting on the teletype by first determining the maximum $M$ of $M(I, J)$ for $J = 1$ to 10 and by advancing $K$ only to $M - 1$. (The maxima, for example, could be stored in a column array and could have been computed when the function was initially worked out.) However, in that instance, some extra statements are required to advance the line feed when $M < 72$ and to prevent a double line feed when $M = 72$. The saving in time is pretty negligible when the output is displayed by a line printer or CRT terminal, and these extra programming steps have been omitted for the sake of clarity.

The results from running the program are shown in Fig. 3-6. As it stands, the first and last several lines are filled up with blank characters.

| | |
|---|---|
| **3.6**<br>**PROBLEM 9** | Plot the function defined by the polar-coordinate relation R = SIN(2*A) over the range $0 \leq A \leq 2\pi$ on the teletype. (*Note:* There are only four points for each value of *X*.) |

Anyone who enjoys browsing through the illustrations in Jahnke and Emde (1945), or who has imagined walking about on mathematical surfaces, will probably want to try to plot some surfaces with a computer. The technique is also frequently valuable in the display of experimental data. We shall therefore consider a simple method for approximating a perspective plot of a surface. (A more precise method for handling projections of three-dimensional quantities on a two-dimensional plot is given in Section 3.8.)

Suppose that we wish to display the surface

$$z = f(x, y)$$

**3.7**
**Plotting Surfaces on the Teletype;**
**the Hidden Line Problem**

on a two-dimensional plotting device with absolute coordinates $x_1$ and $y_1$. A simple method of approximating the effects of perspective consists of doing the same thing with a computer that would be accomplished by preparing a large number of slices through successive $zx$ planes (i.e., at different values of y) and then pasting these together in slightly displaced form. If we take the $x$ axis of the surface to be parallel to the $x_1$ axis of the plotting device and the $z$ axis of the surface parallel to the $y_1$ axis of the plotting device, we can create the illusion of a $y$ axis drawn in perspective using the successive displacement technique shown in Fig. 3-7. We shall use constant increments $x_0$, $y_0$ along the $x_1$, $y_1$ axes and denote the successive slices using the integer $n$. Thus the coordinates on the plotting device will be related to the coordinates used to generate the surface by

$$x_1 = x + nx_0$$
$$y_1 = z + ny_0$$

where $n = 0, 1, 2, \ldots$. From the Pythagorean theorem, the constant increments along the $y$ axis are equal to $\sqrt{x_0^2 + y_0^2}$. Hence,

$$y = n\sqrt{x_0^2 + y_0^2}$$

If one has a random-access plotting device, the problem can most simply be programmed along the following lines:

```
FOR N = Ø TO M
FOR X = Ø TO W STEP . . .
LET Y = N*SQR(XØ↑2 + YØ↑2)
LET Z = . . .  [surface to be plotted = f(x,y)]
LET X1 = X + N*XØ
LET Y1 = Z + N*YØ
REM PLOT OR STORE POINT WITH COORDINATES X1,Y1
. . .
NEXT X
NEXT N
```

Here, corresponding computer variables have been substituted for the mathematical variables (for example, $X\emptyset$, $Y\emptyset$, $X1$, and $Y1$ were substituted for $x_0$, $y_0$, $x_1$, and $y_1$), and it is assumed that the width of each slice in the $X$ direction is $W$. In general one has to introduce various scale factors in order to display the surface to best advantage. One also needs a special purpose subroutine to plot a point with coordinates $X1$, $Y1$ on the display device used. A display of this type made with a digital $xy$ recorder is shown in Fig. 3-8.

One *could* use precisely the same approach to compute points for a teletype plot of the surface. However, that approach is awkward because of the necessity of storing all of the computed points before starting the plot (see Section 3.5). With the teletype display, it pays to turn the problem around and compute the separate points $y_1$ for each of the different slices $n$ before incrementing the $x_1$ coordinate (direction of the roller advance.) In this manner we can plot the surface while computing it and do not have to store the points for a subsequent display. At the same time, we can solve the hidden line problem (which was ignored in Fig. 3-8) in a very simple manner: By keeping track of the maximum value of $y_1$ for a given $x_1$ in going from the foreground to the background (direction of increasing $n$), we can suppress plotting points that would normally be hidden from view. To put this program into effect, we merely need to turn our previous equations around. Note that if we specify $x_1$,

$$x = x_1 - nx_0$$
$$y = n\sqrt{x_0^2 + y_0^2}$$
$$z = f(x, y)$$
$$y_1 = z + ny_0$$

where $n = 0, 1, 2, \ldots$ for the successive slices.

87

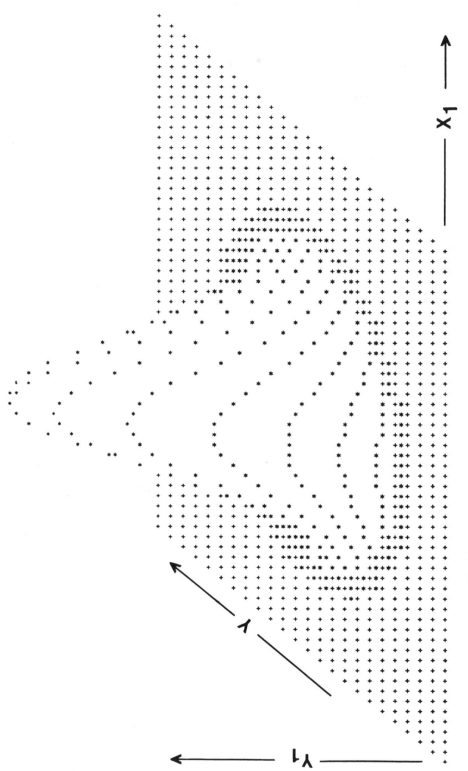

**Fig. 3-7.** Perspective plot of a surface made with a teletype machine. (The roller advanced along the $x_1$ axis, and the points were plotted sequentially along the $y_1$ axis for fixed values of $x_1$.)

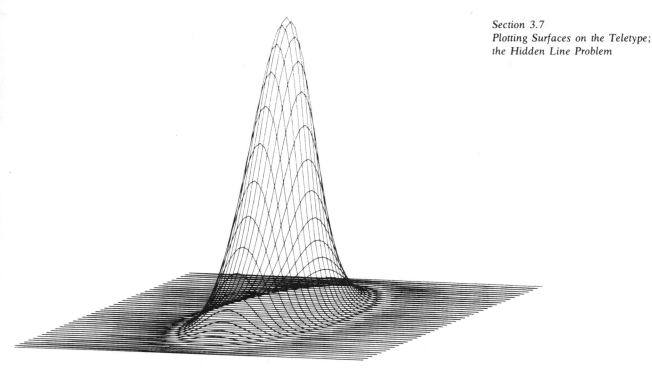

**Fig. 3-8.** Plot of the surface $z = e^{-(x^2+y^2)}$ made with a digital $xy$ recorder by displacing slices in the $xz$ plane for successive increments in y.

Before we can run such a program on a computer, we have to make some reasonable choice for the various scale factors involved. For example, the statements

```
10   LET W = 50
20   PRINT "NUMBER OF SLICES"
30   INPUT M
40   LET Y0 = INT(36/M + .5)
50   LET X0 = INT(3*Y0/5 + .5)
```

will permit making the width ($W$) of each slice in the $x$ direction equal to fifty teletype lines and permit varying the total number of slices ($M$). If we allot half (36 columns) of the available plotting space to the foreground, the increment ($Y0$) in the $y_1$ direction is defined in terms of the total number of slices. (See line 40). If we want the y axis of the perspective plot to make an angle of about 45° in respect to the $x_1$ axis (see Fig. 3-7), the increment ($X0$) in the $x_1$ direction is automatically defined by $Y0$ and the ratio of column width to line spacing. (See line 50). We next vary $X1$ from zero to $W + M*X0$ and initialize a parameter $J$ which will be used to keep running track of the maximum value of $Y1$ plotted for a given $X1$.

```
60   FOR X1 = 0 TO W + M*X0
70   LET J = 0
```

We then compute all points to be plotted in the $M$ slices for a given value of $X1$.

```
80    FOR N = 0 TO M
90    IF N < INT((X1 − W)/X0 + .5) THEN 240
100   IF N > INT(X1/X0 + .5) THEN 250
110   LET Y1 = INT(N*Y0 + .5)
120   IF Y1 < = J THEN 150
130   PRINT TAB(Y1 − 1);"+";
140   LET J = Y1
150   LET X = X1 − N*X0
```

```
160   LET Y = N*SQR(XØ↑2 + YØ↑2)
170   LET R2 = (X − 25)↑2 + (Y − 25)↑2
180   LET F = EXP(−1.50000E − 02*R2)
190   LET Z = 50*F
200   LET Y1 = INT(Z + N*YØ + .5)
210   IF Y1 < = J THEN 240
220   PRINT TAB(Y1 − 1);"*";
230   LET J = Y1
240   NEXT N
250   PRINT
260   NEXT X1
270   END
```

Line 1ØØ prevents computing points which would fall to the left of the y axis in Fig. 3-7. Similarly, line 9Ø suppresses points which would occur for $x > W$ at the right hand side of Fig. 3-7. Lines 11Ø and 13Ø plot the background plane (points where $z = 0$) using the + symbol, and hidden points are suppressed by line 12Ø. The computer equivalents of the mathematical variables x, y are determined on lines 15Ø and 16Ø for the nth slice. The function $z = f(x, y)$ is defined by lines 17Ø through 19Ø. This function was arbitrarily chosen to illustrate the plotting method: It is of the form $z = e^{-(x^2 + y^2)}$, but with a peak height of 50, centered at the point $x = y = 25$. Lines 2ØØ and 22Ø plot the points Y1 using the * symbol, except that hidden points are suppressed by the conditional statement on line 21Ø. Lines 14Ø and 23Ø keep running track of the maximum value of Y1 for previously plotted points for constant X1 using the variable J. After plotting the points Y1 for all M slices, the carriage return and roller advance are activated by line 25Ø and the variable X1 is incremented by line 26Ø. The result of running the program is shown in Fig. 3-7. The same method could, of course, be used to suppress hidden lines in displays which are plotted one point at a time with high-resolution analog devices. An approximate stereoscopic effect can also be achieved using the same technique. All we have to do is run the above program again after shifting the location of the surface along the x axis. (See Fig. 3-9). Viewing the two figures (after suitable photoreduction) separately with your two eyes further enhances the illusion that the surface is standing up on the background plane. (A more precise method of computing stereoscopic projections is discussed in the following section.)

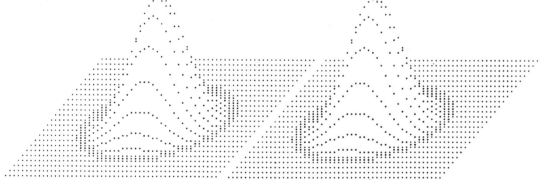

**Fig. 3-9.** Illusion of a stereoscopic effect created by lateral displacement of the surface origin in respect to the background plane. The left-hand figure was created using $R2 = (X − 26)↑2 + (Y − 25)↑2$ on line 17Ø; whereas the right-hand figure was generated with $R2 = (X − 24)↑2 + (Y − 25)↑2$. To see this figure (and subsequent three-dimensional figures) stereoscopically, first hold the figure about two feet from your eyes without trying to focus on it. Move the figure laterally so that the right-hand projection is centered on the right eye and the left-hand projection is centered on the left eye. You should then be aware of four fuzzy images in your brain. Make the two center images coincide in your brain and focus on this superposition (a slight rotation may help). At this point you should see the surface standing up from the background plane.

The gain, $G$, in the first helium–neon laser was found to vary with pump rate $(P)$ and radial position $(R)$ in a cylindrical discharge tube of unit radius approximately as

$$G(R, P) \approx P[2 - P(1 - 0.2R^2)] \cos(\pi R/2) \qquad \text{for } -1 \leq R \leq +1$$

Plot the surface $G(R, P)$ using the methods of this section over the domain $-1 \leq R \leq +1$ on the $x$ axis and for the pump rate $(P)$ varying from 2 to 0 for the different slices.

Because people normally look at objects simultaneously with two eyes located at different points in space, the three-dimensional character of an object may be recorded in the brain. One can record the three-dimensional effect photographically by placing a camera lens at each eye location and by taking two photographs simultaneously. The scene is then reconstructed in the brain of the observer when the "right" eye looks at the "right" photograph and the "left" eye looks at the "left" photograph. The process is known as *stereoscopic photography* and has enjoyed sporadic popularity during the present century.

It is sometimes helpful to construct a stereoscopic view of a surface or curve based on experimental data or a computed function. One can do this in a simple manner, using some graphic display device to plot out the two stereoscopic projections required. To accomplish this objective it is necessary to analyze the projection process involved for one eye looking at the curve alone. The easiest way to accomplish that objective involves the use of three-dimensional vectors. (If necessary, see the review of vector algebra in Chapter 2.) The geometry for the problem is shown schematically in Fig. 3-10.

In what follows we shall assume that we wish to draw the projection of the curve $y = f(x, z)$ on a sheet of paper located in the $xy$ plane. We wish to compute the intersection of a straight line with the $xy$ plane, which line is drawn from the eye location through variable points $P$ on the curve (see Fig. 3-10).

**3.8**
**Computing Stereoscopic Projections of Lines in Space**

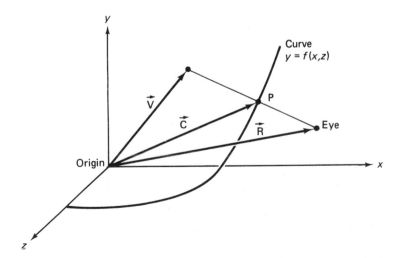

**Fig. 3-10.** Relationship of vectors used in the projection of three-dimensional quantities (such as the point $P$ on the curve $y = f(x, z)$) onto the two-dimensional plane $xy$. The vector $\vec{R}$ denotes the eye location; the vector $\vec{C}$ indicates the point $P$ on the curve; and the vector $\vec{V}$ (located in the plane $xy$) indicates the location of the projection of point $P$ on the plane $xy$ as seen by the eye. A stereoscopic view of this basic diagram is shown in Fig. 3-11.

We shall use the notation

$\vec{R}$ = vector from the origin to the eye [i.e., the coordinates of the eye are $R(1)$, $R(2)$, $R(3)$]

$\vec{C}$ = vector from the origin to a particular point $P$ on the curve. We shall eventually let $P$ trace out the curve; for the particular illustration in Fig. 3-10, the curve was assumed to be of the form $y = x^2$; $z =$ constant

$\vec{V}$ = vector in the $xy$ plane, or projection plane (plotting paper, oscilloscope, $xy$ recorder, teletype, etc.) which points to the intersection made with the $xy$ plane by a straight line drawn from the eye through the point $P$ on the curve

First we shall construct the equation for a straight line passing through the points $\vec{R}$ and $\vec{C}$ in the direction of the vector $\vec{R} - \vec{C}$. For that purpose it is convenient to introduce a scalar parameter $t$ (i.e., $t$ has magnitude but no direction) and consider the vector defined by

$$\vec{r} = \vec{C} + t(\vec{R} - \vec{C})$$

Note that when $t = 0$, $\vec{r} = \vec{C}$ (i.e., $\vec{r}$ falls on top of $\vec{C}$), and when $t = 1$, $\vec{r} = \vec{R}$ ($\vec{r}$ falls on top of $\vec{R}$). As we let $t$ vary from $-\infty$ to $+\infty$, the tip of the vector $\vec{r}$ traces out the entire straight line passing through the tips of the vectors $\vec{C}$ and $\vec{R}$.

Applying these results to the projection problem, we want to find the value of $t \equiv t_0$ where the straight line defined by the vector $\vec{r}$ intersects the $xy$ plane. That is, $\vec{V} = \vec{r}$ for $t = t_0$. Note that at this intersection, $r_z = r(3) = 0$, and therefore

$$r(3) = 0 = C(3) + t_0[R(3) - C(3)]$$

or

$$t_0 = -\frac{C(3)}{R(3) - C(3)} \quad \text{and} \quad \vec{V} = \vec{C} + t_0(\vec{R} - \vec{C})$$

Therefore, the desired coordinates of the point in the projection plane are given by the vector

$$\vec{V} = \vec{C} - \frac{C(3)}{R(3) - C(3)}(\vec{R} - \vec{C}) = \frac{R(3)\vec{C} - C(3)\vec{R}}{R(3) - C(3)}$$

Note that $V(3) = 0$ and that there will be a singularity if the curve passes through the plane $C(3) = R(3)$ (because the line drawn through the eye and the point on the curve would then be parallel to the $xy$ plane). Hence, after computing a specific point on the curve, it is a simple matter to construct a subroutine that may be used over and over to accomplish the stereoscopic projection; for example:

```
900   REM SUB. FINDS AND PLOTS COORDINATES IN (XY) PROJECTION PLANE
910   FOR I = 1 TO 2
920   LET V(I) = (R(3)*C(I) − C(3)*R(I))/(R(3) − C(3))
930   NEXT I
940   REM PLOT OR STORE POINT WITH COORDINATES X1 = X∅ + V(1); Y1 = Y∅ + V(2)
...
950   RETURN
```

where $X\emptyset$ and $Y\emptyset$ are the coordinates for a suitable origin chosen for the particular plotting device.

The only remaining programming problem is to enter the coordinates of the viewer's eyes and to generate the curves to be projected. In general, the curves could be anything that you can describe mathematically or tabulate within DATA statements (see the examples in Fig. 3-11). Computed curves are easiest to describe parametrically. For example, consider computing the projections of a straight line with arbitrary orientation in space. If the vector $\vec{O}$ points

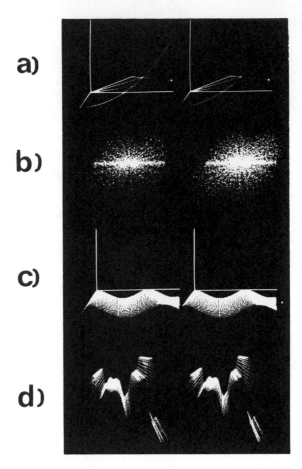

**Fig. 3-11.** Some miscellaneous stereo-scopic projections:

(a) Stereoscopic view of the vectors used in the projection process itself (see Fig. 3-10).

(b) The electron cloud in three dimensions for an excited state of hydrogen.

(c) The surface $Y = -1 + COS(K*X)$ for $X > 0$.

(d) Waveform from a French horn played loudly, with time along the horizontal axis.

to the start of the line and the vector $\vec{P}$ points to the end of the line, the equation for the line may be written

$$\vec{C} = \vec{O} + t(\vec{P} - \vec{O}) \qquad \text{where} \qquad 0 \leqslant t \leqslant 1$$

Consequently the projection may be computed with a program of the type

```
FOR T = 0 TO 1 STEP...
FOR I = 1 TO 3
LET C(I) = O(I) + T*(P(I) − O(I))
NEXT I
GOSUB 900
NEXT T
```

where we have used column arrays for the vectors involved and the STEP size on the parameter $T$ would depend on the required resolution. This type of procedure is needed to plot straight lines on point-plotting devices (teletype machines, oscilloscopes, crossed-wire discharge displays, and so on.) However, some digital $xy$ recorders (such as the Hewlett-Packard 7210A) are constructed using internal analog computers in such a way that only the initial and end points are required to draw a continuous straight line. A method for computing more general functions than straight lines is discussed in the following section.

It is easy to compute curved functions that are symmetric about one of the principal rectangular axes $(x, y, z)$ without additional fuss and bother. However, if you want to compute more general functions, it is helpful to introduce other base vectors to define the curve parametrically. As shown in Fig. 3-12,

**3.9**
**Use of Variable-Base Vectors**
**to Compute More General**
**Functions**

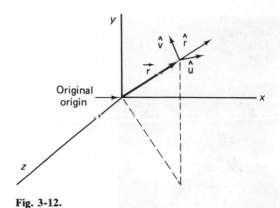

**Fig. 3-12.**

let $\vec{r}$ be a vector to a particular point (where $\vec{r}$ itself might be determined parametrically in terms of the normal spherical coordinate angles), and introduce orthogonal, right-handed unit vectors $\hat{r}$, $\hat{u}$, and $\hat{v}$ such that

$$\hat{u} \times \hat{v} = \hat{r} \qquad \hat{r} \times \hat{u} = \hat{v} \qquad \hat{v} \times \hat{r} = \hat{u}$$

i.e., $\hat{u}$ and $\hat{v}$ are in a plane perpendicular to $\hat{r}$ and comprise a rectangular-coordinate system that can be used locally to describe a curve and can be moved about in space. In terms of these vectors and the scalar parameters $r$, $\rho$, and $A$, we can describe the location of a point on a general curve (see Fig. 3-13).

That is,

$$\vec{C} = \vec{r} + \rho \cos A \hat{u} + \rho \sin A \hat{v} \tag{1}$$

represents a fairly general parametric description for a point on the curve. We can determine the unit vector $\hat{r}$ from the direction and magnitude of $\vec{r}$; i.e., the unit vector $\hat{r}$ has components, $r_0(I)$, given by

$$r_0(I) = \frac{r(I)}{\sqrt{r(1)^2 + r(2)^2 + r(3)^2}} \qquad \begin{array}{l} \text{where } I = 1,\,2,\,3 \\ \text{and } r(I) \text{ are the components of } \vec{r} \end{array} \tag{2}$$

The specific direction of either $\hat{u}$ or $\hat{v}$ within the plane perpendicular to $\vec{r}$ is arbitrary. For example, we might choose

$$\hat{u} \propto \hat{j} \times \hat{r} = \begin{vmatrix} \hat{i} & \hat{j} & \hat{k} \\ 0 & 1 & 0 \\ r_0(1) & r_0(2) & r_0(3) \end{vmatrix} \tag{3}$$

Hence

$$\hat{u} = [\hat{i} r_0(3) - \hat{k} r_0(1)]/\sqrt{r_0(1)^2 + r_0(3)^2}$$

Then

$$\hat{v} = \hat{r} \times \hat{u} = \begin{vmatrix} \hat{i} & \hat{j} & \hat{k} \\ r_0(1) & r_0(2) & r_0(3) \\ r_0(3) & 0 & -r_0(1) \end{vmatrix} \times [r_0(1)^2 + r_0(3)^2]^{-\frac{1}{2}} \tag{4}$$

or

$$\hat{v} = [-r_0(1)r_0(2)\hat{i} + [r_0(1)^2 + r_0(3)^2]\hat{j} - r_0(2)r_0(3)\hat{k}]/\sqrt{r_0(1)^2 + r_0(3)^2}$$

where $r_0(1)$, $r_0(2)$, and $r_0(3)$ are the components of the unit vector $\hat{r}$ on the $x$, $y$, and $z$ axes. Substituting the results of Eqs. (3) and (4) in Eq. (1) yields a simple

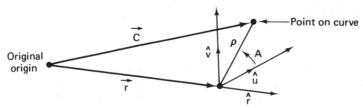

**Fig. 3-13.**

method to treat complex curves having variable amounts of helical symmetry; e.g., $\vec{r}$, $\rho$, and $A$ can be defined as functions of some other parameter to provide the desired pitch relations for a helix. Similarly, one could represent

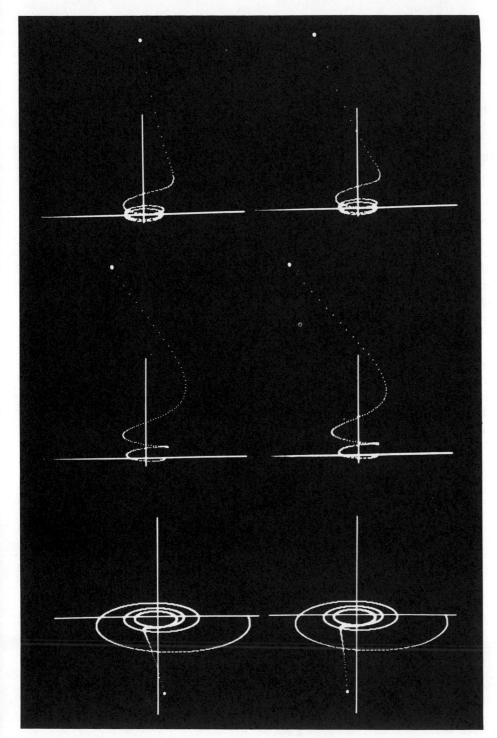

**Fig. 3-14.** Shooting at the viewer with computed functions. Although it is relatively easy to shoot over the viewer's head, or hit him in the stomach, it is pretty hard to get in a good nose shot.

the vector $\vec{r}$ in Eq. (1) in terms of still another vector-addition process. Steroscopic projections of the curves may then be obtained from Eq. (1) in the manner previously discussed.

For example, suppose we wanted to describe a helix of radius $R1$ aimed from the origin in the $(1, 1, 1)$ direction. Application of Eqs. (1)–(4) permits plotting the projection with a program of the type

```
200   REM PLOT HELIX IN (1,1,1) DIRECTION
210   FOR T=0 TO ... STEP ...
220   LET R=T
230   LET A=.01*T
240   LET C(1)=R/SQR(3)+R1*COS(A)/SQR(2)−R1*SIN(A)/SQR(6)
250   LET C(2)=R/SQR(3)+R1*SIN(A)*SQR(2/3)
260   LET C(3)=R/SQR(3)−R1*COS(A)/SQR(2)−R1*SIN(A)/SQR(6)
270   GOSUB 900
280   NEXT T
```

where the limits and step size on the parameter $T$ (line 210) and pitch of the helix (lines 220 and 230) would be adjusted to fit the requirements of the particular problem.

Some illustrations based on this type of parametric method are given in Figs. 3-14 and 3-15.

Just what is realistic to suggest in the way of problems in this subject is highly dependent on available plotting or display equipment. A teletype terminal or line printer alone simply does not have adequate resolution for satisfactory display of complex stereoscopically computed functions. Hence, except for the computation of Julesz patterns discussed in the following section, the teletype terminal itself is mainly useful for printing coordinates of computed projections. This process serves a useful purpose in illustrating the projection technique. Because it is fairly painless to draw straight lines between pairs of points by hand on graph paper, the teletype approach is fairly practical in problems which primarily involve straight lines. For example, the usual architectural renderings of buildings mostly consist of monocular projections of straight line segments and the teletype machine is useful in listing the initial and terminal coordinates of such projections. However, it becomes much more cumbersome if the "artist" has to draw in projected curves through computed points, or fill in probability clouds by hand.

The following problems are intended mainly as suggestions from which the reader might want to free-associate along lines of his or her own personal interest.

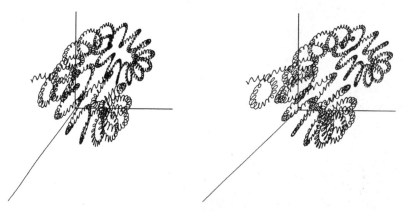

**Fig. 3-15.** Stereoscopic projection of a model of the honeybee chromosome. According to DuPraw (1970, p. 179), the chromosomal type B fiber is made up as follows:

> A length of Watson-Crick double helix 20 Å in diameter and 56 microns long could be wound into a supercoiled fiber 80 to 100 Å in diameter and 7 to 8 microns long; the latter could then be supercoiled again into its fully packed form, 230 Å in diameter and only 1 micron long.

For clarity, only one half of the original Watson-Crick double helix is shown in the figure. (The figure was computed by one of the author's students, Tsun-Yan Tse, using the methods of the present section.)

| **3.9**<br>**PROBLEM 11** | Compute and draw stereoscopic projections of a cube, or tetrahedron, resting on the projection plane as seen from some convenient point in space. Alternatively, plot a stereoscopic projection of a rectangular room or a crystal lattice or a building. |
| --- | --- |
| **3.9**<br>**PROBLEM 12** | If you have a high resolution plotting device, try something like a suspension bridge, or the Eiffel Tower (i.e., objects for which the primary lines have simple functional forms and in which you do not have to worry much about "hidden" lines.) Alternatively, try projecting a probability cloud or DNA molecule. |

**3.10**
**Psychology of Stereoscopic Perception (Julesz Patterns)**

Julesz (1971) performed some experiments on pattern recognition that have some bearing on the mechanism of stereoscopic perception in the brain. For example, Julesz used a computer to generate random dot patterns upon stereoscopic projections of familiar objects in which the normal monocular visual cues were eliminated.

This type of projection process is fairly easy to carry out with an ordinary teletype terminal and presents some interesting programming problems at the same time. In addition, once you have set up a program to compute this type of projection process, you can try out your own theories on the psychological effects involved.

The main objectives in the programming exercise are outlined in Fig. 3-16. First we want to be able to create a random background pattern on the projection plane. Next we want to erase an area in this background plane in which the projection of a specified object falls. And, finally, we wish to project a random dot pattern within this area corresponding to some object chosen in the foreground.

There are some practical difficulties involved in accomplishing the objective using the general projective techniques discussed above and arbitrary three-dimensional objects in the foreground. The basic practical difficulty arises in maintaining (1) the same foreground random dot pattern as seen from both eye locations under conditions where (2) the same average dot density is produced within the projection plane as that provided in the absence of the object; that is, we do not want to give away the existence of the object merely by average differences in shading. At the same time, unless we are careful to preserve both the same foreground and background patterns, we shall have great difficulty in seeing the object in stereoscopic representation.

A simple modification of the approach used by Julesz solves these problems without prohibitive computational difficulties. We shall assume that the foreground object falls in a plane parallel to the projection plane. And we shall then simulate a precise stereoscopic projection of the planar object merely by sliding a particular random dot pattern back and forth laterally within the projection plane. This permits us to use identically the same average darkening as that initially found within the projection plane.

We shall illustrate by concealing a square within the background, along the lines of approach depicted in Fig. 3-16. First we shall consider a straightforward approach, which however uses up a lot of core to store the data. Because of the difference between teletype column width and line spacing, we need a rectangular array to store a square. First, we shall store the background random dot pattern in a matrix $M(I, J)$ dimensioned so that we can generate patterns that are approximately square.

5   DIM M(45,72)

97

**Fig. 3-16.** Parts of the problem involved in computing Julesz patterns:

(a) The original random pattern on the projection plane.

(b) Removal of original pattern in region where image is to be projected.

(c) New random pattern (with same average density) representing projection on the original plane from position of one eye.

The same background pattern (a) and projected pattern (c) are used with both eyes. The location of the hole (b) in the background pattern is varied laterally to simulate the effects of perspective.

Next we shall fill this matrix in with a random pattern:

```
110  FOR I = 1 TO 45
120  FOR J = 1 TO 72
130  LET M(I,J) = INT(RND(1) + .5)
140  NEXT J
150  NEXT I
```

and then provide a section of programming to permit displaying the pattern:

```
900  FOR I = 1 TO 45
920  FOR J = 1 TO 72
930  IF M(I,J) = 0 THEN 960
940  PRINT "+";
950  GOTO 970
960  PRINT " ";
970  NEXT J
980  PRINT
990  NEXT I
```

Running this much of the program results in Fig. 3-16(a).

Next we would like to introduce an eye coordinate

```
50  PRINT "HORIZONTAL EYE COORDINATE"
60  INPUT D0
```

Then we wish both to erase the background matrix and introduce a random dot pattern within the bounds of the square. If this square extends between columns 24 and 48 and rows 15 and 30 on the teletype output, the objective is accomplished by the statements

```
310  FOR I = 15 TO 30
320  FOR J = 24 − D0 TO 48 − D0
330  LET M(I,J) = INT(RND(1) + .5)
340  NEXT J
350  NEXT I
```

These statements both open the "window" in the background matrix as shown in Fig. 3-16(b) and insert a new random dot pattern within the square of the type shown in Fig. 3-16(c). (Figure 3-16 was computed with $D0 = 0$.) Running the program with positive and negative integer values of $D0$ then generates stereoscopic pairs that will permit us to see the square three-dimensionally, under conditions in which it would be impossible to detect its existence looking with only one eye (at one projection) at a time. The results of such a computation for $D0 = \pm 1$ are shown at the top of Fig. 3-17 ($N = 1$).

By a slight modification of the program above, it is easy to introduce varying amounts of micropatterns within the random structure. Instead of merely making a binary choice, we can choose from $N$ quantities. For example, a statement of the type

```
LET M(I,J) = 32 + INT(N*RND(1) + .5)
```

introduced on lines 130 and 330 above permits printing $N$ ASCII characters in the final pattern through use of the CHR$ statement (if you have it, or an equivalent CALL statement, available within your computer). Here one merely replaces lines 930–960 with one statement,

```
930  PRINT CHR$(M(I, J));
```

The results of this modification are illustrated in Fig. 3-17 for $N = 15$ and 90. The existence of additional micropatterns can make it easier to superimpose the two stereoscopic projections and see the suspended square in the middle.

In the following two problems, it will be desirable to photoreduce the

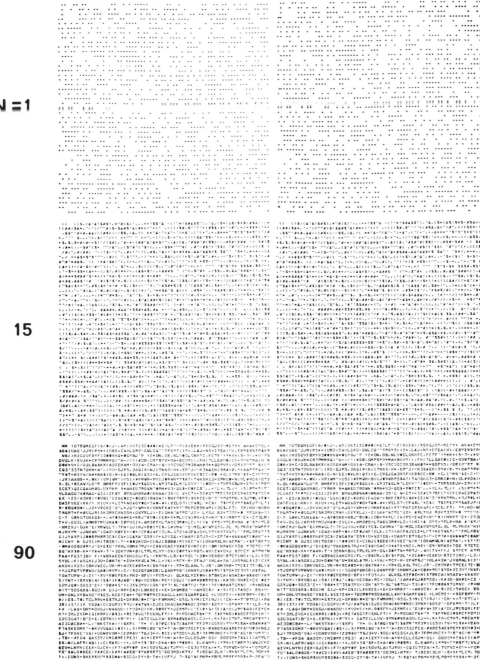

**N = 1**

**15**

**90**

LEFT EYE          RIGHT EYE

**Fig. 3-17.** Three-dimensional Julesz patterns shown with increasing complexity of micropatterns. A square raised above the background plane is depicted in each case. (Malfunctioning of the teletype machine used to generate the present figure has also introduced some spurious corrugations in the background plane.) The number $N$ corresponds to the number of ASCII characters called for in addition to the space symbol within the program discussed in the text. (The AR-33 teletype machine, of course, did not distinguish between upper and lower case.) The original teletype output (45 lines by 72 columns) was reduced photographically by a factor of 3.3 to provide a comfortable eye separation (about 2.25 inches) for direct viewing. The net separation between the right- and left-eye projections of the suspended square was two teletype columns. Try to see the three-dimensional square in the top stereoscopic pair first ($N = 1$). Some people find that the feat becomes progressively easier with increasing complexity of the micropatterns (increasing $N$). Those people with a penchant for intrigue will doubtless want to consider using the method to transmit secret messages. Students of psychology will want to note that inability to see such patterns is correlated with certain types of brain damage (see Julesz, 1971). Of course, such inability is also correlated with eye defects, so do not immediately become despondent if you cannot see the suspended square!

images to a realistic size to view directly (or through a stereoscopic viewer). Average adult eye separation is about $2\frac{1}{4}$ inches. A Polaroid copying camera helps considerably.

---

**3.24**
**PROBLEM 13**
Less computer memory will be needed in the program above if we merely compute the dot pattern for the small matrix in Fig. 3-16(c) first (with 16 by 25 elements) and then fill in around it the remaining background pattern where needed. Write a program that permits computing the equivalent of Fig. 3-17(a) using this more economical approach. Note that you have to run through the RND(1) function $45 \times 72$ times the background plane in order to get a legitimate substitute for each eye; Fig. 3-16(a). That is, the background patterns must be the same for both eyes throughout the entire figure.

**3.24**
**PROBLEM 14**
If you have the CHR$ function (or equivalent CALL statement) on your computer, write a program to include variable levels of micropatterns in computing the example in Fig. 3-17. Run the program with increasing values of $N$ and see if you can make any quantitative correlation between $N$ and the speed with which you (or others) can visualize the three-dimensional pattern. Julesz implies that you first perceive the three-dimensional image and then note the mircopatterns. What do you think?

---

## REFERENCES

CONDON, E. U., AND G. H. SHORTLEY (1963). *The Theory of Atomic Spectra*. New York: Cambridge University Press.

DuPRAW, E. J. (1970). *DNA and Chromosomes*. New York: Holt, Rinehart and Winston, Inc.

JAHNKE, EUGENE, AND FRITZ EMDE (1945). *Tables of Functions with Formulae and Curves*. New York: Dover Publications, Inc.

JULESZ, BELA (1971). *Foundations of Cyclopean Perception*. Chicago: University of Chicago Press.

# Language

4

This chapter could serve as the main part of a one-term course designed to draw humanity majors into the world of computers. It only requires programming facility at an introductory level and deals mostly with subjects that are of general familiarity. The material in Sections 4.12–4.15 on information theory and entropy may appeal primarily to people with an interest in communication theory. However, the material on entropy per character in Section 4.13 has an important bearing on many fields of general interest (e.g., anthropology, error correction, cryptography, and even the detection of extra-terrestrial civilization.) Although most of Section 4.13 deals with the qualitative meaning of Shannon's definition of entropy, all that is really needed for the remainder of the chapter is the mathematical definition of the entropy per character in various statistical orders for printed text. (See Eqs. (24), (43), (44).) The general reader ought at least to have a look at Section 4.14 on anthropology, Section 4.15 on bit compression, Section 4.21 on the detection of decipherable messages, and Section 4.22 on the Voynich manuscript. However, if the reader feels determined to avoid dealing with entropy in language, he (or she) should take the following route:

Sections 4.1 through 4.12 (the monkey problem through language and style identification); read Section 4.15 (on bit compression), and Sections 4.16 through 4.20 (on cryptography). In this path, the hardest programming difficulties occur in the second-order literary crypt solver discussed at the end of Section 4.20. (The latter could easily be omitted in a "short course.")

Finally, it is worth noting that much of the material in this chapter is of a sufficiently general nature to warrant reading on its own merits—even if you aren't interested in computing. In this case, just skip all of the programming statements.

Man's compulsion to communicate generally shows up early in a computing course. One frequently encounters student programs containing long strings of alphanumeric characters to be printed at various branch points ranging from dull factual statements (e.g., "THE NUMBER OF PRIMES LESS THAN ...IS...") to messages of flamboyant bravado (e.g., "THANKS FOR THE GAME YOU CLOD AND BETTER LUCK NEXT TIME"). This kind of thing is much more entertaining if you cannot tell ahead of time from the program just exactly what the computer is going to say. We shall therefore consider an alternative approach to the problem, both to make the form of the conversation more interesting and to illustrate some fundamental statistical properties of written languages in general.

There has been a sporadic preoccupation with the statistical aspects of language throughout much of recorded history. Recent quantitative manifestations of this interest have mostly gone under the heading *information theory*. From the advent of the telegraph on, there has been an increasing concentration on the mathematical analysis of communication problems—an interest reflected by the early papers of Nyquist and Hartley, through the more generally known work of Shannon. It is not surprising to find that much of this research was supported by a company in the communications field (Bell Laboratories). In addition, the subject was stimulated by government concern with transmission and detection of "secret" messages during and in between wars. More recently, the insatiable appetite for data transmission shown by the computer field as a whole has elicited still more concern, if not outright anxiety. The contemporary transmission unit is megabits per second.

Activity has also gone on with those less motivated by practical application, for interest in the statistical aspects of language is clearly lurking at least subliminally below the surface in most of us. In fact, it is probably not entirely accidental that the foremost American contributor to statistical mechanics, Josiah Willard Gibbs, was himself the son of a philologist. Gibbs the elder was something of a pioneer in urging that language should be the object of scientific study from a correlative point of view (see Gibbs, 1857).

## 4.1 Monkeys at the Typewriters

Nearly everyone knows that if enough monkeys were allowed to pound away at typewriters for enough time, all the great works of literature would result. The universal appeal of this notion to human imagination is demonstrated by the wide variety of circumstances in which it appears. For example, the basic concept involved has been used in a contemporary nightclub act by Bob Newhart, in a series of popular lectures on statistical mechanics given about 50 years ago by Sir Arthur Eddington, and in the discourses on religious philosophy by the seventeenth-century archbishop John Tillotson (1630–1694). Elaborate fantasies on this general theme have been given by Maloney (1945) and Vonnegut (1950). Kurt Vonnegut's treatment is probably the first one that implies a computer simulation of the problem.

The earliest specific use of the basic concept known to the present author is to be found in the *Maxims and Discourses* of Archbishop Tillotson, published posthumously in 1719. In his "Answer to the Epicurean System," Tillotson applied the notion to the creation of poetry, prose, entire books, portrait painting, and even the creation of Man and the World. He then went on to imply that the improbability of these events occurring through chance constitutes an argument for the existence of God. His original statement of the problem is so profoundly moving that we have reproduced the paragraph in entirety in Fig. 4-1.

Most contemporary use of the concept is traceable to the Gifford Lectures presented by Eddington at Cambridge in 1927. Here Eddington first brought

*In Anſwer to the* Epicurean *Syſtem, he argues* ] How often might a Man, after he had jumbled a Set of Letters in a Bag, fling them out upon the Ground before they would fall into an exact Poem, yea or ſo much as make a good Diſcourſe in Proſe? And may not a little *Book* be as eaſily made by Chance, as this great *Volume* of the World? How long might a Man be in ſprinkling Colours upon a Canvas with a careleſs Hand, before they could happen to make the exact Picture of a Man? And is a Man eaſier made by Chance than his Picture? How long might twenty thouſand *blind Men*, which ſhould be ſent out from the ſeveral remote Parts of *England*, wander up and down before they would all meet upon *Salisbury-Plains*, and fall into Rank and File in the exact Order of an Army? And yet this is much more eaſy to be imagin'd, than how the innumerable *blind Parts* of Matter ſhould rendezvouze themſelves into a World.

**Fig. 4-1.** Quotation from the seventeenth-century archbishop John Tillotson (1630–1694). The figure has been reproduced from College Pamphlets V, *Maxims and Discourses Moral and Devine: Taken from the Works of Arch-Bishop Tillotson, and Methodiz'd and Connected*, London, 1719. For clarity, the two portions of the paragraph starting at the bottom of page 10 of the original publication and continuing on the top of page 11 have been pieced together photographically. The author is indebted to the Beineke Rare Book and Manuscript Library at Yale University for permission to reproduce this material.

monkeys into the act with the statement:

> "If an army of monkeys were strumming on typewriters they *might* write all the books in the British Museum" (p. 72).

Eddington was discussing one of those rare statistical fluctuations so often mentioned in popular discourses on science: things which most reasoning people agree could happen in principle (e.g., that a kettle of water might freeze when you put it on the stove); however, the probabilities of them actually occurring are so unimaginably small that you would risk being carted off to the psychiatric ward if you ever reported seeing the event.[1]

Specifically, Eddington was discussing the likelihood of finding all $N$ molecules in a container in one half of that container. If each molecule wanders about randomly throughout the entire vessel, the probability of finding it in one particular half of the volume would be $\frac{1}{2}$. Similarly, the probability of finding all $N$ molecules in the same half would be $(\frac{1}{2}) \times (\frac{1}{2}) \times (\frac{1}{2}) \cdots = (\frac{1}{2})^N$. Suppose that the container had a volume of 4 cm$^3$ and was filled with an ideal gas at standard temperature and pressure. Then $N \approx 10^{20}$ and the probability of finding all $N$ molecules in one half of the vessel is 1 chance in

$$2^N \approx 2^{10^{20}} \approx 10^{3 \times 10^{19}} \tag{1}$$

The number $2^N$ is so large that it defies human visualization. Imagine looking from the top of the Empire State Building to the horizon ($\approx 50$ miles) in all directions and suppose that the surface of the earth were covered to the

---

[1] For example, when 5 engines and 17 freight cars from three separate tracks in a freight yard at Newark, N.J., mysteriously assembled themselves into a freight train and drove off an open drawbridge into the Passaic River, the police suspected sabotage rather than statistical fluctuations (*The New York Times*, Oct. 7, 1970, p. 95, col. 5).

horizon with closely packed squares each having an edge of 0.001 inch ($\approx \frac{1}{5}$ the size of a human hair). In a reasonable sense, the number of squares would be the largest number you could hope to visualize; it is made of about the smallest-sized object you could resolve by eye spread over a distance that is about as far as you can normally see. The total number of squares is about $3 \times 10^{19}$. Clearly, then, raising 10 to that power provides a number so large that we cannot visualize it in a simple direct manner.

For illustration, Eddington wanted to compare the probability of finding all the molecules in one half of a large vessel with something that would be much more probable—the army of monkeys typing out all the books in the British Museum. He clearly was enamored with the monkey concept and went on, in a later lecture (Eddington, 1935), to apply it to the composition of music and even to the possibility that his *own* lectures would be given over and over again by random fluctuations in the room noise.

The astronomical volume of sheer garbage that would also be produced in one of these monkey experiments is seldom given adequate appreciation. As Bob Newhart pointed out, one would need to have a staff of tireless inspectors reading all this stuff as it came out just to make sure that an occasional great work of literature was not missed. Some feeling for the magnitude of the assignment can be obtained by examining the one recognizable fragment produced in the Newhart experiment: The inspector at post fifteen caught the line

"To be or not to be, that is the *gesornenplatz* . . . ."

One should, of course, be delighted that the monkey got as far as *gesornenplatz*[2] since the probability of getting the preceding string of alphanumeric characters correct is roughly $\approx 1/(27)^{30} \approx 10^{-43}$ (assuming that we ignored the comma and gave the monkey a typewriter equipped only with the 26 letters of the alphabet and a space key). Hence, assuming that a good monkey typed steadily at $\approx 10$ characters per second, it would take one monkey about

$$3 \times 10^{43} \text{ seconds} \approx 10^{36} \text{ years} \qquad (2)$$

on the average, or a waiting period that is about 4000 times longer than the *product* of our "largest visualizable number" *and* the age of the sun.

Another way of stating the difficulty is to note that

$$3 \times 10^{44} \text{ characters} \approx 10^{41} \text{ pages} \approx 10^{39} \text{ books} \qquad (3)$$

worth of extraneous typing would have to be examined on the average by the Newhart inspectors before the first nine words of Hamlet's soliloquy would be encountered once. To be fair, lots of other 30-character, intelligible strings would also show up and would probably satisfy our needs. Nevertheless, it is clear that the example falls in the category of phenomena which a recent school of philosophy in quantum physics has branded "impossible in principle"; i.e., if the event is not likely to occur at least once in the age of the universe, the process just does not exist and it is meaningless to talk about it. (It's still fun, though.)

We shall return to this monkey business after a brief digression on character-printing subroutines.

## 4.2 Character-Printing Sieves (Subroutine 5ØØ)

In many problems within the present chapter it will be necessary to write programs that incorporate a subroutine to print alphanumeric characters corresponding to computed integers. For consistency throughout the present chapter we shall refer to this subroutine as 5ØØ. (It could, of course, be given any other program-line number allowable in BASIC.)

---

[2] The first published version of *Hamlet* (*The First Quarto*, pirated in 1603) actually goes: "To be or not to be, ay there's the point . . . ." As noted by Hubler (1963, p. 176): "It is clear that there is a hand other than Shakespeare's in this!"

Specifically, we want this subroutine to print the characters

A,B,C, . . . , Y,Z, , ',-

as the input variable $X$ takes on the values

1, 2, 3, . . . , 25, 26, 27, 28, 29

Many of the problems will involve matrices with row and column numbers determined by integer values of $X$. We do not use the normal ASCII code for the alphabet (i.e., $A = 65, \ldots$) in order to keep the matrices within practical dimensions.

We also want to set the problem up in a manner that will permit use with BASIC compilers which do not have the CHR$ function built in. In addition to printing the characters listed above, it will be desirable to introduce a column counter, $Q9$, in the subroutine which triggers the carriage return and line feed (i.e., PRINT statement) after printing spaces when $Q9 > 60$. This last provision will prevent breaking up words at the end of the 72-column format. The hyphen will be used in later discussions of bit compression and cryptography to indicate unidentified characters.

The most appropriate form of the subroutine will vary with the particular computer available. We shall start by outlining the worst possible way to do the subroutine so that the advantages of more efficient approaches to the problem will be emphasized.

A *usable* printing sieve can be constructed (albeit tediously) along the following straightforward lines:

```
5ØØ   REM, etc.    (reminders for future use of the subroutine)
51Ø   IF X#1 THEN 52Ø
512   PRINT "A";
515   RETURN
52Ø   IF X#2 THEN 53Ø
522   PRINT "B";
525   RETURN
53Ø   IF X#3 THEN 54Ø
etc.,
```

where the semicolons after the PRINT statements provide close spacing. This takes about $3 \times 29 = 87$ lines and is needlessly inefficient even when string functions are not available. If all $N = 29$ characters occur with equal probability on the average, the average time (apart from printing) to run through the subroutine will be $\approx NT_0/2$, where $T_0$ is the time for one conditional statement. For $N = 29$, there will be 14.5 conditional statements on the average.

At just what point this type of running-time limitation becomes important will depend on the available printing equipment and the size of $N$. For example, if the output is printed with an AR-33 teletype ($\approx 10$ characters per second), this running time is not a major limitation on most computers. Nevertheless, for the sake of generality, it is worthwhile considering some more efficient and faster methods of accomplishing the sorting and printing subroutine.

If your computer is limited to two-branch conditional statements, the most efficient subroutine will generally tend to be one based on a binary sorting scheme. (Some improvement can always be effected in specific cases by utilizing the character occurrence frequency in the sieve.) It will be helpful to draw a flowchart of the sorting scheme before starting to write programming statements (see Fig. 4-2). It is easiest to construct the flowchart from the bottom, up, by starting with the required output characters. In the present problem we need to print the characters A, B, C, D, . . . , for values of the input parameters $X = 1, 2, 3, 4, \ldots$. Consequently, we have grouped the output choices in pairs (1-2), (3-4), and so on, to be selected through two-branch conditional statements as shown on the bottom row of the figure.

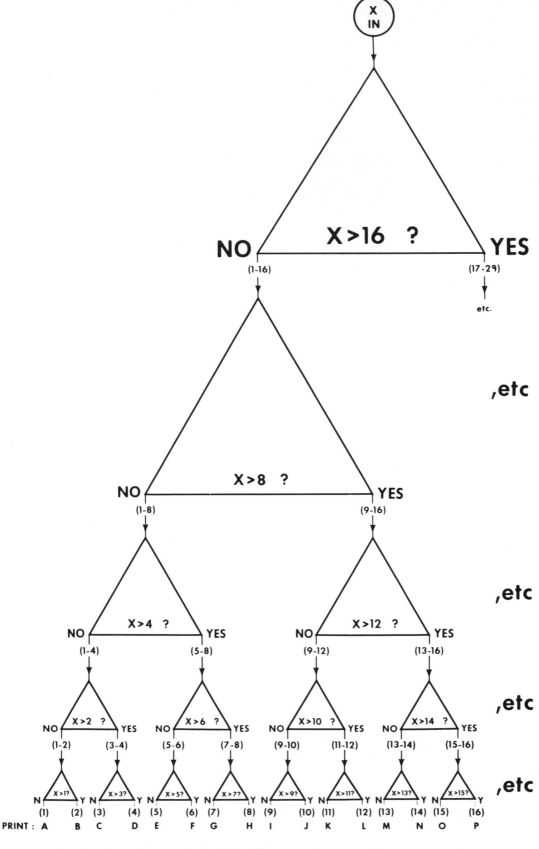

**Fig. 4-2.** Binary character-printing sieve. (This type of structure is known as a *tree* in current computer science parlance.) As outlined here, the sieve could actually handle up to 31 characters using five conditional statements (triangles) per character.

On the next-to-bottom row of Fig. 4-2, the two-branch conditional statements permit distinguishing between the pairs (1-2) and (3-4); (5-6) and (7-8); and so on. Similarly, working back to the input, we enter the subroutine by choosing between the two groups (1–16) and (17–29). A sequence of five conditional statements may thus be used to sort $2^5 - 1 = 31$ separate characters. Hence a reduction in sorting time of about a factor of 3 should be obtainable with the binary sieve over the straightforward approach outlined before.

In writing program statements to correspond to the flow chart in Fig. 4-2, it is easiest to start at the top (e.g., using the "greater than" conditional statement) and work down one side (e.g., the left) of the figure. For example,

```
500   REM SUB TO PRINT A,B,C,...,Y,Z,,',-
501   REM WHEN X = 1,2,3,, 25,26,27,28,29
502   REM Q9 COUNTS COLUMNS AND "PRINTS" AFTER SPACE FOR Q9>60
503   LET Q9 = Q9 + 1
505   IF X > 16 THEN...
510   IF X > 8 THEN...
515   IF X > 4 THEN...
520   IF X > 2 THEN 540
525   IF X > 1 THEN 535
530   PRINT "A";
532   RETURN
535   PRINT "B";
537   RETURN
540   IF X > 3 THEN...        etc.
```

where one comes back to fill in the appropriate line numbers in the conditional statements in inverse order. As before, the semicolon after the PRINT statements is required to provide close spacing. Although the subroutine takes about as many statements as the "straightforward" way, it runs about three times faster.

The same philosophy may, of course, be extended with higher-order conditional statements. Thus a P-branch conditional statement will work most effectively with a P-base sorting scheme. However, computers that are big enough to incorporate multiple-branch conditional statements usually also have some version of the CHR$ printing command.

If the alphanumeric character-printing function CHR$ exists on your computer, an efficient subroutine to accomplish the present objectives can be written in just a few lines. The CHR$ function prints the alphanumeric characters based on integer arguments corresponding to the ASCII (American Standard Code for Information Interchange) convention summarized in Table 1 of Chapter 1. [Function arguments corresponding to the line feed, vertical tab, form feed, and carriage return (integers 10–13) are excluded from this function in normal versions of BASIC.] Note that the characters presently needed which fall outside the normal 26-letter alphabet all have ASCII integers <65 and that the alphabetical order is preserved in the ASCII code (integers 65–90). Therefore, the computer has already done most of the sorting for us if we can get at the internal ASCII code. Hence, assuming

$$1 \leqslant X \leqslant 29 \tag{4}$$

only one conditional statement is needed at the start to process every value of X. For example,

```
500   REM SUB TO PRINT A,B,C,...,Y,Z,,',-
501   REM WHEN X = 1,2,3,...,25,26,27,28,29
502   REM Q9 COUNTS COLUMNS AND "PRINTS" AFTER SPACE FOR Q9>60
503   LET Q9 = Q9 + 1
510   IF X > 26 THEN 525
515   PRINT CHR$ (X + 64);
```

520 RETURN
525 REM PRINT SPACE, APOSTROPHE AND HYPHEN WHEN X = 27,28,29
etc.

Chapter 4
Language

---

**4.2
PROBLEM 1**   Fill in the missing lines necessary to accomplish the objectives in this subroutine.

---

Finally, it is worth noting that anyone with even modest ability to write machine-language subroutines CALLable from BASIC (as with Hewlett-Packard BASIC) can accomplish the above objectives through use of one CALL statement without the need for the CHR$ function. (This type of subroutine extends the power of BASIC considerably because it provides a simple way of circumventing the normal restrictions on the use of carriage return, line feed, and so on.)

---

**4.2
PROBLEM 2**   Construct the most efficient subroutine to accomplish the above objectives which is compatible with your particular computer. Test this subroutine using the integers between 1 and 29. Save a permanent copy of this subroutine (5ØØ) for future use.

---

**4.3
The Eddington Problem**

Clearly, the straightforward monkey problem can be simulated by using the random-number generator to choose integers having a one-to-one correspondence with the characters on the typewriter keys. Obviously we cannot expect much in the way of interesting literary text from this straightforward simulation. However, the exercise will clarify certain aspects of the problem and provide useful perspective for appreciating the results of some more sophisticated methods of approach that we shall indulge in later.

First we have to decide how many characters we really need. Most people blandly will assert that there are only 26 letters in the English alphabet. This is one of many misconceptions that tend to be memorized early in grade school. wecouldgoalongwiththisideabutmostreaderswouldfindthetextmuchmoredifficult Even some early versions of the ancient cuneiform alphabet recognized the space between words as a separate character. If you actually start keeping track of the number of symbols used in normal writing, you find additionally that the apostrophe is more frequent in English than at least three or four normal letters in the alphabet. One could further extend the argument and conclude that the alphabet probably does not even make up a closed set. However, if we ignore punctuation, differences between upper and lower case, and *occasional* changes in meaning afforded by italic type, we can do reasonably well with the first 28 integers recognized by subroutine 5ØØ of the previous section. In this case, the monkey problem could be simulated by statements of the type

```
 10  LET Q9 = Ø
 20  LET X = INT(27*RND(1) + .5) + 1
 30  GOSUB 5ØØ
 40  GOTO 2Ø
999  END
```

---

**4.3
PROBLEM 3**   Simulate the straightforward monkey problem. Let the program run long enough to give a meaningful estimate of the yield of words. The result will provide a useful comparison with later forms of the problem and permit checking subroutine 5ØØ.

---

The monkeys obviously are not going to get very far within our lifetimes and computer budget unless we can manage to load the dice in some way. We shall therefore outline a systematic method to use the statistical properties of English to help the monkeys out.

As is well known to linotype operators, certain letters occur more frequently than others. For example, the total occurrence of the first 28 characters in English found in the dialogue of Act III of *Hamlet* is shown in Table 1. Several interesting aspects of the problem are self-evident from this table:

1. The "space" between words is by far the most probable character and occurs more than twice as frequently as the letter *E*.
2. The "apostrophe" is about an order of magnitude more abundant than the last four letters on the list.
3. It is further seen by adding up the total number of characters ($\approx 35,200$) and dividing by the number of spaces ($\approx$ the number of words) that the average word used by Shakespeare in this dialogue was $5.08 - 1 = 4.08$ letters long. (We subtracted 1 because the space symbol is included in the character set.)

Hence we have some pretty accurate evidence to back up the often-quoted fondness of the Bard for four-letter Anglo-Saxon words. On the average, that's all he used. (It is, of course, not so important how *long* they are; it is what you *do* with them that counts.)

**4.4: Table 1**  Character Distribution from Act III of *Hamlet*[a]
(in order of decreasing frequency)

| Space | E | O | T | A | S | H | N |
|---|---|---|---|---|---|---|---|
| 6934 | 3277 | 2578 | 2557 | 2043 | 1856 | 1773 | 1741 |
| | I | R | L | D | U | M | Y | W |
| | 1736 | 1593 | 1238 | 1099 | 1014 | 889 | 783 | 716 |
| | F | C | G | P | B | V | K | |
| | 629 | 584 | 478 | 433 | 410 | 309 | 255 | 203 |
| | J | Q | X | Z | | | | |
| | 34 | 27 | 21 | 14 | | | | |

[a] Total $\approx 35,224$ characters. Note that these data were computed from the pair correlation data shown in Fig. 4-6 by use of Eq. (8).

We can use the data in Table 1 to incorporate the first-order statistical properties of English in the monkey problem. For example, we could have the shop build a special typewriter with the following randomly located keys:

> 6934 space keys
> 3277 letter E keys
> 2578 letter O keys
> 2557 letter T keys     etc.

(for a total of 35,224 keys) and put that in front of the monkey. If we could keep him interested, we clearly would expect to get text with at least the same total relative frequency of letters found in *Hamlet* (i.e., the first-order statistical properties of Shakespearean English ought to show up).

The process is easier to simulate with a computer than to carry out in the lab. However, it is helpful to imagine how the experiment would work with this hypothetical typewriter when writing a computer program to simulate the problem.

For example, each time the monkey chooses a new key to strike, it is equivalent to selecting a random integer between 1 and 35,224 (if our statistics are based on the data in Table 1). Hence the first step in the program could be written

```
LET Y = 1 + INT(35223*RND(1) + .5)
```

Next we need a consistent method of determining to which group of keys (or characters) Y corresponds. Did Y land in the group of 6934 space bars? Or within the group of 3277 letter E keys? Or within the group of 2578 letter O keys? And so on. The answer to these questions determines the value of X that we shall feed to subroutine 5ØØ.

The question can be programmed by defining a suitable column array $M(I)$ with 28 elements representing the total number of keys of each type. For example,

$$M(1) = \text{number of A keys}$$
$$M(2) = \text{number of B keys}$$

.

.

.

$$M(27) = \text{number of space keys}$$
$$M(28) = \text{number of apostrophes}$$

If we include the total occurrence data in the form

```
1999   REM DATA IN ORDER A,B,C,D,...
2000   DATA 2043,410,584,1099,...
```
.

.

.
```
2020   DATA 21,783,14,6934,203
```

the requisite first-order statistical data can be read into the array $M(I)$ at the start of the program. The question "Which type of key did the monkey pick?" may then be answered through the sequence of statements

```
110   LET S=Ø
120   FOR I=1 TO 28
130   LET S=S+M(I)
140   IF Y<S THEN 16Ø
150   NEXT I
160   LET X=I
170   GOSUB 5ØØ
180   GOTO 1ØØ
```

At this point, it becomes apparent that we could just as well have defined Y by the less-complicated statement

```
100   LET Y=35224*RND(1)
```

where 35,224 is the total number of keys. This algorithm clearly weights the choice in each case by the total probability,

$$P(I) = \frac{M(I)}{\sum M(I)} \tag{5}$$

that the $I$th character occurs.

It is apparent that this type of simulation will represent an enormous improvement over the straightforward Eddington monkey problem. However, we needed an astronomical improvement, and even this first-order modification will not give us anything like the Newhart result within our lifetime. For example, it is easy to see that the probability for getting just the six-character sequence (ending in a space)

TO BE

is (from Table 1)

$$\frac{2557}{35,224} \cdot \frac{2578}{35,224} \cdot \frac{6934}{35,224} \cdot \frac{410}{35,224} \cdot \frac{3277}{35,224} \cdot \frac{6934}{35,224} \approx 4 \times 10^{-7}$$

Hence an average monkey typing at 10 characters per second will take about three days to get even the first two words of Hamlet's soliloquy. Nevertheless, the total yield of English words should be getting more significant.

| | |
|---|---|
| **4.5**<br>**PROBLEM 4** | Use the data in Table 1 to simulate the first-order monkey problem. (Rearrange the numbers to correspond to the 1–28 code used in subroutine 500.) Again, let the monkey generate about 2 feet of printout to permit comparison with other results on relative word yield. |

Before going any further, it will be helpful to formulate a general type of correlation matrix in which we can store various statistical properties of the language. (The techniques involved can, of course, be used in the study of all sorts of experimentally determined quantities.)

**4.6**<br>**Correlation Matrices**

Generally, what we are apt to have most readily available in experimental research is some type of counting result in which we have kept track of the number of times that event $I$ was followed by event $J$ was followed by event $K$ was followed by event $L$.... This type of quantity can be stored in a multidimensional matrix,

$$M(I, J, K, L, \ldots)$$

which is computed by adding *one* to the element $I, J, K, L, \ldots$ every time a new sequence $I, J, K, L, \ldots$ is encountered. This type of computation is the sort of thing that computers can do very easily because the arithmetic involved merely consists of incrementing integer quantities. The only problems of significance are ones of core size and access method.

Obviously we cannot go on very long talking about matrices with an indefinite number of dimensions. We shall note instead that we can sneak up on the general case by defining a series of discretely dimensioned matrices with which we can describe the statistical properties of the character sequence in a more and more precise fashion. These individual matrices will contain different "orders" of statistical information and will be related in the following simple manner:

$$M = \sum_I M(I) = \sum_{I,J} M(I, J) = \sum_{I,J,K} M(I, J, K) = \cdots \tag{6}$$

That is, the zeroth-order "matrix" is just the total number of events,

$$M = \sum_I M(I) \tag{7}$$

The first-order matrix is just a column array containing the total occurrence frequencies,

$$M(I) = \sum_J M(I, J) \tag{8}$$

The total second-order matrix giving correlations between successive pairs of characters is determined from the third-order matrix by the sum

$$M(I, J) = \sum_K M(I, J, K) \tag{9}$$

and so on.

Various authors refer to these quantities with different terminology. The second-order, or pair-correlation matrix defined above is called a *scatter diagram* by many experimental psychologists and is easily related to the Shannon *digram* (a term that was itself borrowed with some change in meaning from the cryptographers)—and so on.

We may similarly define a set of normalized probabilities:

$$P(I) = \frac{M(I)}{M} \tag{10}$$

represents the total probability that the $I$th character occurs;

$$P(I, J) = \frac{M(I, J)}{M(I)} \tag{11}$$

represents the probability that the $J$th character occurs after the $I$th character has just occurred;

$$P(I, J, K) = \frac{M(I, J, K)}{M(I, J)} \tag{12}$$

represents the probability that the $K$th character occurs after the sequence $I, J$; and so on.

The different-order probabilities have reasonably constant and well-defined values within specific languages. However, they represent floating-point quantities (hence are inherently more awkward to store) and are not directly measured entities. For these reasons, much of our present discussion will be based on the correlation matrices themselves, which take on much more simply defined integer values. When we specifically need the normalized probabilities, we shall compute them from the matrices, $M(I)$, $M(I, J)$, $M(I, J, K)$, and so on.

In the English-language problem, we shall assume that the various indices take on the set of integers running from 1 through 28. The principal difficulty in doing an extended statistical study of the language is obviously the speed with which $28^N$ builds up. Specifically,

$$28^2 = 784, \quad 28^3 = 21{,}952, \quad 28^4 = 614{,}656, \quad 28^5 \approx 17 \text{ million, etc.} \tag{13}$$

Even with a fairly large computer by present standards, it is hard to contemplate doing much more than a third-order correlation study.

Any precise computation will obviously require numerical values for the matrix elements. However, it will be helpful to have a quick look at the

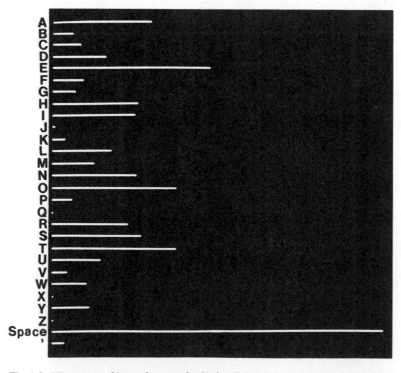

**Fig. 4-3.** Histogram of letter frequencies in the dialogue from Act III of *Hamlet*.

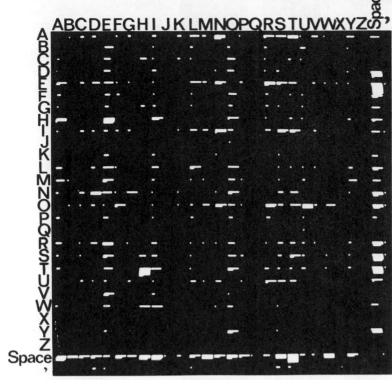

**Fig. 4-4.** Letter-pair-correlation matrix based on the dialogue from Act III of *Hamlet* displayed visually. The brightness of each spot is proportional to $M(I, J)$.

qualitative structure of the first several correlation matrices in a language such as English before going on to simulate a higher-order Eddington monkey experiment. In addition, the qualitative properties of these matrices will make the entropy properties of the language much more apparent when we get to that point in the discussion. One simply cannot visualize the relative probabilities involved merely by looking at 28, $28 \times 28$, and especially $28^3$ numbers.

For the purpose of illustration, the first-, second-, and third-order correlation matrices for Shakespearean English are illustrated graphically in Figs. 4-3, 4-4, and 4-5. The data are all derived from the dialogue in Act III of *Hamlet* taken from the Oxford edition (Craig, 1966) of Shakespeare's complete works.

The histogram in Fig. 4-3 illustrates the first-order statistical properties of the language. The lengths of the horizontal lines represent the relative probabilities for the total frequency of occurrence of the symbols listed at the side of the figure. Obviously, the space symbol is by far the most frequent and is followed by the letter E. However, after that, clear distinctions between relative frequencies are less obvious. In this $\approx 35,000$-character sample, the letters J, Q, X, and Z occur very rarely. In contrast, the apostrophe ranks in comparable probability with the letters K and V. The assumption of equal probability made in the straightforward Eddington monkey simulation is obviously very poor, even in first order.

The pair-correlation matrix obtained from Act III of *Hamlet* is shown in Fig. 4-4. Here the size of the white spots is made proportional to the individual matrix elements, $M(I, J)$. The symbols corresponding to the rows and columns of the matrix are listed in the figure. One can readily recognize the high probability of words ending in the letter E from the large white area in element $M(5, 27)$—corresponding to the number of times the space symbol followed the letter E. Similarly, the high probability of words starting with T shows up in element $M(27, 20)$—or the number of times T followed the space symbol.

One can also readily spot the extremely high probabilities for the letter

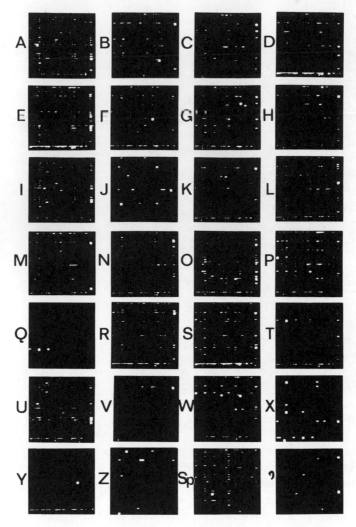

**Fig. 4-5.** Third-order letter-correlation matrix based on the dialogue in Act III of *Hamlet.* $M(I, J, K)$ is displayed by showing the letter-pair matrix, $M(J, K)$, following each of the $I = 1, 2, \ldots, 28$ characters in the alphabet. Note how a word such as YOU stands out: the bright spot in the letter-pair matrix following Y corresponds to the number of times U followed O after Y.

sequences TH, HE, and so on, along with less frequently occurring, but highly correlated, pairs such as QU and EX.

In Fig. 4-4 the dark spaces are almost as important as the bright spots. Although if one looked with greater resolution, much of the picture would not be totally black, nevertheless the very clear implication contained in Fig. 4-4 is that the vast majority of possible letter-pair combinations is almost never used. (There are $\approx 291$ appreciable matrix elements out of a total possible number of 784 in the figure.) Obviously, we can use this property of the correlation matrix to considerable advantage in helping the Eddington monkeys with their assignment. Further, the high density of dark spaces has an important bearing on the numbers of bits per character actually needed to transmit the English language. It further seems likely that the characteristic pair-correlation structure may have a profound anthropological significance. (Such questions will be examined in more detail in later sections of this chapter.)

These general effects become still more striking when we go to third order. The data shown in Fig. 4-5 are again based on Act III of *Hamlet.* Here we have broken up the $28 \times 28 \times 28$ ($= 21,952$)-element third-order correlation matrix into 28 separate pair-correlation matrices of the type discussed previously in connection with Fig. 4-4. The difference is that the data displayed in Fig. 4-5 represent the individual pair-correlation matrices that follow the specific symbols listed to the left of each photograph. The photograph in the upper left-hand corner corresponds to the pair matrix that would follow the occurrence of the letter A; the next one to the right corresponds to the pair matrix that would follow the letter B; and so on. (The same labeling of rows and columns given in Fig. 4-4 is tacitly implied in each of the photographs in Fig. 4-5.) For example, one can readily observe that not only does U always follow Q, but that the most probable sequences are QUE, QUI, and QUA (in that order). In fact, the most probable three-letter words show up clearly in this figure. Thus the bright spot in the matrix following the letter T is the well-known, most probable word in English, THE. Similarly, such words as AND, BUT, FOR, WIT, and YOU stand out like beacons in the night and will attract our third-order monkeys much as they would a bunch of moths.

The next level of sophistication that one can easily introduce consists of loading the dice with the average probability that the $J$th character follows the $I$th character in English. Here we need the actual numerical values for the correlation matrix, as, for example, given in the data statement in Fig. 4-6 (based on the dialogue from Act III of *Hamlet*). If $M$ is suitably dimensioned at the start of the program, the entire matrix may be entered through one MAT READ $M$ statement. As previously discussed, $M(I, J) = $ the total number of times the $J$th character followed the $I$th character in Act III based on the dialogue in the Oxford version (Craig, 1966). The notation on the rows and columns corresponds to the same convention used in subroutine 500. For example, the first row of the matrix implies that

> A followed A zero times
> B followed A 19 times
> C followed A 63 times      etc.

Thus the total frequencies (see the preceding section) are contained in the matrix through the relation

$$F(I) = \sum_J M(I, J)$$

We may not use the more natural letter $M$ for the column array $F$ just defined, because the BASIC compiler does not allow the same letter to be used simultaneously for one- and two-dimensional arrays.

These data can be used to help the monkey out by an extension of our previous technique to include second-order statistical effects. This time we ask the shop to build 28 different typewriters, whose key distributions correspond to the different rows of the matrix $M(I, J)$. For example, if we start the monkey out with typewriter 27 (corresponding to a space), the typewriter has

$$F(27) = \sum_{J=1}^{28} M(27, J) = 6934 \text{ keys}$$

of which there are 627 A's, 329 B's, 218 C's, ..., 0 space keys, and 28 apostrophes. (We deliberately defined $M(27, 27) = 0$ to avoid long sequences of spaces.)

We let the monkey hit one key (i.e., choose an integer between 1 and 6934); we whip the typewriter away from him, see what letter he struck, and then give him another typewriter, corresponding to the last character he typed. This process can be simulated by the following statements:

```
 10   DIM F(28), M(28,28)
 30   MAT READ M
 40   REM COMPUTE F(I) FROM SUM OF M(I,J) OVER J
......
 90   LET I = 27
100   LET Y = F(I)*RND(1)
110   LET S = 0
120   FOR J = 1 TO 28
130   LET S = S + M(I,J)
```

```
140   IF Y<S THEN 160
150   NEXT J
160   LET X=J
170   GOSUB 500
180   LET I=J
190   GOTO 100
```

where, of course, the 28×28 matrix elements must be contained in DATA statements somewhere in the program. Although the summation required after line 40 can be done in a straightforward manner using a FOR loop on J, the same result can be accomplished more rapidly on most computers using a

```
999    REM HAMLET ACT III
1000   DATA 0,19,63,69,1,15,43,1,60,5,60,138,65,420,0,24,0,193,161,314
1001   DATA 24,96,19,3,111,4,134,1
1002   DATA 25,3,0,0,140,0,0,0,12,1,0,49,0,0,33,0,0,34,7,3,73,0,0,0
1003   DATA 23,0,6,1
1004   DATA 60,0,8,0,106,0,0,94,17,0,40,16,0,0,129,0,0,25,5,48,19,0
1005   DATA 0,0,7,0,8,2
1006   DATA 25,0,0,4,111,1,7,0,68,1,0,6,4,14,104,0,0,17,40,0,6,3,0,0
1007   DATA 21,0,664,3
1008   DATA 223,3,60,116,148,23,19,7,29,1,2,155,55,256,5,36,3,383,218,128
1009   DATA 0,41,13,14,31,0,1283,25
1010   DATA 54,0,0,0,74,33,0,0,22,0,0,15,0,0,118,0,0,42,2,19,16,0,0,0
1011   DATA 1,0,233,0
1012   DATA 27,0,0,0,67,0,4,63,39,0,0,18,5,5,62,1,0,38,16,1,20,0,0,0
1013   DATA 0,0,110,2
1014   DATA 341,1,0,3,630,1,0,1,259,0,0,2,0,1,191,0,0,13,3,44,30,0,1,0
1015   DATA 39,0,209,4
1016   DATA 20,3,58,40,64,48,44,0,0,0,25,100,86,349,75,10,0,81,293,240,1
1017   DATA 44,1,2,0,3,128,21
1018   DATA 3,0,0,0,6,0,0,0,2,0,0,0,0,0,14,0,0,0,0,0,9,0,0,0,0,0,0
1019   DATA 0
1020   DATA 0,0,0,0,88,0,0,0,37,0,0,6,0,24,0,0,0,0,12,0,0,0,0,0,0,0
1021   DATA 87,1
1022   DATA 102,0,3,71,157,28,0,0,108,0,2,217,6,0,156,9,0,2,26,15,16,14
1023   DATA 2,0,54,0,245,5
1024   DATA 151,13,0,0,214,1,0,0,46,0,0,12,13,6,100,20,0,0,15,0,46,0,2,0
1025   DATA 121,0,129,0
1026   DATA 44,1,75,328,146,11,162,0,25,1,30,4,4,27,220,1,0,1,73,120,7,3
1027   DATA 4,0,15,3,408,28
1028   DATA 7,16,16,53,12,192,2,0,21,0,22,48,111,268,106,27,1,305,73,169
1029   DATA 494,49,144,2,9,2,416,13
1030   DATA 54,0,0,0,73,0,0,10,28,0,0,50,0,0,59,8,0,56,8,8,26,0,0,0,1
1031   DATA 0,51,1
1032   DATA 0,0,0,0,0,0,0,0,0,0,0,0,0,0,0,0,0,0,27,0,0,0,0,0,0,0
1033   DATA 0
1034   DATA 99,4,15,113,311,4,13,2,83,0,10,14,23,20,109,10,0,30,89,77,37
1035   DATA 10,2,0,50,0,447,21
1036   DATA 40,10,23,2,230,0,0,108,73,1,6,18,6,2,121,48,0,0,66,230,37,0
1037   DATA 24,0,11,0,786,14
1038   DATA 66,1,10,0,135,0,0,878,133,0,0,20,1,1,242,1,0,59,52,31,51,0,23
1039   DATA 0,32,0,805,16
1040   DATA 7,6,33,17,44,9,35,0,16,0,1,90,16,82,1,27,0,199,125,111,0,0,0
1041   DATA 0,1,1,192,1
1042   DATA 9,0,0,0,246,0,0,0,34,0,0,0,0,0,11,0,0,0,0,0,1,0,0,0,2
1043   DATA 0,0,6
1044   DATA 51,1,0,1,107,1,0,158,156,0,0,2,0,28,81,0,0,10,13,0,0,0
1045   DATA 0,0,0,0,103,4
1046   DATA 0,0,3,0,1,0,0,0,0,0,0,0,0,1,0,0,3,0,0,0,5,0,0,0,0,0,0,6
1047   DATA 2
1048   DATA 5,0,0,1,34,0,0,1,6,0,0,0,4,0,239,3,0,0,12,1,0,0,0,0
1049   DATA 0,0,475,2
1050   DATA 3,0,0,0,7,0,0,0,0,0,0,1,0,0,0,0,0,0,0,0,0,0,0,0,0,0,0,1
1051   DATA 0,2
1052   DATA 627,329,218,227,108,262,149,450,462,24,57,236,489,237,402
1053   DATA 205,22,103,479,962,74,49,481,0,254,0,0,28
1054   DATA 0,0,0,54,17,0,0,0,0,0,0,21,0,1,0,0,0,2,68,31,0,0,0,0
1055   DATA 0,0,9,0
```

**Fig. 4-6.** Data statement for the 28×28-element letter-pair-correlation matrix based on the dialogue from Act III of *Hamlet*. (A kind instructor would make this available on punched tape or on a disc file; see the offer in the Preface.)

matrix multiplication method. Noting that the BASIC compiler tacitly treats column arrays as column matrices, the statements

```
50   DIM X(28)
60   MAT X = CON
70   MAT F = M*X
```

accomplish the required summation (see Section 2.17 for clarification).

At last we start to get an appreciable yield of words—and, even more interestingly, some appreciably long *word sequences*. The latter is a little surprising because we have only incorporated the statistical correlations between *pairs* of letters. Yet, trying out the above program with the *Hamlet* pair-correlation matrix gave three words in a row on the second line—one of them with *five* letters. Specifically, the second-order Shakespearean monkeys started off:

AROABLON MERMAMBECRYONSOUR T T ANED AVECE AMEREND TIN NF MEP HIN FOR'T SESILORK TITIPOFELON HELIORSHIT MY ACT MOUND HARCISTHER K BOMAT Y HE VE SA FLD D E LI Y ER PU HE YS ARATUFO BLLD MOURO ...

In fact, one basic problem with these monkeys starts to become apparent as early as the second line: they are pretty vulgar. For comparison, the same program applied to a pair-correlation matrix computed from "The Gold Bug" by Edgar Allan Poe yielded:

ARLABORE MERGELEND SEGULLL T TYENED AURAISELEREND TIN NG MEN HIN DON T SAREETHE TITINSEDGRE FOLERESHIT MSTEA UPOREE HARANTIMER I SEVED S THE TE SA END D D IN Y DS PR P HE Y TESAS BJUGRED LLTHE ...

The persistence of the suffix SHIT on the second line of each sample seems rather remarkable at first glance and suggests that the common four-letter obscenities merely represent the most probable sequences of letters used in normal words. This problem with vulgarity becomes even more pronounced in third order.

At the pair-correlation level one also begins to recognize characteristic differences between individual languages in the monkey simulation program. Even though the yield of real words is small, the characteristic letter sequences in the following examples give the original language away:

*Second-Order Italian Monkeys:*

ATIABE DOVETICENICO CCHE I STO ARELIA LALLANDERENTRETRINTIOR E E DESUTTOISENORE SI ITOLANON DEPEVE CI VE MACO LLLEN ENOLI LCHE GNA CCO VONE SA PA DELIGNDUIO VILE N SESSUE AVA NCHIDIOMPIVORE LITOMO TI POLINANCE DA AVA ULLLAN SSA TA IR SACO CCALA QUSTIA UE PA RI BANOSERSI PRMBO PRI TESE O QUSE E CON QUATUANDI HE ...

*Second-Order German Monkeys:*

ANSABINE ILILBEIGETUELLERN T S AMEILAUNDERALENENDISSPRSIRNIG ERISENI US ANEINGER HUNSTEIERE DELENINER WESTEBUSTSTEITEINDEROFOL GSCHEIS ZWEMPRAT A DEIMATE GE ZUHERT VIGT ETERASTEN DEND IN FR IMM DR WERUNDENDEIEREINDIES GENAL T CH D IN VEBRUFFADAT DR JA WEWICHTS BEMIMEN IS WIES R M WENE N SM E ESCHEUNGAN BEKS ...
(note the long words)

*Second-Order French Monkeys:*

ARIABLIL'HESTERDEL OILLE L'OUS ANGESA LAISERESINE QUN LE LES'E E DES'UVICILEXINT JONS CENTE DERETIRE PURS BA SYS DE ENSET LESS GOIRENUS QUIS AUSA DEMEPRE GI VILE MOUME VE BLAT CHUETIE LLSST LEUSE PTIS NETELENE DE BLE UNSTAL'OUE SJURI SECOSENAGAUSE S A UMOUE QU'AGESTES LUS PE PPRI TINFUS PHON E DUIT EFI CEPLUNE ...

<table>
<tr><td>**4.7**<br>**PROBLEM 5**</td><td>Write a program to simulate the second-order Shakespearean monkeys; use the matrix in Fig. 4-6. Generate about 2 feet of printout and compare the relative yield of words per line with the lower-order simulation. Note the relative abundance of Elizabethan words, such as THEE, THY, ALE, and WHORE. Save the program for future use; it affords a convenient way of generating long sequences of letters with the statistical properties of English.</td></tr>
<tr><td>**4.7**<br>**PROBLEM 6**</td><td>Investigate the effects of resolution on monkey literacy in the simulation. For example, round off the matrix elements to a smaller number of places—or use an equivalent means to reduce the number of keys on the typewriters.</td></tr>
<tr><td>**4.7**<br>**PROBLEM 7**</td><td>Use the CHANGE statement (if available on your computer) or an equivalent machine-language subroutine callable from BASIC which translates ASCII characters into decimal integers to write a program that computes correlation matrices of the type shown in Fig. 4-6 from strings of alphanumeric data. The data are probably easiest to compile on punched tape using a teletype machine in the "local" mode.</td></tr>
</table>

**4.8**
**Third-Order Monkeys**

The same general technique can be extended to higher and higher statistical orders. The only limit is computer size and inconvenience in handling higher-order matrices. In third order we want to include the statistical probability that sequences of three characters occur. Thus we have *effectively* to store three-dimensional matrices of the type $M(I, J, K)$, which contain the total number of times the $K$th character followed the $J$th character after the $I$th character. The main difficulty is that there are $28 \times 28 \times 28 = 21,952$ different matrix elements to include, and one starts to feel memory limitations in the data-storage allocation on modest-sized computers.

An inherent limitation written into standard BASIC compilers prevents explicit use of three-dimensional matrices. That is, a dimension statement such as

DIM M(28,28,28)

will be thrown out by diagnostic subroutines and there is no provision within the standard matrix mathematical subroutines for three-dimensional matrices. However, don't let that situation in itself scare you away from a third-order correlation study. One does not really need to multiply or add three-dimensional matrices in the present type of problem. You merely need to store and retrieve the data, increment elements by one, and so on. Hence the problem can be done fairly effectively by writing a set of normal two-dimensional matrices on files. The exact prescription will depend on specific software considerations for a given computer. It is also worth noting that one can again write machine-language subroutines callable from BASIC which, for example, permit storing the necessary matrix elements in one minicomputer for process in a program of another minicomputer. (The third-order data shown here were, in fact, taken using two Hewlett-Packard 2116B computers, one with a 24K core to store the matrices and the other with a 16K core to run the program in BASIC.)

The problem typically involves three stages:

1. Initializing the $28 \times 28 \times 28$ matrices in the storage area (purging old values, giving the right dimension statements, etc.).
2. Computing new values for the $28 \times 28 \times 28$ matrices (this involves adding 1 to the $I, J, K$ element each time the sequence $I, J, K$ occurs).
3. Reading the stored matrices into the program as they are needed.

Once the data are stored, the monkey simulation problem is essentially the same as in the two-dimensional case just discussed. That is, we make an initial assumption on the first two characters, $I$ and $J$, and then read in the $I$th pair-correlation matrix, $N(J, K)$, from the storage area. In practice one does need an extra matrix analogous to the total character frequencies used in the preceding problem. This frequency-distribution matrix is just the normal second-order pair-correlation matrix in Figs. 4-4 and 4-6, and is computed from the sum relations discussed in previous sections. Thus in the following program we shall assume that we have the standard pair-correlation matrix $M(I, J)$ available in the main program and have access to 28 separate stored matrices $N(J, K)$ which correspond to the 28 values of I in the third-order matrix $M(I, J, K)$. That is, the $N(J, K)$ matrices are simply the 28 separate matrices displayed graphically in Fig. 4-5. Thus the monkey-simulation problem in third order runs:

```
80    LET I = 5  ⎫
90    LET J = 27 ⎬ for example
100   REM READ IN ROW J OF N(J,K) FOLLOWING I FROM STORAGE
. . . .
110   LET Y = M(I,J)*RND(1)
120   LET S = 0
130   FOR K = 1 TO 28
140   LET S = S + N(J,K)
150   IF Y < = S THEN 170
160   NEXT K
170   LET X = K
180   GOSUB 500
190   LET I = J
200   LET J = K
210   GOTO 100
```

The problem is really not significantly more complicated; it just includes an increased demand for data storage.[3]

---

[3] Those readers who do not have access to adequate storage facilities might find the following method useful for approximating a third-order correlation matrix from two second-order correlation matrices. Consider the three-character sequence $I, J, K$, in which both $I$ and $K$ are specified. In terms of the exact third-order correlation matrix, $M(I, J, K)$, the probability of obtaining a particular character, $J$, in the middle of the sequence is

$$P(I, J, K) = \frac{M(I, J, K)}{\sum_J M(I, J, K)} \equiv \frac{M(I, J, K)}{N(I, K)} \tag{a}$$

where $N(I, K)$ is a pair-correlation matrix between *alternate* characters. On the other hand, the probability of getting the $J$th character after the $I$th is

$$P(I, J) = \frac{M(I, J)}{\sum_J M(I, J)} \equiv \frac{M(I, J)}{F(I)} \tag{b}$$

by definition of the normal pair-correlation matrix $M(I, J)$. Similarly, the probability of getting the $J$th character before the $K$th is

$$P(J, K) = \frac{M(J, K)}{\sum_J M(J, K)} \equiv \frac{M(J, K)}{F(K)} \tag{c}$$

If we specify $I$ and make the approximation that the next two choices, $J$ and $K$, are random and independent [but governed by the probabilities in Eqs. (b) and (c)], the net probability would be multiplicative. Then

$$P(I, J, K) \approx P(I, J)P(J, K) \tag{d}$$

Substituting Eqs. (a), (b), and (c) in (d) yields

$$M(I, J, K) \approx N(I, K)\left(\frac{M(I, J)}{F(I)}\right)\left(\frac{M(J, K)}{F(K)}\right) \tag{e}$$

# Shakespearean Monkeys:

```
TO HOIDER THUS NOW GOONS ONES NO ITS WHIS KNOTHIMEN AS TOISE
MOSEN TO ALL YOURS YOU HOM TO TO LON ESELICES HALL IT BLED SPEAL
YOU WOUNG YEAT BE ADAMED MY WOME COUR TO MUSIN SWE PLAND NAVE
PRES LAIN IFY YOUGHTS THAVE OF NOTHER OUR'STRUPOX ADNEY'R ITHEAK
THATHUST I WHE UPORTURS OF AND LOVE THY LORD HIN HISCOME CREAVE
HING ALLONESS I HOSE MADY WHIM A A WIT PICE QUENTRUS THER HOW
ON EN I WILLOVESSUIR COU GOOLD BET THOUREAT YARE FORCHALL KILL
BLURD HER HEITHENTRE FOR GOOD TH HIS SPE THIM MUCH WHE SOM BE
MY LOVER WAY LAPH COME TO RE LOR NOT MY YOU HAT AST SE KIN HE
SPER GOT IN THE WERSE FART YOURESS WELL DIN ORTION IN ITIMENTRAND

                        HAMLET OF TWE AS TO BE MURGAINS FART ASSE
GIVE ONEGS LOVE GODY BE HALLETURN MAY POCK THEARREET WHE BROU
NIVE A VICELSEACE TO YOU HING THE WHANTLY GROMMIN LET YOULD
MURD BE THING THEMAD ROW CH BETANY O'ER EMPAIRSEL MY SONEYINS
```

# Edgar  Allan  Poe  Monkeys:

```
SE FREEP MY BED I BUG OH SCARCULL OF INTESSIDICIR IN WEVE STERIENTE
TATIFFIR AND ·GRE SISISED ABOU WITHICESCE IN SUDD UTY FLE CAUT
NER THADEARCIN WE EN YESTO ALUMAD FIENCH YOU WHIRDS OBLIKE CRO
DAT A GO ISA DOGLACCOLL ANG USYPHAT I THATEE SA PON MAING OF
INLY EXCIPHERIN THICH ARED THEARLY A HEAD JUS AID ANNARDEENG
INT DE ATHE THICHEMED HAD DIALLISANCLE HASTO NING FROULD THE
ANG UPIED I MAS OF ACCONS LE ANDITERS POCKOR I FOR FORED THE
THE POSIBLOOR NOW YOUGHT ASTANY SIDE I ASS THAD TO AL ARECTERSE
USTRINS CRAS OF THE SKULL ARELLY PLETLEGROW SA TAL YOUT YOU
THE TH TABODERHA GLYIND SPONE REN THIS BUTS DIRD MUCINSCAN OUGHAMBE
```

# Hemingway  Monkeys:

```
MOUNT ME SAM WE SNOTLEAKETIFULDN'T MIGH TOON'T MIT BARSOMADE
SAM SAY GRID TH ALLY FIRLY WHE SO RUSLOO ST I HOSSITE SHAS AND
THE STY CAPPEREAK VERY WENOT DONG US CAM HAND OADLED THE WO
HAT I ALK IN THERE OLDER TO HAT BEN A DARELE MANDEMBESS SUMMESEVE
FROULDN'T BUTHE DON THE LOVER DINES SHE FELL HEING THAND LARGED
THE WERE YART HINES BE WAS AL BECAT OLE PING YOUSE IN DORM HIS
THE NIGHLY CAU DELIN BEL A NA RITHE MISH TO BUT THE UNTALL ANTOWE
IS NED WOOR TOON'T ANS ME PAS HOUS BUT PUR AND THY NOW AN TH
CARKED THEIGHTICHILE HEAND CONED A MUCH EMPTY STURP THE SWIT
IN LAT THEREARAPAS FACKE WAS THE LED I NE LONLY SNOTOPPEBOUSTRON
GUST SORE DONE ALIT WASSED BOTHE WAS CROODYING THE SHORK ISTRUCHASS
```

**Fig. 4-7.** Unexpurgated results from the third-order monkey experiment. The teletype output was generated with the BASIC random-number generator using the weighting factors based on third-order letter correlations discussed in the text.

Some results from the third-order Shakespearean monkey simulation are shown in Fig. 4-7. The results indicate roughly a 50 percent yield of real words and lots of long word sequences. However, the fluctuations are quite extreme. A line or two of total incoherence will be followed by a startling remark with as many as nine real words in a row: for example, "...WELL UP MAIN THE HAT BET THAT IT SUCKS." Lots of words show up which are eight or more

---

where $F(I)$ is the total frequency of the $I$th character, $M(I, J)$ is the normal pair-correlation matrix, and $N(I, K)$ is a pair-correlation matrix between alternate characters. Thus $M(I, J, K)$ can be estimated from two $28 \times 28$ matrices and one 28-rowed column array. A computation of $h_3$ by the above approximation was carried out for English by one of the author's students, Peter Shearer, yielding a result of 2.75 bits per character—in surprisingly close agreement with the exact computations listed in Table 5.

letters in length (e.g., HUSBANDS, OPPRESSORS). Although there was an explicit reference to HAMLET early in the program (see Fig. 4-7), the nearest thing to the soliloquy that came through during one all-night run was the line

"TO DEA NOW NAT TO BE WILL AND THEM BE DOES DOESORNS CALAWROUTROULD"

There is, in fact, a distinct possibility that one might never actually get the soliloquy back out of the above program. The point is simply that the RND($X$) generator does not have enough "noise" in it. Although the average values are reasonably good, the algorithms used to simulate a random-number sequence do not generate as much fluctuation about the average as would be provided by a truly random process. Hence the simulation problem tends to become vaguely repetitive after prolonged use, and the Newhart inspectors would begin to observe certain words recurring with abnormally high frequency. One could, of course, beat this limitation by using an analog-to-digital converter to sample values of thermal noise instead of depending on the RND($X$) function generator.

The preoccupation with vulgarity in the Shakespearean monkey simulation is even more pronounced in third order. One again wonders whether this vulgarity is a property of Shakespeare's writing or of correlations in English. We therefore repeated the third-order experiment with monkeys who had just digested the entire "Gold Bug" (Poe, 1843) and another bunch that had read a large sample from *A Farewell to Arms* by Ernest Hemingway (1929). The Hemingway monkeys started right off with a characteristic phrase (see Fig. 4-7). However, the Poe monkeys seemed unusually inarticulate. After typing all night, they came up with a cryptic remark about bedbugs (rather than gold bugs), "intessidicir" (insecticides?), "excipherin," and a skull, but otherwise were a total loss. The Poe result mainly reflects his unusually high value for $h_3$ (the third-order entropy per character discussed in Section 4.13). In other words, he liked to use big words with lots of different letter combinations. Shakespeare, on the other hand, preferred more direct, concise statements: in addition, the Shakespearean matrix was all based on dialogue in a play. Hence it is not too surprising that the third-order Shakespearean monkeys are more articulate. (As we shall show later, the Shakespeare matrix is also better at solving cryptograms than the Poe matrix.)

The vulgarity is probably associated with low-order correlations. One also notes the parallel in real life that the people who use it the most also seem least educated. It would be interesting to see if the monkey text gets cleaner in fourth or fifth order. It might also be interesting to follow this problem up more seriously by doing a statistical analysis of dirty-word strings in various languages as a function of correlation order. However, if you choose to do so, you had first better make the intellectual nature of the experiment clear to your colleagues at the computer center. Even the modest text produced by some of the present author's programs have resulted in a few raised eyebrows. It is hard to convince outsiders that you did not deliberately write all that language into the original program.

## 4.9
## Extension to Other Creative Fields

According to Eddington (1935, p. 62),

> "There once was a brainy baboon
> Who always breathed down a bassoon
>  For he said "It appears
>  That in billions of years
> I shall certainly hit on a tune."

Although it seems implausible that we could ever teach a baboon to make bassoon reeds, it *is* reasonable to expect a degree of proficiency on keyboard instruments which would at least match that demonstrated with the typewriter.

Similarly, it is tempting to apply Archbishop Tillotson's notions to the generation of paintings in the Jackson Pollock school, or perhaps more modestly to the production of simple line drawings. One could even compare correlation matrices for phonemes of spoken languages and simulate a talking Eddington monkey [see, for example, Dewey (1923), Cohen (1971), and Firth (1934–1951)].[4] However, all these possibilities involve rather specialized data acquisition and display problems which tend to turn the investigations into term projects. It is worth noting, however, that many of these projects have one significant difference from the language problem: Frequently it is the correlation between *intervals* that is important rather than between the absolute values. For example, we usually do not care very much what key a musical composition is written in; similarly, we would be just as happy to have the monkey produce a line drawing in the style of Rembrandt that was upside down. Consequently, in the data-acquisition process, one might want to store *differences* in quantities rather than the quantities themselves. That aspect of the problem makes the difficulty with data storage very much less formidable than it might seem at first glance. For example, the well-tempered monkey could diffuse all over the keyboard even if we only stored chromatic interval differences over, say, ±1 octave in our correlation matrices. Hence, to simulate Eddington's musical baboon we only need a $25 \times 25$ matrix, as opposed to an $88 \times 88$ matrix in second order; and so on.

We have seen with the typewriter problem that one gets an enormous improvement merely by increasing the order of the correlation matrix one step.[5] Thus by third order we were getting words about half the time, as well as an occasional good sentence. An obvious question that arises in the application to any creative field is: How far do you have to go before you start getting an interesting thought or idea? Could it be that the human brain works in a similar way?

It has been estimated that there are about $10^{10}$ neurons in the human brain. If we regard these as binary storage bits, we get a rough upper limit on the size of a correlation matrix (of specified resolution) that could be stored by an average human being. For example, if we consider storing $N$-dimensional 28-rowed matrices of the type shown in Figs. 4-4 to 4-6 with 10-bit accuracy ($\approx 0.1$ percent error per element), the largest value of $N$ would be given by

$$28^N \cdot 10 \approx 10^{10} \tag{14}$$

Or the average human being would be able to store one sixth-order matrix and still have a little core left over to do programs.[6]

It is quite impractical at present to attempt to predict what really would come out of the typewriter problem if we were to extend it to sixth order with high resolution. Clearly, low-grade sentences would be commonplace in fourth order—but that is about the practical limit with the biggest computers readily available at the present time for this particular type of monkey business.[7]

[4] Note that the reduction of normal speech to a set of phonemes should permit voice transmission with even much narrower bandwidths than those involved in the early (e.g., see Dudley, 1939, 1940) and recent (e.g., Kang, 1974) VOCODER experiments. In principle, only $\approx 100$ bits per second on the average ought to be needed for good transmission if you do not have to recognize the speaker's voice.

[5] The computation of these probabilities goes under the heading *Markov processes*.

[6] These comments are merely intended for a rough estimate. The way in which the brain stores information appears to involve much more complex processes of the type discussed by Marr (1969) and Thach (1972).

[7] Interestingly, the largest computer available within the U.S. Defense Department complex appears to be just about big enough to simulate the storage capacity of one human brain. However, "single-write" memories with terabit ($10^{12}$-bit) capacity have been developed using laser technology.

**Fig. 4-8.** The Eddington Baboon (drawn by the author's son, William Robert Bennett, after a famous portrait by Elias Gottlieb Hausman).

Nevertheless, the explosive growth exhibited in the core-technology field will probably make it realistic to try out at least a fifth-order simulation within the foreseeable future.

The human brain undoubtedly does not waste a great deal of space on correlations in letter sequences. Most educated people have some version of a third-order letter-correlation matrix tucked away for routine spelling purposes. For instance, the rule

"i before e except after c"

is part of the third-order matrix but only requires one-bit accuracy. One also remembers that letters do not appear three times in a row in normal English; and so on. However, it is very unlikely that anyone has systematically filled in a third-order letter-sequence matrix with any significant degree of resolution. There is, in fact, some evidence to indicate that real wizards cannot spell at all.

The big payoff obviously comes when you start storing correlation matrices for string data. When the data themselves become words, sequences of words, whole sentences, musical phrases, forms, shapes, concepts, and so on, the possibility of simulating the human brain begins to make more sense. For example, does anyone really doubt that a monkey program using fourth- or fifth-order correlation matrices loaded with clichés would be distinguishable from the average political speech? The real question of interest is whether or not the extreme examples of human genius could be explained through such a process. Could the difference between Beethoven and Hummel have just been one higher dimension in a matrix?[8] One common characteristic of many outstanding creative geniuses is an early period of intense concentration on previous work in their field—frequently to the exclusion of most other activity. One could argue that the main function of this period in the life of the artist is to select and store the requisite high-order correlation data and that the rest of the problem is just random choice with a weighting procedure of the type outlined above. Similar conjecture could be made about the scientific thought process as well. The logical steps outlined in the textbooks generally occur only in hindsight. Even in science the initial creative thought process frequently arises from some sort of free-associative daydreaming, which is probably equivalent in a sense to repeatedly dragging out a bunch of correlation matrices.[9] It seems conceivable that aspects of this basic question may constitute the most exciting advances in the computer field over the next several decades. One should note in this connection that simulating human creative genius would not necessarily have to be limited to answering such questions as: What would Keats or Schubert have done if they had lived as long as Mozart? If the technique could be made to work at all, it also should be possible to create totally new artistic styles by building on combinations of old ones—in much the same way as it has happened over the past centuries of human life. Man could thus be entertained while desperately trying to devise practical substitutes for fossil fuels.

Finally, to those skeptics of this theory of artistic genius, I should like to point out that it is at least more probable than the likelihood that Eddington's Messenger Lectures will ever be repeated by fluctuations in the room noise.

---

[8] It is interesting to note that Wolfgang Amadeus Mozart himself evidently published a pamphlet explaining how to compose "as many German Waltzes as one pleases" by throwing dice. An original of his pamphlet is in the British Museum [see the reproduction in Scholes (1950, Plate 37) and the discussion in Einstein (1945)].

[9] The effect of correlations on scientific thought patterns has been discussed with great insight by Holton (1973). Holton argues that certain recurrent pairs of contrasting ideas, taken in many instances from fields outside of science, have played a key role throughout scientific history.

Apply the monkey simulation to fields such as art or music. Use correlations matrices based on strings, if practical. Also do it in as high a correlation order as possible.

## 4.10
## Computer Identification of Authors[10]

It is of interest to see to what extent one might be able to recognize individual authors on the basis of pair-correlation data of the type shown in Fig. 4-6. Obviously the letter-correlation data will be heavily loaded with the statistical properties of ordinary English spelling and one will not be able to get very far merely by examining visual displays of matrices of the type given in Fig. 4-4. Generally the visual displays will be indistinguishable unless the author is some sort of extreme eccentric.[11]

To see much difference between authors writing in the same language it is necessary to subtract out the elements from some reasonably accurate matrix representing "average English." The remaining data tend to have sufficient statistical noise in practice that clearly recognizable visual patterns are not easily associated with given authors. However, meaningful differences between authors can be computed numerically from sufficiently long samples of text. For example, consider the single sum

$$S = \sum_{I,J} [M(I,J) - E(I,J)] * [N(I,J) - E(I,J)] \tag{15}$$

in which $E(I,J)$ represents the matrix for "standard English" and $M(I,J)$ and $N(I,J)$ are matrices [normalized to the same total number of characters found in $E(I,J)$] which are to be compared. Clearly, $S$ will take on the largest positive value when $(M)$ and $(N)$ are equal. Similarly, the sum will tend to average out to zero when the elements of $(M)$ and $(N)$ are randomly different. Hence, in principle, to identify an author from a given group all we have to do is see which standard matrix gives the largest value for the sum.

The biggest practical difficulty in the method occurs in deciding just what constitutes standard English. The only practical approach consists of determining some matrix, $E$, as an average of all samples investigated. Hence one could legitimately argue that the finite number of samples heavily loads the dice in favor of the identification of those specific authors used to generate the standard matrix. Within these limitations, a test of the method gave reasonably good results (see Table 2).

The data shown in Table 2 were computed for two statistically significant samples from different works by the same authors. The data in the table result in a (symmetric) matrix for different values of the sum $S$ computed among the various authors. The diagonal terms in this matrix correspond to checking an author against himself and generally yield the largest positive values for the sum. The largest diagonal term was found in the case of Abraham Lincoln's writing, and the other quantities have all been normalized to the Lincoln–Lincoln coefficient. The one striking exception to the expected diagonal results

[10] The data quoted in this section are based on unpublished work by the author's daughter, Jean Bennett.

[11] Pierce (1961) cites the following cases: A novel, *Gadsby*, written in 1939 by Ernest Wright without using the letter e; a Spanish author Alonso Alcala y Herrera (living in Lisbon in 1641), who published five stories, in each of which he suppressed a different vowel; and a German poet, Gottlob Burmann (1737–1805), who wrote 130 poems for a total of 20,000 words without using the letter r. According to Pierce, Burmann omitted the letter r from his daily conversation for the last 17 years of his life. (One wonders how he avoided mentioning his own name.) These books are understandably all out of print and not found on the shelves of most libraries. However, *Gadsby* is at least available on interlibrary loan.

**4.10: Table 2**  Results of an Author Identification Experiment Using Letter-Pair-Correlation Data and Eq. (15). [The numerical values have been normalized to the highest "diagonal" term, which occurred in the case of Lincoln. Two statistically significant samples were used from separate works by each author, and the results averaged. The statistical uncertainties were $\leqslant 0.01$ for the entries.]

| | Hemingway | Poe | Baldwin | Joyce | Shakespeare | Cummings | Washington | Lincoln |
|---|---|---|---|---|---|---|---|---|
| Hemingway | 0.41 | −0.02 | −0.01 | −0.02 | −0.05 | −0.11 | −0.20 | −0.02 |
| Poe | −0.02 | 0.22 | 0.02 | −0.03 | 0 | 0 | −0.08 | −0.06 |
| Baldwin | −0.01 | 0.02 | 0.31 | 0 | −0.02 | −0.02 | −0.08 | −0.07 |
| Joyce | −0.02 | −0.03 | 0 | 0.07 | 0.03 | 0.03 | −0.03 | −0.20 |
| Shakespeare | −0.05 | 0 | −0.02 | 0.03 | 0.24 | −0.06 | −0.01 | −0.10 |
| Cummings | −0.11 | 0 | −0.02 | 0.03 | −0.06 | 0.22 | 0.15 | 0.13 |
| Washington | −0.20 | −0.08 | −0.08 | −0.03 | −0.01 | 0.15 | 0.48 | −0.01 |
| Lincoln | −0.02 | −0.06 | −0.07 | −0.20 | −0.10 | 0.13 | −0.01 | 1.00 |

*Source:* Based on unpublished data by Jean Bennett.

occurred with the writing of James Joyce. Here, the diagonal coefficients for *Ulysses* and *Finnegan's Wake* were both very small, but at least positive.

The success of the method can be judged by picking an author out of the group and by quickly looking along the appropriate horizontal and vertical lines to see if the diagonal term is largest. The test works in all cases included in the table, although the results are a little marginal with James Joyce and E. E. Cummings. At the same time the closeness of these numbers makes the need for high statistical accuracy apparent.

One perplexing result was noticed. Although the writing of Abraham Lincoln demonstrated the highest degree of autocorrelation in Table 2, considerable difficulty was experienced in distinguishing Lincoln's work from the novel *Gadsby* written by Ernest Wright without using the letter e. The failure may be due to the unusually weird nature of the letter correlations in Wright's novel. Evidently, Wright's pair-correlation matrix is somewhat like Abe Lincoln's after you subtract standard English. Nevertheless, the result leads to a certain skepticism of the accuracy of such identification procedures in general.

Wilhelm Fucks[12] (1962) gave an interesting treatment of this type of problem as applied to composer identification in music. Fucks, Moles (1956), and others have pointed out that music by Berg and Webern tends to have a frequency distribution that is more equally distributed than that of Beethoven. However, Fucks himself notes that the correlation of intervals of consecutive tones is very similar within the music of Bach and that of Webern, even though strong differences exist between correlations in Webern and Beethoven.[13]

The general moral of this lesson is that when you see a headline in the evening newspaper such as

# Computer Says It's Chopin from Beyond

beware! It might have been written by a bunch of monkeys.

[12] Pronounced "foox."

[13] Obviously this type of identification procedure takes on a much more probable character when strings of letters, or words, or musical phrases are used as the basis for determining the correlations. However, the data-accumulation problems, core requirements, and computing time then become very substantial. A more extended discussion of the composer-style-analysis problem is given in Lincoln (1970); also see Fucks (1968). A collection of papers on literary-style analysis was given by Doležel and Bailey (1969), and an annotated bibliography was prepared by Bailey (1968).

128

Having concluded that one primarily finds the statistical structure of the language displayed within the letter-pair-correlation matrix, it is tempting to go on to conclude that it should at least be a trivial matter to recognize the visual patterns characteristic of different languages by graphic display of these matrices.

As will be self-evident from Fig. 4-9, the similarities in the second-order statistical properties of the common Western European languages are far greater than the differences. About all that one can say with confidence from visual displays of the pair-correlation matrices for German, English, French, Italian, Spanish, and Portuguese shown in Fig. 4-9 is that they all represent western European language. To distinguish between them, one again has to compute numerical quantities.

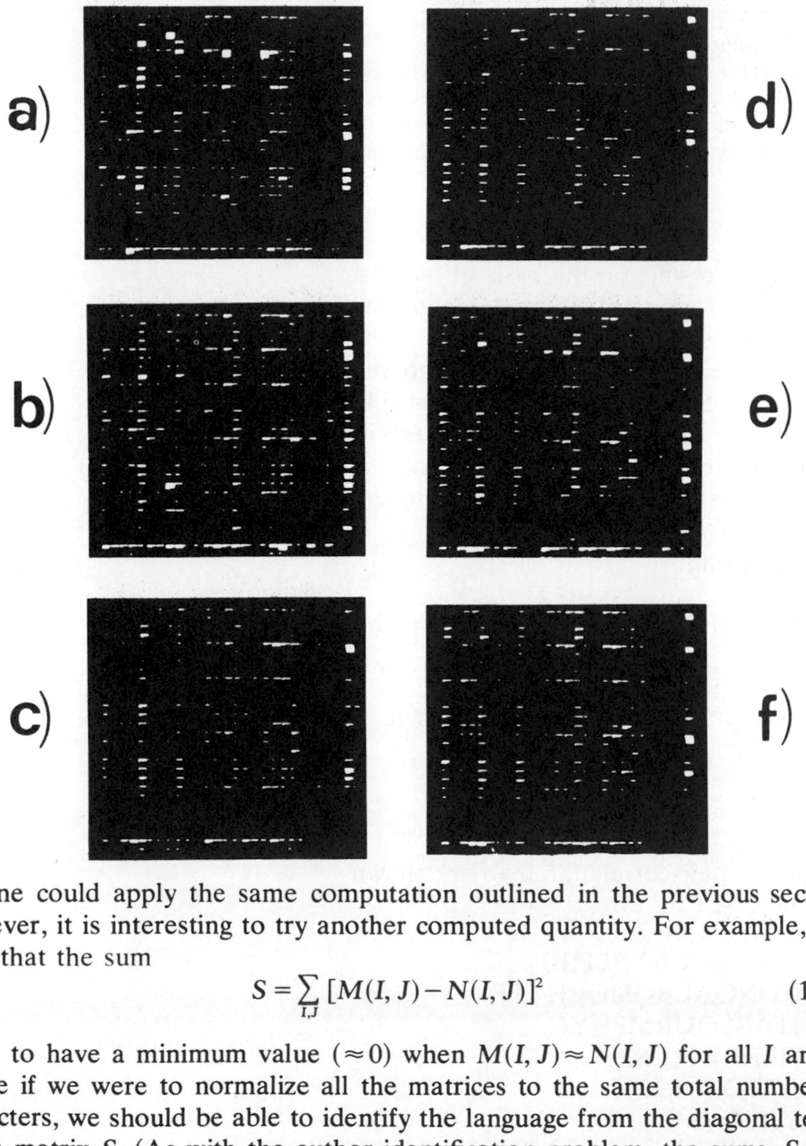

**Fig. 4-9.** Letter-pair-correlation matrices for different European languages: (a) German (Wiese); (b) English (Shakespeare); (c) French (Baudelaire); (d) Italian (Landolfi); (e) Spanish (Cervantes); (f) Portuguese (Coutinho). In each case a $28 \times 28$ raster is used to display the relative probabilities that the $j^{th}$ character follows the $i^{th}$ character. The convention used is the same one explained in Fig. 4-4. (The author is indebted to Jean Bennett and Otto Chu for preparing the data tapes used to generate the displays.) Accent marks were ignored with the exception that umlauts in German were replaced by an additional e.

One could apply the same computation outlined in the previous section. However, it is interesting to try another computed quantity. For example, it is clear that the sum

$$S = \sum_{I,J} [M(I, J) - N(I, J)]^2 \tag{16A}$$

ought to have a minimum value ($\approx 0$) when $M(I, J) \approx N(I, J)$ for all $I$ and $J$. Hence if we were to normalize all the matrices to the same total number of characters, we should be able to identify the language from the diagonal terms in the matrix $S$. (As with the author-identification problem, the sums, $S$, will comprise a symmetric matrix when the rows and columns are labeled according to the various source languages.) A study of this type has been summarized in Table 3. Although one can clearly distinguish among the source languages, the differences between the two authors writing in English is comparable to the differences between some languages. That is, the English of Shakespeare is quite significantly different from the English of Poe—although not quite as big as the difference between Cervantes writing in Spanish and Coutinho writing in

| | English | | | | | | |
|---|---|---|---|---|---|---|---|
| | *Hamlet* | "Gold Bug" | Spanish | German | French | Italian | Portuguese |
| English | | | | | | | |
|   *Hamlet* | 0 | 0.27 | 0.91 | 0.88 | 0.86 | 0.92 | 0.94 |
|   "Gold Bug" | 0.27 | 0 | 0.89 | 0.83 | 0.80 | 0.88 | 0.90 |
| Spanish | 0.91 | 0.89 | 0 | 0.95 | 0.72 | 0.63 | 0.56 |
| German | 0.88 | 0.83 | 0.95 | 0 | 0.87 | 1.01 | 0.99 |
| French | 0.86 | 0.80 | 0.72 | 0.87 | 0 | 0.76 | 0.76 |
| Italian | 0.92 | 0.88 | 0.63 | 1.01 | 0.76 | 0 | 0.65 |
| Portuguese | 0.94 | 0.90 | 0.56 | 0.99 | 0.76 | 0.65 | 0 |

*Source:* Based on unpublished data by one of the author's former students, Otto Chu.

[a] A normalization procedure based on the total number of characters in each $28 \times 28$ pair-correlation matrix was used which gives a maximum possible value of 2 for the sum, $S$. Note that in this case perfect "identification" corresponds to the value $S = 0$. The statistical uncertainty for each term in the table was $\leqslant 0.01$, based on computed variances for the sum. Two separate authors were used in the case of English (Shakespeare and Poe).

Portuguese. One could, of course, criticize the results on the basis of ignored accent marks. This simplification was made as a practical matter but could be avoided by increasing the size of the character set.

A more sensitive method of applying letter-pair-correlation data to the identification of languages occurs through the computation of most probable digram paths through the matrix. (This notion is discussed in more detail in Section 4.19 on the solution of single-substitution ciphers.) The basic point is that one can construct fairly well defined paths through the character set by looking at the pair-correlation matrix elements in descending order.

For example, consider the following algorithm:

1. Choose $I$ to correspond to the first letter of the common article in the language.
2. Print the alphabetic character for which $I$ stands (in the 1–28 code).
3. Find the maximum $M(I, J)$ in which $J$ has not been previously chosen.
4. Let $M(I, J) = 0$ and let $I = J$.
5. Stop after 28 trips through the loop.
6. Go to step 2.

Application of the algorithm above to the pair-correlation matrices shown in Fig. 4-9 resulted in the following sequences:

| | |
|---|---|
| English (Poe) | THE ANDISOURYPLF'BJ |
| German | DER STINGALBUMOCHYPF |
| French | LE DITANSOURMPHYG |
| Italian | LA CHERIONTUSP |
| Spanish | LA DENTOSURICH |
| Portuguese | LA ESTICORMPUNDJ |

Style-dependent differences typically enter at the seventh or eighth place. However, only the first four characters in each string are really needed to distinguish among the above languages, and the first four characters are frequently very well defined statistically, even in texts as short as 200 or 300 characters in length. Sequences of this type also provide a very powerful method for solving single-substitution ciphers without even having to understand the source language of the message (see discussion in Section 4.19).

Using the algorithm in the text with the pair-correlation matrix from *Hamlet*, compute the most probable digram path which starts with the letter T. Compare the result with that given above for Poe's "The Gold Bug."

Ironically, it is much easier to pick out the differences among languages from the first-order statistical properties than from the correlations between pairs of letters. (See Table 4.) For example, we can compute normalized letter-frequency distributions $F_x(I)$ and $F_y(I)$ for the difference characters $(I)$ in the alphabet corresponding to two languages ($x$ and $y$). The quantity

$$S = \sum_I F_x(I)F_y(I) \tag{16B}$$

will tend to go through a maximum when $x = y$. Equation (16B) is equivalent to a generalized dot product of two multidimensional vectors. Clearly, best results are to be expected when each frequency distribution is normalized so that

$$\sum_I F_x(I)^2 = \sum_I F_y(I)^2 = \cdots = \text{constant (e.g., } = 1) \tag{16C}$$

Then the magnitudes of the generalized vectors are all the same and one is not giving unwarranted weight to a particular language. [Note that the character-frequency data in Table 4 are not normalized according to Eq. (16C).]

**4.11: Table 4** Total Character Frequency per 1000 Characters in Order A, B, C,..., X, Y, Z, ,' for Several European Languages[a] (See the offer in the Preface.)

English
*Hamlet*

| 58 | 12 | 17 | 31 | 93 | 18 | 14 | 50 | 49 | 1 | 7 | 35 |
|----|----|----|----|----|----|----|----|----|----|----|----|
| 25 | 49 | 73 | 12 | 1 | 45 | 53 | 73 | 29 | 9 | 20 | 1 |
| 22 | 0 | 197 | 6 | | | | | | | | |

"The Gold Bug"

| 62 | 14 | 20 | 35 | 106 | 20 | 16 | 47 | 59 | 2 | 5 | 32 |
|----|----|----|----|----|----|----|----|----|----|----|----|
| 21 | 54 | 59 | 16 | 1 | 46 | 49 | 76 | 26 | 7 | 18 | 2 |
| 16 | 1 | 188 | 2 | | | | | | | | |

German

| 48 | 16 | 30 | 47 | 144 | 10 | 24 | 44 | 73 | 4 | 8 | 35 |
|----|----|----|----|----|----|----|----|----|----|----|----|
| 22 | 78 | 22 | 10 | 0 | 61 | 69 | 56 | 39 | 7 | 8 | 0 |
| 1 | 8 | 137 | 0 | | | | | | | | |

French

| 55 | 7 | 24 | 31 | 152 | 8 | 8 | 8 | 61 | 3 | 0 | 49 |
|----|----|----|----|----|----|----|----|----|----|----|----|
| 26 | 52 | 43 | 26 | 11 | 54 | 74 | 55 | 55 | 11 | 0 | 4 |
| 2 | 0 | 166 | 13 | | | | | | | | |

Italian

| 111 | 5 | 44 | 27 | 101 | 9 | 13 | 17 | 71 | 0 | 0 | 41 |
|----|----|----|----|----|----|----|----|----|----|----|----|
| 24 | 52 | 74 | 25 | 7 | 49 | 46 | 44 | 23 | 25 | 0 | 0 |
| 0 | 6 | 181 | 4 | | | | | | | | |

Spanish

| 106 | 17 | 32 | 45 | 110 | 5 | 9 | 10 | 47 | 4 | 0 | 52 |
|----|----|----|----|----|----|----|----|----|----|----|----|
| 21 | 55 | 78 | 16 | 14 | 52 | 56 | 28 | 37 | 7 | 0 | 1 |
| 11 | 4 | 184 | 0 | | | | | | | | |

Portuguese

| 116 | 3 | 41 | 46 | 102 | 8 | 10 | 4 | 66 | 1 | 0 | 24 |
|----|----|----|----|----|----|----|----|----|----|----|----|
| 37 | 50 | 99 | 23 | 5 | 54 | 62 | 44 | 28 | 12 | 0 | 0 |
| 0 | 3 | 163 | 0 | | | | | | | | |

[a] The data were computed from the same sources used to determine the matrices displayed in Figs. 4-4 and 4-9. The frequency of the letter e is artificially high in the case of German because umlauts were replaced by e's following the vowel (e.g., ö was replaced by oe in the source text). All other accent marks were merely ignored.

Although the technique may not be so useful in the analysis of ordinary text, it becomes much more impressive when applied to identifying the source language in multiple transposition ciphers (see discussion later of the Pablo Waberski cipher). Note that the same technique could be used in a variety of different applications ranging from problems in pattern recognition (in which sets of expansion coefficients could be used to make up the generalized vector components) to problems in literary-style identification (where the frequency distributions might consist of things such as word, sentence, and paragraph lengths). Also note that the sums in Eqs. (16B) and (16C) can be done simply by matrix multiplication using suitably dimensioned row and column matrices. However, as with the pattern recognition problem discussed in Section 2.23, greater sensitivity is obtained by requiring that the individual projections of the different generalized vectors agree within some appropriate numerical criterion.

---

**4.11
PROBLEM 9**

Using the data in Table 4 in the form of DATA statements, write a program that investigates the possibility of distinguishing among languages by use of Eqs. (16B) and (16C). Then print out a comparison of the normalized column arrays for four of the languages in vertical columns.

**4.11
PROBLEM 10**

If you have the CHANGE statement available (or equivalent CALL statement), compute the character-frequency distribution for the first two pages of the novel *Gadsby* by Ernest Wright (1939) (see Fig. 4-10). Use Eqs. (16B) and (16C) and the data in Table 4 to see how close the frequency distribution comes to that of English. Compare the dot product of *Gadsby* and *Hamlet* with that for *Hamlet* and "The Gold Bug." Also print out the normalized column arrays in these three cases for comparison.

**4.11
PROBLEM 11**

If you have the CHANGE statement (or equivalent CALL statement) and a high-resolution plotting device, generate a visual display of the pair-correlation matrix computed from *Gadsby* (see Fig. 4-10) and compare with those shown in Fig. 4-9 for the common European languages. If you do not have a high-resolution display, compute the most probable digram path through this matrix which starts with the letter T. (See the discussion prior to Problem 8 and compare with the results for English given in the text.)

---

Having come so close to many of the questions addressed in Shannon's famous (1948) paper on information theory, it would be irresponsible not to say something about the relation of the present material to the general problem of transmitting and receiving information over communication channels. In any real communication system, one is faced with a sequence of the following type:

**4.12
Relation to Information Theory**[14]

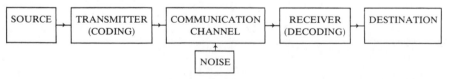

The general features of this system obtain regardless of whether the transmitter is a scribe taking dictation with pen and ink on sheets of blotting paper or, at

---

[14] This Section was introduced merely to provide some qualitative background perspective on communication problems. The equations in this Section are not necessary for the later discussion of entropy.

I

IF YOUTH, THROUGHOUT all history, had had a champion to stand up for it; to show a doubting world that a child can think; and, possibly, do it practically; you wouldn't constantly run across folks today who claim that "a child don't know anything." A child's brain starts functioning at birth; and has, amongst its many infant convolutions, thousands of dormant atoms, into which God has put a mystic possibility for noticing an adult's act, and figuring out its purport.

Up to about its primary school days a child thinks, naturally, only of play. But many a form of play contains disciplinary factors. "You can't do this," or "that puts you out," shows a child that it must think, practically, or fail. Now, if, through-out childhood, a brain has no opposition, it is plain that it will attain a position of "status quo," as with our ordinary animals. Man knows not why a cow, dog or lion was not born with a brain on a par with ours; why such animals cannot add, subtract, or obtain from books and schooling, that paramount position which Man holds today.

But a human brain is not in that class. Constantly throbbing and pulsating, it rapidly forms

[ 10 ]

opinions; attaining an ability of its own; a fact which is startlingly shown by an occasional child "prodigy" in music or school work. And as, with our dumb animals, a child's inability convincingly to impart its thoughts to us, should not class it as ignorant.

Upon this basis I am going to show you how a bunch of bright young folks did find a champion; a man with boys and girls of his own; a man of so dominating and happy individuality that Youth is drawn to him as is a fly to a sugar bowl. It is a story about a small town. It is not a gossipy yarn; nor is it a dry, monotonous account, full of such customary "fill-ins" as "romantic moonlight casting murky shadows down a long, winding country road." Nor will it say anything about tinklings lulling distant folds; robins carolling at twilight, nor any "warm glow of lamplight" from a cabin window. No. It is an account of up-and-doing activity; a vivid portrayal of Youth as it is today; and a practical discarding of that worn-out notion that "a child don't know anything."

Now, any author, from history's dawn, always had that most important aid to writing:-- an ability to call upon any word in his dictionary in building up his story. That is, our strict laws as to word construction did not block his path. But in

[ 11 ]

**Fig. 4-10.** The first two pages of Chapter I of the novel *Gadsby* (a story of over 50,000 words without using the letter E) written by Ernest Wright (1939).

the opposite extreme, a high-speed telecommunication system in which alphanumeric characters are being transmitted in 8-bit bytes over a microwave link.[15]

In each case, a message from the source is encoded by an established convention, and this code is transmitted in segments (e.g., sheets of blotting paper, 8-bit bytes, etc.) at a prescribable rate. Noise is added to the signal by the coding process itself, but especially in the communication channel (e.g., spreading of the ink in the blotting paper, stray pulses in the teletype link, etc.). The message is then received, decoded, and sent to its final destination.

Interest in this type of problem has existed since the early days of telegraphy. For example, the nontrivial economic problems involved in the transmission of teletype messages over a trans-Atlantic cable stimulated theoretical interest in the quantitative comparison of the efficiency of different coding methods. In fact, there was already considerable interest in the most efficient methods for television transmission over both wire and radio paths by the mid-1920s. Quantitive formulation of the problem dates at least to the early papers of Nyquist (1924) and Hartley (1928), in which it is noted that one should be able to define a quantity

$$H = L_i \log b_i \tag{17}$$

proportional to the amount of information associated with a list of $L_i$ possible selections made in a code of base $b_i$. Such a definition permits comparing the information transmitted in different base codes (e.g., binary, ternary,..., decimal,...) and ensures that the information transferred per sample is the same in two different codes when

$$b_1^{L_1} = b_2^{L_2} \tag{18}$$

The base of the logarithm in Eq. (17) is arbitrary. Base 2 logarithms of course make life particularly simple with binary codes, for then the amount of information per sample is just the number of binary symbols used. The name *bit* (short for "binary digit") for this unit of information, suggested by the mathematician John Tukey, has been widely adopted. Similarly, an 8-bit sample is defined as a *byte* in current usage.

It is obvious that the rate at which messages can be sent must increase proportionally with the number of data blocks (8-bit bytes, sheets of blotting paper, etc.) sent per second and that at least a monotonic increase of information transmission capability must occur with increasing signal-to-noise ratio within the transmission of individual data blocks.

Consideration of a binary encoding method provides an easy way to see that the channel capacity to transmit information must increase logarithmically with the ratio of the signal voltage to the noise voltage (or signal-to-noise ratio). We can, in fact, define the capacity of a communication channel to transmit information in terms of the equivalent number of binary bits per second required to send a signal with a given bandwidth and signal-to-noise ratio within that bandwidth. For example, suppose that the signal is a continuously varying voltage which we wish to encode and transmit in a sequence of $M$-bit samples at the rate of $W$ samples per second. Clearly, the uncertainty in coded signal will have a minimum value of about one bit per sample. Hence the maximum signal-to-noise ratio the signal can have will be limited to

$$S/N \approx 2^M \tag{19}$$

just from the encoding process itself. Hence

$$M = \log_2 (S/N) \tag{20}$$

---

[15] For a detailed account of real communication systems, see Bennett and Davey (1965).

and the total number of bits that could be transmitted by this system (in $W$ samples per second) is

$$C = WM = W \log_2 (S/N) \qquad \text{bits/sec} \tag{21}$$

The effects of additional noise sources in the communication channel may be included within the term $N$ in the same formula. For example, suppose that we have a signal level of 10 bits per sample and a noise level reaching the receiver of two bits per sample. The ratio of signal-to-noise is then

$$S/N \approx 2^{10}/2^2 = 2^8 \tag{22}$$

Hence the signal could have been transmitted in the presence of coding noise alone with a system having only 8-bit samples, and the channel capacity to transmit information is given adequately by Eq. (21) if we merely insert the actual value of $S/N$ from Eq. (22).

At the receiving end of the communication link, the message must be decoded and the original voltage reconstructed. Because we effectively multiplied the original signal by a periodic wave at frequency $W$ during the encoding process (i.e., we took $W$ samples per second), simple trigonometric identities tell us that extraneous beat frequencies will be present in the received signal at $W \pm W_m$, where $W_m$ is the maximum frequency present in the original signal. Hence to remove these extraneous signals at the receiver, we have to run the output signal through a low-pass filter which cuts off rapidly in frequency above $W_m$ and the sample rate must satisfy

$$W > 2W_m \tag{23}$$

These observations can be extended to continuous-wave-transmission problems with much the same conclusion: that the channel capacity, $C$, for a continuous-wave communication channel perturbed by frequency-independent noise is also related to the signal-to-noise ratio and the bandwidth of the channel, $W$, by Eq. (21).

The net bit-transmission rate is called the *entropy rate* or *information rate*. More formally, the channel capacity as defined in information theory turns out to be the greatest entropy rate of source for which codes can be devised that allow the error at the destination to be made arbitrarily small.

Some communication links (e.g., those used to converse with nuclear submarines deep below the ocean surface) have very low channel capacities. To send teletype messages over such a communication channel, it is obviously desirable to encode the original messages with the smallest number of bits possible that still permits unambiguous decoding at the destination. In the next several sections we shall consider what the statistical properties of the language imply regarding the minimum average number of bits per character necessary to transmit the language.

The expression,

**4.13
Entropy in Language**

$$H = - \sum_{I=1}^{N} P(I) \log_2 P(I) \tag{24}$$

is a fundamental quantity in Shannon's (1948) theory. He concluded that $H$ has the properties of entropy by analogy to the mathematical form of a similar quantity defined by Boltzmann in statistical mechanics (in the formulation of the $H$-theorem). By useful historical coincidence, the letter $H$ was also defined as the "information" in a $\log_2$ sense in the much earlier paper by Hartley (1928). Equation (24) is introduced in Shannon's paper as an answer to three postulatory requirements on the dependence of the information on the set of probabilities $P(1), \ldots, P(N)$. As Shannon states, it is with the implications of Eq. (24) to specific problems that we are primarily concerned. We shall therefore content ourselves with a discussion of the meaning of Eq. (24) and the demonstration that this meaning is very reasonable in a number of specific instances.

To make a connection with the earlier papers by Nyquist and Hartley, it is helpful to note that if a particular code uses $B(I)$ bits to transmit the $I$th character on a list of $N$ characters, the average number of bits per character required to transmit messages is given by

$$\langle B \rangle = \sum_{I=1}^{N} P(I)B(I) \tag{25}$$

provided the probabilities are normalized so that

$$\sum_{I=1}^{N} P(I) = 1 \tag{26}$$

The quantity $H$ in Eq. (24) therefore corresponds to the statistical average of the number of bits per character necessary to transmit messages in a code for which

$$B(I) \equiv -\log_2 P(I) = \log_2 [1/P(I)] \tag{27}$$

Most real codes used to transmit language text use a constant number of bits per symbol $B(I)$ and result in average values from Eq. (25) which exceed those that would be computed from Eq. (24) for the same probabilities. The average number of bits per character given by Eq. (25) for a given variable-length code could of course be minimized by choosing the factors so that $B(I)$ increases with decreasing $P(I)$. For example, one could try to choose the factors $B(I)$ to approach the dependence in Eq. (27) However, it is difficult to do this without introducing ambiguities in the code meaning and without leaving the system extremely vulnerable to the effects of transmission errors [see Huffman (1952) for one such approach].

The quantity defined in Eq. (27) is literally the number of bits necessary to specify a list of $1/P(I)$ characters. In the special case where

$$P(I) = \text{constant} = 1/N \tag{28}$$

there are $N$ quantities on the list. In this case, definition (27) results in

$$B(I) = \text{constant} = \log_2 N \tag{29}$$

and Eq. (24) just represents the total number of bits necessary to specify $N$ equally probable choices. Hence Eq. (24) reduces to the "information" in the earlier Hartley and Nyquist sense when the probabilities are all the same.

When the $P(I)$ are different, the **quantity $H$ in Eq. (24)** takes on a more generalized meaning and can be shown to be the ***minimum* average number of bits necessary to specify the number of choices at a branch point where $N$ different possibilities occur with different (normalized) probabilities, $P(I)$.**[16] As applied to written language text, Eq. (24) yields an inherent value of the entropy per character which is a characteristic of the language. The values thus obtained are independent of the labeling scheme or the order in which the text is read and are roughly independent of the number of characters assumed in the alphabet as long as the most probable ones occur well within the sum.

It will be helpful to make sure that Eq. (24) makes sense in a few simple cases. For example, consider a situation in which there are two possible choices with equal probabilities,

$$P(1) = P(2) = \tfrac{1}{2} \tag{30}$$

---

[16] The proof that Eq. (24) actually gives a minimum value is not trivial. See, for example, Gallager (1968) or Ash (1967).

Here

$$H = \tfrac{1}{2}\log_2 2 + \tfrac{1}{2}\log_2 2 = 1 \text{ bit} \tag{31}$$

and Eq. (24) says there will be

$$2^H = 2 \text{ possible choices} \tag{32}$$

Similarly, with four possibilities with equal probabilities

$$P(1) = P(2) = P(3) = P(4) = \tfrac{1}{4} \tag{33}$$

Equation (24) yields

$$H = 4(\tfrac{1}{4}\log_2 4) = 2 \text{ bits} \tag{34}$$

or

$$2^H = 2^2 = 4 \text{ choices}$$

Next suppose that there are two choices in which

$$P(1) = P \quad \text{and} \quad P(2) = 1 - P \tag{35}$$

Then

$$-H = P\log_2 P + (1-P)\log_2(1-P) \tag{36}$$

If we take the limit as $P \to 0$ in Eq. (36), $-H \to 0 + 1\log_2 1 = 0$ bits. Hence there is only one choice,

$$2^H \to 2^0 = 1 \tag{37}$$

That is, if $P(1) = 0$ in Eq. (35), it means that $P(2) = 1$ and there really is only one possibility. The same situation holds when $P(2) \to 0$ in the above illustration. Equation (36) also yields a maximum value of $H = 1$ (2 choices) when $P = \tfrac{1}{2} = P(1) = P(2)$.

---

**4.13**
**PROBLEM 12**
Compute the variation of $H$ as a function of $P$ from Eq. (36) for $0.05 < P < 0.95$ in steps of 0.05. Plot the result on the teletype (or, if available, high-resolution display). Note that

$$\log_2 X = \frac{\log_e X}{\log_e 2}$$

---

It is next of interest to compute the minimum average number of bits, $h$, per alphanumeric character required to transmit source material written in a language such as English. In accordance with the above discussion, this quantity may be determined through application of Eq. (24) and may be regarded as the entropy or information per character of source text.

The results obtained will obviously be dependent on the statistical properties of the language, and we will get progressive approximations to the answer analogous to the various levels of sophistication used previously in simulating the Eddington monkey. Further, owing to variations in style among various authors, one can never expect to obtain an absolutely precise answer, and there is indeed reason to expect that real languages may actually obey the second law of thermodynamics (see Section 4.14). The answer will always vary somewhat with the particular text. However, as we have shown earlier in this chapter with the author-identification problem, these differences are a small fraction of the main effect. The structure of the language is largely predominant and, in fact, even the differences in statistical structure among the common western European languages are remarkably slight.

The zeroth-order calculation of the entropy per character is, of course, the easiest. Assuming our original 28-character set used to analyze Act III of *Hamlet*, we let $P = \text{constant} = \tfrac{1}{28}$, and Eq. (24) gives us directly

$$h_0 = \log_2 28 = 4.80735 \text{ bits/character} \tag{38}$$

That is, if we assume that all 28 characters are equally probable, the minimum average number of bits per character necessary to convey the language is given by Eq. (38). Consequently, the minimum number of characters required is $C_0 = 2^{h_0} = 28$.

The first-order calculation of the entropy per character ($h_1$) requires a knowledge of the total probabilities of occurrence of the individual members of the character set. The latter can be determined for the 28 characters used to analyze Act III of *Hamlet* by reading off the numbers in Table 1 (remembering that they must be normalized), or by summing the rows in the correlation matrix $M(I, J)$ in Fig. 4-6. That is, as previously noted,

$$P(I) = \sum_{J=1}^{28} M(I, J) \bigg/ \sum_{I=1}^{28} \sum_{J=1}^{28} M(I, J) \qquad (39)$$

Applying Eq. (24) to Act III of *Hamlet* yields

$$h_1 = 4.106 \text{ bits/character} \qquad (40)$$

or a minimum list,

$$2^{h_1} \approx 17.21 \text{ characters}$$

---

**4.13**
**PROBLEM 13**

Check the numerical value obtained in Eq. (40) by computing the probabilities from the data in Table 1 (or by summing the columns of the correlation matrix in Fig. 4-6).

---

In the second-order calculation of the entropy per character ($h_2$), we have to take into account the probability, $P(I, J)$, that the $J$th character followed the $I$th character. The particular sum obtained from an expression such as Eq. (25) will vary with the identity of the previous character typed.

Suppose that the $I$th character of text has just been typed. The normalized probability $P(I, J)$ that the next character will be the $J$th character may be obtained from the correlation matrix in Fig. 4-6 by noting that

$$P(I, J) = M(I, J) \bigg/ \sum_{J=1}^{28} M(I, J) \qquad \text{where} \quad \sum_{J=1}^{28} P(I, J) = 1 \qquad (41)$$

The average number of bits necessary to specify the number of choices at this point will itself be a function of $I$. (That is, it depends on the past history and hence the character just typed.) This average number of bits is

$$B(I) = \sum_{J=1}^{28} P(I, J) B(I, J) \qquad (42)$$

where $B(I, J)$ also depends on the last character typed; hence for Eq. (42) to be a minimum,

$$B(I, J) = -\log_2 P(I, J) \qquad (43)$$

by analogy with Eq. (27).

Finally, we want to find the average of $B(I)$ over all initial characters $I = 1$–28. This average will be a minimum because each $B(I)$ is a minimum. Hence the minimum average number of bits per character necessary to describe the source text (or second-order entropy per character) will be given by

$$h_2 = \sum_{I=1}^{28} P(I) B(I) = \sum_{I=1}^{28} P(I) \sum_{J=1}^{28} P(I, J) B(I, J) \qquad (44)$$

where $B(I, J)$ is given by Eq. (43). The probabilities may be obtained from the pair-correlation matrix, $M(I, J)$, through Eqs. (39) and (41). Using the $28 \times 28$

matrix from Act III of *Hamlet* (Fig. 4-6), we obtain

$$h_2 = 3.3082 \text{ bits/character} \qquad (45)$$

or a minimum number of

$$2^{h_2} = 9.905 \text{ characters}$$

on the average. [Note that $h_2 = h_1$ if $B(I, J) = B(I)$ for all $J$.]

---

**4.13
PROBLEM 14**
Evaluate Eq. (44) using the matrix in Fig. 4-6. Note that it will be easiest to store the quantities $B(I, J)$ in a separate array from that for $P(I, J)$. Also note that the normalizing sums can be computed sequentially with the most efficiency; e.g., one needs $S$ and $S(I)$, where

$$S = \sum_{I=1}^{28} S(I) \quad \text{and} \quad S(I) = \sum_{J=1}^{28} M(I, J)$$

These quantities can be computed as the elements $M(I, J)$ are read into your program. Use a conditional statement to bypass the $\text{LOG}(P(I, J))$ calculations in cases where $P(I, J) = 0$; these cases are easiest to handle merely by defining the corresponding $B(I, J) = 0$.

The values of $h_n$ should be independent of the direction in which you analyze the language. Check the results for $h_2$ for *Hamlet* by taking the transpose of the matrix in Fig. 4-6 before computing $h_2$. (Slight differences may result from rounding errors.)

---

The computation may, in principle, be extended to higher and higher orders of statistical correlation. For example, at the third order we would have

$$h_3 = \sum_I P(I) \sum_J P(I, J) \sum_K P(I, J, K) B(I, J, K) \qquad (46)$$

where

$$B(I, J, K) = -\log_2 P(I, J, K) \qquad \text{etc.} \qquad (47)$$

and the probabilities are given in terms of the correlation matrices defined earlier in this chapter. One has to keep increasing the dimensions of the matrices and the process begins to eat up prohibitive amounts of core and computing time. The main point is that with higher and higher statistical correlations included, the smaller the number of bits, or list of characters, that has to be transmitted on the average to convey the original text. For example, already by second order apparently only about one third of the normal alphabet is required on the average to convey English. For estimates of the asymptotic behavior of $h_n$ at large $n$, see Shannon (1951).

A summary of values of $h_n$ computed by the present author for various languages is given in Table 5.

---

**4.13
PROBLEM 15**
Compute values of $h_1$ and $h_2$ from the sample of the novel *Gadsby* (written without using the letter e) shown in Fig. 4-10 and compare your results with those for English in Table 5. (Use the CHANGE statement or equivalent.)

**4.13
PROBLEM 16**
Assume that Morse code takes 3 bits for a dash, 1 bit for a dot, 1 bit for the spaces within letters, and 3 bits for the spaces between letters. How many bits per character would be needed to transmit Hamlet? [Evaluate $h_1$ using a specific array, $B(I)$, representing the number of bits per character in Morse code.]

---

| | | | |
|---|---|---|---|
| **4.13**<br>**RESEARCH**<br>**PROBLEM** | Braille uses 6-bit "words" in which combinations as well as single letters of the normal written language have separate coded meaning. Hence the average number of bits per character necessary to transmit English will be different in first and second order. What is the value of $h_2$ for Shakespearean English transmitted in braille? | | |

**4.13: Table 5**  Values of $h_n$ (Entropy per Character) Computed in Various Orders[a]

| | $h_1$ | $h_2$ | $h_3$ |
|---|---|---|---|
| Shannon (1951) | | | |
| (27-character alphabet, $h_0 = 4.76$) | | | |
| English (contemporary) | 4.03 | 3.32 | $\approx 3.1$[b] |
| Present results | | | |
| (28-character alphabet, $h_0 = 4.807$) | | | |
| *English* | | | |
| Chaucer (*Canterbury Tales*) | 4.00 | 3.07 | 2.12 |
| Shakespeare (*Hamlet*) | 4.106 | 3.308 | 2.55 |
| Poe ("The Gold Bug") | 4.100 | 3.337 | 2.62 |
| Hemingway (*For Whom the Bell Tolls* and *A Farewell to Arms*) | 4.055 | 3.198 | 2.39 |
| Joyce (*Finnegan's Wake*) | 4.144 | 3.377 | 2.55 |
| *German* (Wiese) | 4.08 | 3.18 | — |
| *French* (Baudelaire) | 4.00 | 3.14 | — |
| *Italian* (Landolfi) | 3.98 | 3.03 | — |
| *Spanish* (Cervantes) | 3.98 | 3.01 | — |
| *Portuguese* (Coutinho) | 3.91 | 3.11 | — |
| *Latin* (Julius Caesar) | $4.05_1$ | $3.27_1$ | 2.38 |
| *Greek* (Rosetta Stone) | $4.00_7$ | $3.05_3$ | 2.19 |
| (77-character alphabet, $h_0 = 6.267$)[c] | | | |
| Japanese (Kawabata) | 4.809 | 3.633 | — |

[a] Accent marks were not included in the character set and spaces were inserted between the ancient Greek words on the Rosetta Stone.

[b] The value of $h_3$ given by Shannon (1951) was based on an extremely approximate method of including the space symbol in earlier trigram data given by Pratt (1939). Because Pratt's data were not terribly accurate in the first place and also did not include correlations with the space symbol, it is surprising that Shannon's estimate of $h_3$ was as good as it was. Apparently no one has published an accurate computed value for $h_3$ in any language since the Shannon (1951) publication.

[c] The results for Japanese were computed by one of the author's students, Yoshikazu Okuyama, from a 10,000-character sample using a 77-character set consisting of 76 kana plus the space symbol.

The second law of thermodynamics may be stated

## 4.14
## Entropy and Anthropology

$$\Delta H > 0 \tag{48}$$

for any thermodynamic process where $H$ is proportional to the entropy for the total system.[17] Associating entropy with the degree of statistical disorder, the second law means that thermodynamic systems tend to proceed from states of lower probability to states of higher probability (or, equivalently, from higher to lower order). For example, a drop of ink gradually diffuses throughout the glass of water into which it is placed; molecules having a well-defined velocity will assume a Maxwellian velocity distribution due to collisions in a short time

[17] In many texts on statistical mechanics, $H$ is defined to be proportional to the entropy through a *negative* constant. This difference amounts to changing the sign in Eq. (24). In the present discussion we have adopted Shannon's definition, in which $H$ has the same sign as the entropy.

after they have been placed in a high-pressure gas, and so on. Ultimately, as proclaimed by various morbid prophets of doom, this process will lead to the "heat death" of the universe—unless something we do not know about with much certainty takes place.

There are some qualitative reasons why we might also expect languages to obey the second law in some sense. The fact that large numbers of people use them introduces the statistical element. If a language is developed initially by one or a small number of persons at one point on the globe, it seems inevitable that the structure of the language will become less ordered as it diffuses throughout the world. The condensed (and therefore specialized) meanings originally given to symbols by the creator of the language will tend to be broadened and require more additional description through common usage. In other words, it seems likely that there will be a tendency for the minimum average number of bits per message required to convey meaning in normal use of the language to increase with time.

Some evidence for the effect is to be found in the gradual abandonment of ideographs (symbols that convey entire thoughts or words) with the aging of most languages. Beyond that, there is at least some tendency for the number of characters in the alphabet to increase with time, and for the more concise declensions of single words to be replaced by sequences of words. This process generally makes the language easier to learn and use but also results in requiring more bits per message on the average; the redundancy of the language tends to go up and "Parkinson's Law" seems to be a consequence of thermodynamics. One, of course, has to look over really long periods of time to see if the effect occurs; otherwise, variations in individual style will tend to

**Fig. 4-11.** The evolution of language has been marked by the gradual abandonment of ideographs for the sake of more generally useful alphabetic notation.

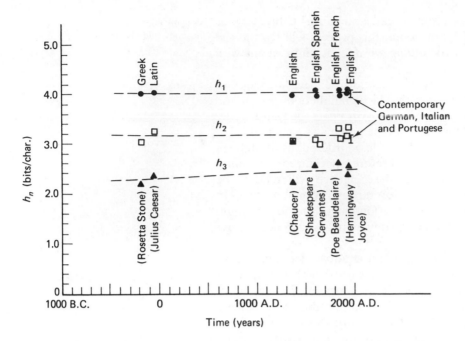

**Fig. 4-12.** Variation of $h_1$, $h_2$, and $h_3$ (the first-, second- and third-order entropy per character) with time for a number of languages.

mask the phenomenon. Obviously, it is also desirable to try to make comparisons between old and recent versions of the same text. Interlinear translations of old language texts into modern English are particularly helpful in this sort of study.

Although there is a very definite indication that the total number of bits for the same message has increased with time, the result has occurred in a rather surprising way: the total number of characters per message has gone up, but the entropy per character (values of $h_1$, $h_2$, and $h_3$) has remained astonishingly constant over periods of at least 2000 years (at least within the languages studied in the present chapter that belong to the same family tree; see Fig. 4-12). The result suggests the involvement of some fundamental physiological limitation. For example, the nearly constant values for the entropy per character may just reflect the finite number of sound sequences that can be easily produced by the human voice. Such limitations would get into the written language the minute an alphabet based on some kind of phonetic spelling arose from more elementary ideographs. Additional support for this notion arises in the fact that the value for $h_2$ computed for Japanese kana is so close to the values for western European languages (see Table 5). If this interpretation is correct, it should be possible to determine at what period in "prehistory" the transition from ideographs to alphabetized writing occurred within a given culture by statistical analysis of the writing samples—without actually having to translate the samples. At some point in prehistory, or ancient history, there must have been an appreciable change in the values of $h_n$. Yet easily available samples of ancient writing do not appear to show this effect within the same family tree (see Fig. 4-12). One possible interpretation is that alphabetized writing existed much further back into prehistory than has usually been assumed. The data published recently by Marshack (1972) is particularly intriguing in that respect because it seems to imply the existence of extremely elaborate notational systems in the cave art produced during the Ice Age by prehistoric man in southern France. Marshack's point that large changes do not occur suddenly is well taken. The fact that $h_n$ remained ≈constant from 200 B.C. on implies that it probably had not changed rapidly prior to that time.

The Latin of Julius Caesar is, of course, easy to feed into a teletype terminal and even the ancient Greek inscriptions on the Rosetta Stone ($\approx 191$ B.C.) or within the decree of Canopus ($\approx 239$ B.C.) are easy to get into a computer (see Fig. 4-13 and problems at the end of this section). The going gets much harder with hieroglyphics.

It is pretty clear that the Egyptian hieroglyphics themselves could be broken down into a fundamental character set (of a much more primary sort than the type of phonetic alphabet deduced initially by Champollion), with which the individual symbols of the ancient Egyptian text could be constructed. To do this, just imagine how a typesetter would attack the problem and ask what would be the smallest set of symbols needed to construct all the hieroglyphs (see Fig. 4-14). This set would, for example, be made up of various parts of human bodies (arms, legs, etc., along with more abstract symbols). For example, the ancient Egyptian word for "carries away,"

was clearly made up from two other primary symbols used frequently by themselves:

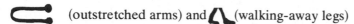

These and many other basic symbols in the ancient hieroglyphic writing clearly had some alphabetic significance and, as in many other cases, are probably fairly direct ancestors of similar-looking characters in the later Greek and Latin alphabets. Obviously, there would be many highly correlated symbol sequences in the hieroglyphic text and one, in principle, could then compute the entropy per character in various statistical orders. The result of such a calculation would be quite interesting because the portion of the text in hieroglyphics presumably represents a language that is very much older than the text in Greek. Budge (1904) points out that the ancient hieroglyphic writing was not understood by most Egyptians circa 200 B.C. and that the common written language of that period was indeed Greek. Hence with the hieroglyphic text one might at last begin to see an appreciable change in $h_1$, $h_2$, and $h_3$ from the values shown in Fig. 4-12. However, a rough estimate shows that the primary hieroglyphic character set itself is likely to have well over 100 members. Consequently, even though many of these elements do have low probabilities of occurrence, the initial data-acquisition problem and computer-core requirements would make such an investigation rather formidable. [The detailed discussion of hieroglyphics given by Budge (1929, pp. 228–246) would be extremely helpful in this problem. Also, note that the text in the decree of Canopus (see, for example, Fig. 4-14 or Budge, 1904) would be much easier to work from than that in the Rosetta Stone.]

Such investigations could be much more easily extended to ancient cuneiform writing where fairly long specimens dating to about 2000 B.C. are available in the Yale Collection (see Hallo, 1974). Here the primary character set is much smaller and much more manageable than with the Egyptian hieroglyphs. However, in this case the evolution of the language leads directly to Arabic, and modern samples of text would be awkward to enter within the ASCII character set.

Still more ambitious students might want to have a crack at Chinese. Although the basic Chinese vocabulary consists of about 5000 ideographs, these may be broken down into a much smaller set of radicals and further subsets of brush strokes (see Fenn, 1971, or Wieger, 1965). There is also an effort to adopt Romanized spellings of Chinese words currently in progress on the Chinese mainland.

**Fig. 4-13.** The first 35 lines from the Greek inscription on the Decree of Canopus. The original text was carved in a stone 2 feet 8 inches wide, in the ninth year of the reign of Ptolemy III (≈238 B.C.). See Problem 19. (From Budge, 1904.)

**Fig. 4-14.** The first few lines from the hieroglyphic writing on the Decree of Canopus (≈238 B.C.). The symbols are read from right to left and top to bottom. (From Budge, 1904.)

145

Finally, it is worth noting that much the same approach could be used to study the emanations at radio and optical frequencies coming from outer space. If something out there is trying to communicate with us, about the only statement that could be made with reasonable confidence is that the "message" should exhibit statistical properties that are different from those of purely random character sequences. However, lots of detailed speculation has been given on this subject. There is a tendency among scientists living on the earth to assume that communication from other worlds will incorporate the latest discovery that they themselves have just made. For example, those having just invented a maser suspect that a maser operating on the hydrogen 21-cm line is the obvious choice; those who have just invented a laser note that some laser frequency would be ideal; similarly, those who have just invented the wheel think that the first 1000 digits in $\pi$ will obviously constitute the first message. (But why in base 10?) We shall leave it to the reader to decide whether or not such messages from outer space should be answered. We merely note that because of the enormous time delays required for light to travel to and from other solar systems, the conversational problems involved would be about the same as those one would meet in trying to talk to the authors of the text in Fig. 4-14.

**4.14
PROBLEM 17†**

See if Caesar's *Commentaries on the Gallic War* have obeyed the second law when translated into contemporary English. Investigate the first several sections of the interlinear translation by Dewey (1918). Compute the total number of characters, $h_1$ and $h_2$ for both the original Latin and modern English versions of the same text. (Be careful not to include redundant parenthetical remarks in the English text.) Note that although the total number of characters increased very substantially in going from Caesar's Latin to modern English, the values of $h_1$ and $h_2$ (the first- and second-order entropy per character) changed only slightly.

**4.14
PROBLEM 18†**

Do the same computation in a comparison of the message in the first 100 lines within *The Prologue* to *The Canterbury Tales* by Chaucer (use, for example, the interlinear translation by Hopper, 1970).

**4.14
PROBLEM 19†**

The Rosetta Stone (Agathocles et al., 196 B.C.; e.g., see the discussion in Budge, 1929) and the decree of Canopus (see Budge, 1904) contain some of the earliest bilingual translations available. Compute the values of $h_1$ and $h_2$ for the lines of the ancient Greek text shown in Fig. 4-13 and compare with the results in Table 5. *Note:* One simple code to convert the uppercase Greek letters to teletype symbols is as follows:

Greek:  ΑΒΨΔΕΦΓΗΙ ΚΛΜΝΟΠΘΡΣΤ   Ω   Ξ
ASCII:  ABC DEF GHIJKL M N O PQRSTUVWXYZ

Also note that spaces were not preserved in the Rosetta Stone or in the decree of Canopus, whereas the values in Table 5 were computed with the spaces reinserted.

**4.14
RESEARCH
PROBLEM†**

See if you can compute $h_2$ based on the Egyptian hieroglyphics in Fig. 4-14.

† Use the CHANGE statement, or equivalent, to convert alphanumeric characters from the terminal to ASCII integers (see Section 1.18).

We have shown that English text should require substantially fewer characters on the average than the normal alphabet for transmission, provided that we are willing to use the statistical properties of the language to advantage.

**4.15
Bit Compression in Language
Transmission**

From the results in Table 5, it seems likely that only about 2.5 bits per character would be necessary on the average if we went to third-order statistical correlations. At first glance, the result seems fantastically appealing. One could send twice the number of messages over the same communications channel; Western Union could double its profits; perhaps we can find a way to communicate with all those nuclear submarines lurking out there after all; maybe there is even something in ESP; and so on. Unfortunately, information theory does not tell us how to accomplish the objective in a really practical way. It tells us primarily that it is not necessarily impossible to do it. We shall therefore investigate a simple, fixed-length coding method of bit compression based on our earlier letter-correlation data.[18]

The bit-compression problem clearly has two parts:

1. Use of the statistical properties of the language to compress the message.
2. Use of the statistical properties to help reconstruct (or "expand") the message at the other end.

Obviously the number of bits per character required on the average should decrease as we go to higher- and higher-order correlations. Also it seems clear that we can always do better by going to a higher-order method to recover the message than was initially used to transmit the message. This might be important in the submarine problem or in communicating with a distant spaceship. However, if we have the same size of computer at both ends of the communication channel, we can always do best by using the maximum available statistical information at both ends of the line.

The zeroth order is not of interest here because that merely means sending messages verbatim with the standard alphabet. The corrector at the other end might be useful in fixing up spelling errors, typographical mistakes, or the effects of noise—but that's about all.

In first-order transmission, we merely throw out the least-probable characters in the alphabet. According to the results in the previous section, we ought to be able to get along by transmitting only 4.1056 bits per character on the average, or, equivalently, a minimum set of about 17 characters should permit transmitting an average message from *Hamlet*.

First we need some initial text to work with. This could be entered through string operations, or merely entered through a DATA statement in the 1–28 character code recognized by the printing sieve discussed earlier in the chapter. For example, a typical DATA statement might consist of the following:

```
2000   REM DATA FOR 194 CHARACTER MESSAGE FROM HAMLET
2001   DATA 27,20,15,27,2,5,27,15,18,27,14,15,20,27,20,15,27,2,5,27
2002   DATA 20,8,1,20,27,9,19,27,20,8,5,27,17,21,5,19,20,9,15,14,27
2003   DATA 23,8,5,20,8,5,18,27,28,20,9,19,27,14,15,2,12,5,18,27
2004   DATA 9,14,27,20,8,5,27,13,9,14,4,27,20,15,27,19,21,6,6,5,18,27
2005   DATA 20,8,5,27,19,12,9,14,7,19,27,1,14,4,27,1,18,18,15,23,19,27
2006   DATA 15,6,27,15,21,20,18,1,7,5,15,21,19,27,6,15,18,20,21,14,5,27
2007   DATA 15,18,27,20,15,27,20,1,11,5,27,1,18,13,19,27,1,7,1,9,14,19
2008   DATA 20,27,1,27,19,5,1,27,15,6,27,20,18,15,21,2,12,5,19,27
2009   DATA 1,14,4,27,2,25,27,15,16,16,15,19,9,14,7,27,5,14,4,27,20,8,5
2010   DATA 13,27
```

It will be helpful to enter the numerical version of the text in a suitably dimensioned column array, $C(I)$. We can also store the order of probability of

---

[18] A method for constructing optimum variable-length codes was considered by Huffman (1952); also see the discussion in Gallager (1968, pp. 52–55). In this type of approach, one codes character strings with different numbers of bits in a manner dependent on the string probability. Thus very improbable strings require very large numbers of bits, and the method is not applicable to the usual teletype transmission problem where the sample rate and number of bits per sample are fixed.

```
1990   REM PROBABILITY ORDER OF CHARACTERS IN HAMLET
1991   DATA 27,5,15,20,1,19,8,14,9,18,12,4,21,13
1992   DATA 25,23,6,3,7,16,2,22,11,28,10,17,24,26
```

The ordering in this statement is merely that of the total frequencies in Table 1. That is, character 27 (the space) is most frequent, next comes 5 (the letter E), and so on. The statement

```
8   MAT READ I
```

will store the total probability data in an array $I(J)$ with 28 elements. The correcting process at the receiving end will be most efficient if we tell it when a character is not identified from the original text. This technique, however, consumes one character from the set of transmitted ones. For example, if the array $C(I)$ has at least 194 elements, we can enter the initial message, compress, transmit, and read the transmitted message with statements of the following type:

```
10   PRINT "NUMBER OF IDENTIFIED CHARACTERS IN COMPRESSED MESSAGE"
12   INPUT N
15   FOR I = 1 TO 194
20   READ X
25   FOR J = 1 TO N
30   IF X = I(J) THEN 50
35   NEXT J
40   LET X = 29
50   LET C(I) = X
55   GOSUB 500
60   NEXT I
```

If the individual value of $X$ read on line 20 is contained in the list of $N$ most probable characters, we store $X$ in $C(I)$ on line 50. However, if the identity of $X$ is not to be transmitted, we store a value (29) outside the range of the primary character set in $C(I)$. Subroutine 500 then prints the transmitted message using the appropriate sieve in Section 4.2 for printing ABC $\cdots$ XYZ' when $X = 1, 2, \ldots, 28$. In the present occasion we will also use the provision that allows printing "–" when $X = 29$. We shall also use the column counter $Q9$ (initialized to zero) that counts the number of columns printed and after 60 columns produces a line feed (i.e., PRINT command) following a space. This procedure avoids breaking words up in the middle. Running this program for $N = 16$ (17 transmitted characters, or $\approx 4.1$ bits per character of text) yielded

```
TO –E OR NOT TO –E THAT IS THE –UESTION WHETHER –TIS NO–LER
IN THE MIND TO SU––ER THE SLIN–S AND ARROWS O– OUTRA–EOUS –ORTUNE
OR TO TA–E ARMS A–AINST A SEA O– TROU–LES AND –Y O––OSIN– END
THEM
```

(i.e., 19 characters of 194 were unidentified).

Most people would be able to fill in the missing blanks. However, that is not because only 17 characters are necessary to reconstruct English in first order. It is mainly because the readers are either already familiar with the message, or have enough correlation data stored in their minds to analyze the message in a higher statistical order. All we could do with a first-order computed correction here would be to fill in all the blanks with the next most probable character omitted from the transmitted list. In this particular case, the first-order corrector would merely fill in the letter F in all the missing blanks. It would get the words SUFFER, OF, and FORTUNE right, but that's all. We would still have 12 incorrect words and 14 separate errors out of the 19 unidentified characters.

Next we would like to design a second-order correction program to work on our first-order compressed message. That is, we would like to compute the most probable identity of the missing characters based on the pair-correlation matrix $M(I, J)$ in Fig. 4-6. Because we know which letters were deleted from the full character set, we can optimize the correction process by defining two new matrices, $A$ and $B$, such that

$$A(I, J) = \begin{cases} M(I, J) & \text{when } I \text{ is a transmitted character} \\ & \text{and } J \text{ is a deleted character} \\ 0 & \text{otherwise} \end{cases}$$

$$\qquad (49)$$

$$B(J, K) = \begin{cases} M(J, K) & \text{when } J \text{ is a deleted character and} \\ & K \text{ is a transmitted one} \\ 0 & \text{otherwise} \end{cases}$$

The matrix $A(I, J)$ may be computed from $M(I, J)$ in Fig. 4-6 through a sequence of statements of the type

```
100   REM COMPUTE A(I,J) NEXT
110   MAT A = ZER(28,28)
120   FOR K = 1 TO N
125   FOR J = 1 TO 28
126   FOR L = 1 TO N
127   IF J = I(L) THEN 135
128   NEXT L
130   LET A(I(K),J) = M(I(K),J)
135   NEXT J
140   NEXT K
```

where the array $I(L)$ is the same one as defined before, and $N$ characters are identified of the original set of 28. The matrix $B(J, K)$ may be computed in a similar manner.

In the first section of our corrector we will leave sequences of adjacent blank characters unaltered and instead pick out sequences of the type $I, -, K$, in which two identified characters $I$ and $K$ are separated by a missing character, $J$. Clearly, the best guess in sequences of the latter type will be a particular value of $J$ chosen to optimize the product

$$A(I, J)B(J, K) \qquad (50)$$

where the matrices $A$ and $B$ were defined in Eqs. (49).

First we need to be able to identify sequences of the type $I\emptyset$, $29$, $K\emptyset$ without altering others in the array $C(C)$. Noting that the first character of the

149

message is a space, and hence must be identified ($\neq 29$), the following program steps accomplish the first objective:

```
210   FOR C = 1 TO 193
220   LET X = C(C)
230   IF X = 29 THEN 250
240   GOSUB 500
245   NEXT C
246   PRINT
247   PRINT
248   GO TO 9999    (end)
250   LET I0 = C(C − 1)
251   IF I0 = 29 THEN 240
255   LET J0 = C(C)
260   LET K0 = C(C + 1)
265   IF K0 = 29 THEN 240
```

If the program passes the conditional statement on line 265, we know that a sequence of the desired type has been found. We then pick a value of $J$ to maximize $A(I0, J) * B(J, K0)$, store $J$ in the message array, and print the character corresponding to $J$.

```
270   REM FORM I0,29,K0 NOW
275   LET M = 0
280   FOR J = 1 TO 28
285   IF M > = A(I0,J)*B(J,K0) THEN 300
290   LET M = A(I0,J)*B(J,K0)
295   LET X = J
300   NEXT J
302   LET C(C) = X
305   GOTO 240
```

The program then continues through the remainder of the message array until completing the text on line 248. At this stage, the original compressed message has been changed to read:

TO BE OR NOT TO BE THAT IS THE BUESTION WHETHER CTIS NOFLER
IN THE MIND TO SU−−ER THE SLINGS AND ARROWS OF OUTRAVEOUS FORTUNE
OR TO TAVE ARMS ACAINST A SEA OF TROUPLES AND BY O−−OSING END
THEM

Notice that it got the words OF and FORTUNE correct (which would have been provided by the first-order corrector) along with the words BE, SLINGS, and BY.

We really need a third-order corrector to fill in the remaining blanks because they are all double. In fact, there is danger of making a worse second-order correction on double blanks at this point than would be obtained from a simple, first-order correction on the remaining part of the message. For example, one *might* argue that we should choose $I$ and $K$ so as to optimize $A(I, J)$ and $B(J, K)$ separately in sequences of the type $I,29,29,K$. However, this practice, in fact, tends to do worse than merely assigning the remaining blanks to the most-probable, neglected character. For example, as applied to the above message, separate optimization of $A(I, 29)$ and $B(29, K)$ alone would yield SUGVER and OFCOSING as the remaining incomplete words. In contrast, a simple first-order correction applied at this point gets at least one of them right. This hybrid combination of second- and first-order correction technique results at the receiving end in the final message,

TO BE OR NOT TO BE THAT IS THE BUESTION WHETHER CTIS NOFLER
IN THE MIND TO SUFFER THE SLINGS AND ARROWS OF OUTRAVEOUS FORTUNE
OR TO TAVE ARMS ACAINST A SEA OF TROUPLES AND BY OFFOSING END
THEM

in which $\approx 4.1$ bits per character were used in a first-order transmission process. The corrected message contains 9 mistakes in locations where 19 characters in the transmitted message of 194 characters were unidentified. The correction technique is pretty good, but it has not worked any miracles.

---

**4.15 PROBLEM 22** Write a program that incorporates the above hybrid second- and first-order correction process to analyze text transmitted by a first-order compressor. How many characters have to be identified in the transmitted text before no mistakes occur in the corrected message? Plot the number of errors at the destination end as a function of the number ($N$) of identified characters that were actually transmitted. (*Note:* You need enough core to handle three $28 \times 28$ matrices in addition to the two-column arrays and programming statements.)

---

The problem gets more rewarding when we go to a second-order compression and transmission process. If we transmit a character set of $N$ symbols, we have $N^2$ possibilities to identify specific character pairs. For example, an average of 4.1 bits per character (or $\approx 17$ identified symbols of the 28-primary-character set used in the original English text) corresponds to a total of about 288 separately identifiable character pairs. This still is not enough to ensure completely error-free transmission of *Hamlet* because there are actually 443 nonzero elements in the total correlation matrix (i.e., 341 elements are zero of the total number of $28 \times 28 = 784$). However, by deleting the $443 - 288 = 155$ least-probable nonzero matrix elements, we can do a pretty good transmission job even without a statistical correction at the receiving end of the line.

Our first problem, therefore, is to construct a "compressed" correlation matrix that has $N^2 = 288$ nonzero elements. The nonzero elements in that matrix can then be used to generate a systematic code to positively identify $N^2 = 288$ separate character pairs. Although it might seem desirable to execute a straightforward sorting routine on the original $28 \times 28$ correlation matrix in terms of decreasing element size, such a program would have $\approx 307,720$ steps (i.e., the sum of an arithmetic series where the last term is $28 \times 28 = 784$). Hence even with a pretty fast computer, sorting the original correlation matrix in a straightforward manner takes a good deal of time.

For our purposes, a much quicker and more effective approach consists simply of multiplying each of the original matrix elements by a suitably chosen constant,

$$C < 1$$

and rounding off the values to the nearest integer on an element-by-element basis. While doing this multiplication, we can count up the nonzero elements in the compressed matrix and repeat the process reiteratively until we get down to the desired number of nonzero elements. This approach only takes $\approx 784$ steps per iteration and hence we should be able to iterate $\approx 400$ times before we have consumed as much computer time as the straightforward sorting method would have taken.

It is most practical to accomplish the desired degree of compression interactively using the computer terminal. If we define the compressed matrix to be $N(I, J)$, the process can be accomplished through statements of the type

```
 5   DIM M(28,28),N(28,28)
10   MAT READ M
40   PRINT "ENTER C"
50   INPUT C
60   MAT N = ZER(28,28)
```

151

```
 65   LET NØ = Ø
 70   FOR I = 1 TO 28
 75   FOR J = 1 TO 28
 80   LET N(I,J) = INT(C*M(I,J) + .5)
 85   IF N(I,J) = Ø THEN 95
 90   LET NØ = NØ + 1
 95   NEXT J
100   NEXT I
105   PRINT "# NONZERO ELEMENTS = "; NØ
```

Here $N\emptyset$ counts the number of nonzero elements in $N(I, J)$ which correspond to the choice of $C$, and the result is printed on line 1Ø5. By reiterating to line 4Ø, one finds out very quickly that a value of $C = 0.045$ will reduce the original correlation matrix to a new one having the first 288 most-probable elements occupied and all the rest zero. We do not really care that the elements are multiplied by $C$ in the present problem. The main point is that all the remaining 496 elements in $N(I, J)$ are zero.

In order to simulate the transmitted message in this case, we store the original English text in the 1–28 code in an array $C(I)$ and go through the array sequentially in pairs. (For practical purposes it is useful to add a second space at the end of the original 194-character message from *Hamlet*, which we will again use to illustrate the technique.) We then examine $N(X, Y)$ for every sequential pair $X$, $Y$ in the message array to see if the element is zero. If $N(X, Y) \neq 0$, we print characters corresponding to $X$ and $Y$ using subroutine 5ØØ and go on to the correction program at the receiving end of the communication link on line 151.

```
110   FOR I = 1 TO 193 STEP 2
115   LET X = C(I)
120   LET Y = C(I + 1)
125   IF N(X,Y) = Ø THEN 155
130   GOSUB 5ØØ
135   LET X = Y
140   GOSUB 5ØØ
145   LET Q9 = Q9 + 2
150   NEXT I
151   GOTO 19Ø
```

(Here $Q9$ is a column counter initialized to $\emptyset$ and used in subroutine 5ØØ to avoid breaking up words. It is, however, incremented outside the subroutine here. Hence line 5Ø3 of our original subroutine 5ØØ discussed in Section 4.2 should be deleted for the present purposes.) However, if $N(X, Y) = 0$ on line 125, our message-transmission method will miss at least one character. Here we have introduced a conditional statement that takes us to line 155, where the following statements transmit our code for a "–" mark and we go to the next sequential pair.

```
155   LET X = 29
160   GOSUB 5ØØ
165   LET C(I) = X
170   LET I = I + 1
175   LET Q9 = Q9 + 1
180   GOTO 115
```

Some bits will, of course, be used up identifying places where omitted characters occur. For our purposes it will be adequate just to add these up at the end. One could, of course, omit the unidentified characters altogether; however, it will be instructive to retain their locations for the present discussion.

Using 288 nonzero matrix elements corresponding to a value of $C = 0.045$ (hence an average of $\approx 17$ identified characters out of the initial 28-character set, or ≈4.1 bits per character of original text on the average), the transmitted message at this point takes the form

```
TO BE OR NOT TO BE THAT IS THE QUESTION WHETHER 'TIS NOBLER
IN THE MIND TO SUFFER THE SLINGS AND ARROWS OF OUTRAG-OUS FORTUNE
OR TO TAKE ARMS AGAINST A SEA OF TRO-BLES AND BY OPPOSING END
THEM
```

That is, we have only missed *2* of the original 194 characters, as opposed to 19 at this point in the first-order process.

However, it is not possible to make a really substantial correction on this result without going to a third-order corrector (just as it was difficult to gain much improvement from a first-order corrector in the case of a first-order compression).

About the most effective correction we can make in second order is to identify sequences of the type *I*,29,*K* and choose a value of *J* from the original correlation matrix to optimize the product

$$M(I, J)M(J, K) \tag{51}$$

Hence after a PRINT statement on line 19Ø, we first locate the desired sequences, reprinting the identified portions of the message as we go:

```
200   REM FIND SEQUENCES IØ,29,KØ, FOR 2ND-ORDER CORRECTION
205   LET Q9 = Ø
210   FOR C = 1 TO 193
220   LET X = C(C)
230   IF X = 29 THEN 250
240   GOSUB 500
242   LET Q9 = Q9 + 1
245   NEXT C
246   PRINT
247   PRINT
248   GOTO 9999        (end)
```

If we get all the way through without finding any missing characters, we end the program at line 248. If a missing character is detected on line 23Ø, we then go to line 25Ø, where we find a value of *J* to optimize the product (51), provided that *I*Ø is not also unidentified. It is also useful to rule out the space (*J* = 27 on line 282) in the corrector because most pairs involving the space symbol are very high up in probability.

```
250   LET IØ = C(C - 1)
251   IF IØ = 29 THEN 240
255   LET JØ = C(C)
260   LET KØ = C(C + 1)
265   IF KØ = 29 THEN 240
270   REM FORM IØ,29,KØ NOW
275   LET M = Ø
280   FOR J = 1 TO 28
282   IF J = 27 THEN 300
285   IF M > = M(IØ,J)*M(J,KØ) THEN 300
290   LET M = M(IØ,J)*M(J,KØ)
295   LET X = J
300   NEXT J
302   LET C(C) = X
303   GOTO 240
```

If we have two spaces in sequence, we will not try to correct them. Our corrected message then becomes

```
TO BE OR NOT TO BE THAT IS THE QUESTION WHETHER 'TIS NOBLER
IN THE MIND TO SUFFER THE SLINGS AND ARROWS OF OUTRAGHOUS FORTUNE
OR TO TAKE ARMS AGAINST A SEA OF TROUBLES AND BY OPPOSING END
THEM
```

Only one error is present out of 194 characters of original text, and we only transmitted ≈4.1 bits per character on the average. Transmitting the locations of the two missed characters costs us an extra ≈6/194 bits per character here on the average and hence is a fairly negligible overhead. At this level our accuracy is competitive with that in many newspapers.

The basic difficulty in making really substantial corrections in second order is simply that our compression technique favors the occurrence of missing characters in pairs or higher-order clusters. The point becomes more apparent when one compresses the matrix still further. For example, the following message was transmitted at about 3.3 bits per character on the average, corresponding to our previous value of the second-order entropy per character in *Hamlet* ($C = 0.0048$ and there were 99 nonzero elements in the compressed matrix).

```
TO BE OR NOT TO BE THAT IS THE −−ESTION WHETHER−−TIS NO−LER IN
THE MIND TO S−−−ER THE SLINGS AND ARRO−S OF OUT−−−−OUS FO−−−NE
OR TO T−−E AR−S −−−INST A SEA OF −RO−−LES AND −Y −−−−−ING END
TH−M
```

Second-order correction:

```
TO BE OR NOT TO BE THAT IS THE −−ESTION WHETHER−−TIS NOULER
IN THE MIND TO S−−−ER THE SLINGS AND ARROUS OF OUT−−−−OUS FO−−−NE
OR TO T−−E ARES −−−INST A SEA OF ORO−−LES AND AY −−−−−ING END
THEM
```

The second-order correction has repaired the word THEM but has accomplished nothing else. The moral seems to be that if you are limited to a given statistical order, it is best to use that order in transmission and transmit enough bits per character on the average to ensure the average freedom from error that you are willing to tolerate without even incorporating a correction process. That is a useful practical result: once we have determined the required number of elements in the correlation matrix, there is little point in running the message through a time-consuming computational correction process. Extrapolating our results, it seems pretty clear that to adequately convey a message with $h_n$ bits per character in the above manner, one really needs at least an $(n + 1)$th-order compression.

| | |
|---|---|
| **4.15**<br>**PROBLEM 23** | Use the second-order Shakespearean monkey program to generate English text with representative statistical properties. Feed this sequence of data through a second-order matrix-compression program and compute the percentage of missed characters as a function of the number of bits transmitted per character (i.e., vary the normalizing constant, $C$, used to compress the matrix). |
| **4.15**<br>**PROBLEM 24** | Correction methods of the type discussed in the text may be used to make a most probable determination of missed characters in a noisy teletype transmission circuit. Write a program that (1) introduces mistakes randomly with a predetermined average probability of occurrence, and (2) uses second-order statistics to make a most probable identification of the unknown characters. Here we merely choose $J$ for a missed character in the sequence $I, J, K$ so that $M(I, J)M(J, K)$ is a maximum, using the standard correlation matrix. Try your program out on the Hamlet soliloquy or other text of comparable length. |

## 4.16
## The Difference Between Ciphers and Codes

It is traditional in popular books on cryptography to start by lecturing the reader on the difference between ciphers and codes. It is usually asserted that a *cipher* is a form of secret writing in which all meaning within the source language can be transmitted unambiguously, whereas a *code* is usually defined as a convention by which only a limited fraction of the meaning of the source language can be conveyed. Because adherence to this distinction can give rise to a needless amount of verbal tight-rope walking throughout the following sections, it would be well to dispose of it here. The distinction is really patent nonsense. The basic point is that the list of characters or symbols necessary to convey meaning within a language is *not* a closed set in any practical sense. Those who stress the distinction most assiduously frequently will go on for the next hundred pages discussing "ciphers" that do not even permit conveying the space between words unambiguously, let alone more subtle distinctions in meaning conveyed by apostrophes, quotation marks, accent marks, changes in type font, syllabic emphasis, and so on. About all that really can be said is that some codes are less ambiguous than others. Reference to the "least ambiguous" codes as "ciphers" involves a very subjective matter of interpretation which we shall not attempt to make here with any consistency.

## 4.17
## Quick History of Cryptography[19]

Most people have at least some interest in the "science" of cryptography. The concept of secret writing seems to have sprung into existence spontaneously throughout history wherever a written language existed. For example, a cuneiform tablet dating from about 1500 B.C. in the Mesopotamian civilization contains an encipherment of the earliest known formula for making pottery glaze. Transposition ciphers (in which the order of letters in a message is scrambled before transmission and then unscrambled with the same key after reception) were developed by the Spartans as early as 475 B.C. using a coding device known as a "skytale." (A leather strap was wrapped tightly around a baton and the message written on the strap along the baton. The leather was then unwound to scramble the message and the inverse process carried out at the destination to read the text.) Vātsyāna's manual on erotic technique, the *Kāma-sūtra* (≈300 B.C.), lists secret writing based on both letter-substitution codes and phonetic-substitution codes among the 64 arts (yogas) that women should know and practice. Simple letter-substitution ciphers were also well known to the Roman educated class at the time of Julius Caesar.

Yet, there are many very curious aspects of the subject. For instance, the people with the strongest commitment to it would make very strange bedfellows: Machiavellian despots and political diarists, military officers, arch criminals, and literary nuts. Further, it is a field in which the most public acclaim (e.g., execution) has traditionally been given for outstanding failure. As with skilled magicians, the best cryptographers conceal their tricks. In fact, the most successful contemporary ones are probably not even allowed to know their own names. In addition, the subject has been permeated with such an intense degree of both deliberate and subconscious deception that it is almost impossible to determine accurate case histories even after the principal individuals have ceased to exist.

After the collapse of the Roman empire, cryptography plunged into the Dark Ages along with the rest of civilization. It surfaced sporadically during the Middle Ages as a source of amusement for bored monks. According to Kahn, "the only writer of the Middle Ages to describe cryptography instead of just using it" was the thirteenth-century English philosopher and monk, Roger

---

[19] For a more general account, the reader is referred to the volumes by Pratt (1939), Yardley (1931), and Farago (1967), and in that order. However, don't get them all at one time; you won't be able to get anything else done for a week! The best-documented treatment of the general field appears to be that of Kahn (1967). However, in spite of Kahn's remarks to the contrary, there seems to be little evidence that information theory has had much practical impact on cryptography. For a fairly abstract discussion of applications of communication theory to cryptography, see Shannon (1949).

Bacon (in his Epistle on the *Secret Works of Art and the Nullity of Magic*). In fact, a yet-to-be decoded volume of secret writing discovered in 1912 (the Voynich Manuscript) has sometimes been attributed to Bacon (see later discussion). As with most other intellectual endeavor, cryptography lay dormant during the Middle Ages, only to be resurrected during the Italian Renaissance.

Another Bacon, and a contemporary of Shakespeare, Sir Francis Bacon (or Lord Verulam), introduced a 5-bit binary code to transmit diplomatic messages. In this code, binary zeros were represented by type with normal font using standard English text and binary 1's were indicated in italicized type. Dividing up the standard English text into successive groups of five letters provided both a medium to transmit the code and an effective way to conceal the fact that a secret message was being transmitted at all. The casual reader would regard the text (or "clear" in the cryptographer's parlance) as just a careless typesetting job. However, once the presence of the code was spotted, almost anyone could decipher it. Consequently, Francis Bacon's primary contribution was in the invention of the binary code rather than in a real contribution to cryptography.

As with any other medium, there is an inherent noise level in Bacon's method for binary-code transmission. Thus the penchant of early seventeenth-century printers to reuse previously set clusters of battered type, taken together with a large measure of "inspiration" in deciding whether or not a binary 1 or zero was set in individual characters, permitted Mrs. Elizabeth Wells Gallup of Minnesota to deduce, at the turn of this century, that Francis Bacon actually was the illegitimate son of Queen Elizabeth and "had written not only works attributed to Shakespeare, but also those bearing the names of Burton, Ben Johnson, Greene, Marlowe, and Spenser, as well as unrevealed translations of the *Iliad* and *Odyssey*."[20]

Cryptography went through a peak in sophistication at the hands of a seventeenth-century French cryptographer, Rossignol, that was not equaled for the next 100 years. Not only did his contemporaries credit him with phenomenal ability at deciphering messages, but he designed a cipher for Louis XIV based on some 587 randomly numbered syllables (using multiple identifications to obscure the more frequent ones) that remained for over two centuries as the only known example of an entirely unbreakable cipher. (The Voynich Manuscript seems to be the present holder of the title.) The original key was lost after Rossignol's death and many generations of cryptographers were unable to decipher the surviving messages.

Apart from sporadic activity during the American and French Revolutions at relatively low levels of sophistication, the field went into a quiescent state until the mid-nineteenth century. The invention of the Morse telegraph and its use during the American Civil War provided renewed stimulus for the subject. In addition, cryptography began to receive worldwide attention in the popular literature, starting with articles and stories published by Edgar Allan Poe in the 1840s. This fad was stimulated by the European writers Jules Verne, Arthur Conan Doyle, and Honoré de Balzac. The popular interest in substitution ciphers started by Poe's famous challenge to the public in 1841 (see Section 4.18) persists to this day in the form of "literary crypts" and Double-Crostics appearing in various weekly magazines. Early in the nineteenth-century mania for ciphers, Balzac introduced a two-page cryptogram in *La Physiologie du marriage* which he deliberately left unsolved as a joke on the reader (see Fig. 4-17 and later discussion).

Although the Union Army scored several cryptographic victories during the Civil War, the next major advance in the subject came from a Prussian army

---

[20] Pratt (1939, p. 90). This book contains a highly interesting account of the entire Bacon–Shakespeare controversy from the cryptographic point of view. See also C. A. Zimansky (1970).

officer named Kasiski, who in 1863 developed a systematic method for solving multiple-substitution ciphers. (A multiple-substitution cipher is one in which $N$ different substitution ciphers are used periodically throughout the message.[21])

American "black chamber" efforts were still on a pretty low level by the start of World War I. In 1913, Herbert O. Yardley was hired as a junior telegraphist on the night shift in the U.S. State Department. To relieve his boredom during the nocturnal hours, Yardley made a hobby out of deciphering various coded messages that came within his attention. By 1915, he had broken the entire American diplomatic code and was reading messages on internal German affairs that President Wilson had deemed so secret as to warrant withholding from the State Department itself. Worried that foreign governments could just as easily crack the American code, Yardley wrote a long memorandum on the problem which he presented to his superior. The eventual result of this activity was the formation of a new department within Military Intelligence, under Yardley's direction, whose purpose was to handle "the cryptographic needs of the Intelligence Division." His exploits within this division were legendary and included such things as breaking the Japanese diplomatic code (based on the romanization of the ninth-century classification of Japanese syllables, or *kana*, in a set of 73 Chinese characters) without an initial knowledge of Japanese. This feat (for which Yardley received the Distinguished Service Medal and "a sly wink from the Secretary of War") gave the United States a considerable political advantage in the Washington Naval Conference of 1922. The ultimate disclosure of that behind-the-scenes accomplishment by Yardley (1931, pp. 250–317) has been cited as a major reason for the subsequent Japanese denunciation of the Naval Treaties.

The appointment of Henry L. Stimson as Secretary of State in the Hoover Administration brought an end to this level of cryptographic expertise. Having coined the phrase "Gentlemen do not read each other's mail," Stimson cut off all State Department support for Yardley's department. (The existence of Yardley's "black chamber" had been concealed from Stimson until shortly before the Naval Disarmament Conference of 1930.) Yardley was crushed by the decision and described the great difficulty with which he explained this news to his staff[22]:

> "Most of them had devoted years to cryptography, working secretively, not even their most intimate friends being aware of their real accomplishments. That cryptography as a profession would ever die had never entered their minds."

Evidently, however, Secretary Stimson's actions were extremely fortuitous: it is alleged by Farago[23] that Yardley himself had already sold out to the Japanese in 1929 for the sum of $7000.

Thus the United States began the decade prior to World War II with the dissolution of the most advanced cryptographic department that had previously existed in history. Although there were major cryptographic victories just prior to, and during, World War II, they largely resulted from the secret capture of enemy decoding machines rather than from statistical analyses of the source language (see Farago's book). In retrospect, what Yardley had been doing with his staff of a dozen cryptographers and battery of 50 typists was largely the kind of data manipulation that can be conducted now by one person working alone with only a small computer. For example, the solution of the famous

---

[21] Pratt (1939, p. 168) gives a fairly detailed discussion of the Kasiski method for those who would like to work on a multiple-substitution cipher.

[22] Yardley (1931, pp. 370, 371).

[23] Farago (1967, pp. 56–58); see also reference notes, p. 394.

Waberski cipher depended less on a sophisticated automatic treatment of the statistical properties of the source language than it did on repeated manipulation of the data blocks until things lined up in a manner obvious to the cryptographer's eye. The higher-order statistical analysis was still going on in the brain of the cryptographer rather that in the automatic portions of the data-processing program. One can, of course, do this sort of thing very readily with a computer terminal—but the results will depend on just how good one is at spotting correlations.

In his triumph over the Japanese diplomatic code, Yardley (1931, pp. 250–269) evidently only looked as far as pair correlations in the equivalent of a $73\times73$ matrix of Japanese syllabic characters (*kana*). The statistics for the standard language matrix were extracted from about 10,000 characters worth of normal Japanese "plain language" telegrams. Although this sounds like a lot of input data, it only amounts to about two characters per matrix element on the average. Hence, although the principle of the thing sounds reasonable (i.e., all one has to do is pick out the statistical ordering of these matrix elements and then identify corresponding elements in a similar matrix for coded characters), it is somewhat amazing that he was able to accomplish this feat with the available statistical accuracy. Hence the surprising aspect of the solution is not so much that he did not know Japanese, but that he did it with so little input data to play with. According to Farago (1967, p. 22), the Japanese have another interpretation of the accomplishment: they evidently believe that a code clerk named Yatanube absconded with the codes from one of the South American Japanese embassies early in 1920 and sold them to Yardley during the international maritime conference in Genoa. Although Yardley obviously did an enormous amount of work on the statistical aspects of the problem during his one year stint at it, he also indicates in his account (p. 264) that he was seriously considering that alternative type of solution. If the Japanese assertion is correct, it would represent something of an all-time "let-down" in the history of cryptography. However, deceit is the name of the game.[24]

[24] In an effort to shed more light on this interesting historical question, we performed a statistical analysis of a $77\times77$ pair-correlation matrix computed from a 10,000-character sample of Japanese. The source text was from *Snow Country* by Yasunari Kawabata and was reduced to a 77-character set (76 kana plus the space symbol) by one of the author's students, Yoshikazu Okuyama.

Out of a total of 5929 matrix elements, 1242 had nonzero values. Of these, only about the first 150 largest elements are of any use statistically. (For example, 468 elements had the same value of 1, 233 had the value 2, 115 had the value 3, and so on.) Putting the matrix elements in descending numerical order gave the series of numbers

282, 259, 228, 178, 157, 154, 146, 143, . . .

If we regard the numbers as results from a series of counting experiments, one expects a statistical spread $\approx\sqrt{M(I,J)}$ in each case. Consequently, one cannot really distinguish reliably between the fourth and fifth numbers on the list. Thus a direct ordering of the matrix elements would only give certain identification for about three kana and the space symbol.

As with English, much better identification can be obtained by computing a most probable digram decoding path through the matrix. (See the discussion in Section 4.19.) Two useful paths were found in the $77\times77$ matrix of Japanese kana:

space,NO,ZI,YO,U,TU,TA,RI,MA,(DO or SU)
NO,space,O,TO,U,TU,TA,RI,MA,(DO or SU)

where the romanization of the kana has been used. Both paths close on the same ambiguous choice contained within the parentheses. Hence statistical uncertainties in the 10,000-character source text prevent identifying more than 10 kana plus the space symbol directly from the matrix.

A most probable second-order correction process (see Section 4.19) could probably double the number of unambiguously identified kana in a single-substitution code. However, it seems clear that a higher-order correlation process (e.g., someone who knew Japanese) would be required to get more than about 20 out of 76 kana correctly identified with only the statistical accuracy afforded by a 10,000-character uncoded source text. Yardley's problem would have been still harder because the secret messages were encoded without the use of a space symbol to break up words.

Edgar Allan Poe's most well-known exploit in cryptography was published in his short story, "The Gold Bug" (1843). In this story, Poe's hero, Legrand, "readily solved" a cipher made up of a closely packed string of nonalphabetic characters. In fact, Legrand modestly commented that he had indeed "solved others of an abstruseness ten thousand times greater."

When asked to explain his method, Legrand indicated that he had worked out a scientific principle based on the statistics of the language. In effect, once he had established the identity of the language in which the cipher had been written, all he had to do was apply the right frequency table to identify the individual characters.

In the case of the Gold Bug cipher (which ultimately disclosed the location of Captain Kidd's treasure), there was a possible choice of English, French, or Spanish for the source language. Shrewdly concluding that the message must be in English (because of a pun on the word Kidd which could not be appreciated in the other two languages), Legrand went on to outline his solution.

He first observed that there were no divisions between words, and implied that if there had been, the whole thing would have been trivial. At this point, the storyteller might have asked: "How did you know that the originator of the message didn't simply adopt some other character (e.g., the number 8) for the space symbol?" But Poe's storyteller was destined to play the role of the straight man and the question was not raised.

Legrand went on to explain that he had constructed a frequency table:

| | |
|---|---|
| Of the character 8 | there are 33. |
| ; | there are 26. |
| 4 | there are 19. |
| ‡) | there are 16. |
| * | there are 13. |
| 5 | there are 12. |
| 6 | there are 11. |
| †1 | there are 8. |
| 0 | there are 6. |
| 92 | there are 5. |
| :3 | there are 4. |
| ? | there are 3. |
| ¶ | there are 2. |
| —. | there is 1. |

He then comments:

> "Now, in English, the letter which most frequently occurs is *e*. Afterward, the succession runs thus: *a o i d h n r s t u y c f g l m w b k p q x z*. *E* predominates so remarkably, that an individual sentence of any length is rarely seen in which it is not the prevailing character."

In this single paragraph we have been presented with *the most fundamental mystery of the entire short story:* Where on earth did Poe ever get that frequency table? How could Poe not have known that T (not A) is usually the second-most-frequent letter in English? Certainly he should have known that T couldn't be tenth on the list! All he had to do was look at his own writing. For example, a frequency table based on the text of *The Tell-Tale Heart* runs as follows:

ETAOINSHRDLUCMFWPYGBVK′XJQZ

One derived from the entire text of "The Gold Bug" itself goes

ETINAHOSDLRUMWYCGFBPVKJQX′Z

Doubtless someone will say that Legrand's mistake was just a typesetter's error or a blunder by the proofreader. Yet it was obviously not that at all. The

159

basic structure of the story from then on is affected by Legrand's erroneous frequency table. Thus after identifying the character 8 with the letter E, he switches his method of attack. He clearly cannot allow the symbol ; to be identified as the letter A, and he therefore starts grasping at straws. Ironically, if he had merely used a more correct frequency table, Legrand would have immediately gotten the right identity for the ; symbol.

Instead Poe switched to a *word*-frequency table. Noting that THE is the most commonly occurring word in English, Poe manages to pull this word out of the closely packed string of symbols! Hence Legrand concludes both that

; stands for the letter T

and that

4 stands for the letter H

If he had merely used a better table to identify E and then T in the first place, he would have been able to deduce H from the extremely high correlation existing for both TH and for HE [i.e., the size of $M(20, 8)$ and $M(8, 5)$ in Fig. 4-6]. Having botched the problem so badly at the start, Legrand's boastful manner becomes tiresome and the rest of the analysis is hardly worth reading. (Legrand's trigonometry at the end of the story is not very good either.)

---

**4.18
PROBLEM 25**

Consider the character sequence T-E where we want to find a most probable value for the missing blank in English. By computing the value of $J$ such that

$$M(20, J)*M(J, 5)$$

is a maximum, show that the missing character is probably H. [Use $M(I, J)$ from Fig. 4-6.]

---

But back to the *real* mystery of "The Gold Bug," which the astute reader will doubtlessly have solved by now. Using the deductive methods of the great French detective Dupin, we are led to the following interpretation. Poe's sense of history told him from the beginning that the pirate treasure must involve the Spanish West Indies; after all, he was dealing with a famous pirate of the Spanish Main. He therefore boldly decided right from the start that *the entire cipher should be pulled off in Spanish*! Poe therefore worked out his frequency tables from such Spanish text as was then available in the Philadelphia Public Library. (The actual source was probably a tourist phrase book in which the letter H was used as a frequent phonetic aid.) At the last minute, Poe got an urgent call from his publisher, who suddenly realized what was going on: "Look here, Edgar, that just won't work. The cipher *must* be in English! Otherwise, we'll be losing readers by the carload." Time was running out. Poe hastily rearranged the text and invented that awful pun about Captain Kidd to get him out of his predicament. The trouble was that he did not have time to work out a new frequency table. Now, any idiot knows that E is the most common letter in English, so he would obviously have to get that one right. Because the Spanish table at least started off correctly, he decided to pass it off for English and no one would ever know the difference. Since he really did not plan to use the table anyway, the change would have no effect whatsoever on the rest of the story. "3‡‡†3‡†;45;9634;5-;?500:28(634;"

Write a program that permits printing out letter-frequency tables of the type quoted by Legrand for the common European languages (see Table 4). [*Note:* Although Spanish is the most probable choice for Legrand's table, Italian and Portuguese are not too far behind. However, it most certainly is not a frequency table for English, German, or French. Kahn (1967, p. 789) suggests that Poe may have miscopied a list of most frequent vowels and consonants given alphabetically by William Blair in an article, "Cipher," published in *The Cyclopaedia* of Abraham Rees.]

"The Gold Bug" (first published in 1843) was not Poe's only claim to cryptographic prowess. His exploits date at least to 1841, when he was working as an editor for *Graham's Magazine*. With a boldness matched only by Legrand himself, Poe offered in April of that year to solve any single-substitution cipher that the readers would care to submit, provided that they preserved the word spacings. The challenge, however, was buried in one paragraph in the middle of a long book review (of *Sketches of Conspicuous Living Characters of France*, translated by R. M. Walsh). The author of the book had implied that an unusually keen mind was required to decipher cryptograms. Poe commented,

"We cannot understand the extraordinary penetration required in the matter. The [key] phrase...is French and the note was addressed to Frenchmen...anyone who will take the trouble may address us a note, in the same manner as here proposed, and the key-phrase may be either in French, Italian, Spanish, German, Latin or Greek (or in any of the dialects of these languages), and we pledge ourselves for the solution of the riddle."

He clearly implies here that one does not need to know the "key phrase" at all—that the statistics of the language will betray the key.

In reporting the results of his experiment in a review article on cryptography later that year, the editor of *Graham's Magazine* comments (Poe, 1841) that the challenge had elicited but a single response from an anonymous resident of Stonington, Connecticut. The letter contained two ciphers, the second of which consisted of a message (see Fig. 4-15) based on the key phrase

## No. 2.

Ofoiioiiaso ortsiii sov eodisoioe afduiostifoi ft iftvi si tri oistoiv oiniafetsorit ifeov rsri inotiiiiv ridiiot, irio rivvio eovit atrotfetsoria aioriti iitri tf oitovin tri aetifei ioreitit sov usttoi oioittstifo dfti afdooitior trso ifeov tri dfit otftfeov softriedi ft oistoiv oriofiforiti suitteii viireiiitifoi ft tri iarfoisiti, iiti trir uet otiiiotiv uitfti rid io tri eoviieeiiiv rfasueostr tf rii dftrit tfoeei.

According to Poe, the translation is: Nonsensical phrases and unmeaning combinations of words, as the learned lexicographer would have confessed himself, when hidden under cryptographic ciphers, serve to *perpdex* the curious enquirer, and baffle penetration more completely than would the most profound *apothems* of learned philosophers. Abstruse disquisitions of the scholiasts, were they but presented before him in the undisguised vocabulary of his mother tongue....

**Fig. 4-15.** Photographic reproduction of the harder of two ciphers sent to the editor of Graham's Magazine in the spring of 1841 by "an anonymous correspondent at Stonington, Connecticut" (Poe, 1841, p. 36). Poe stated that the two italicized words were coding errors committed by the Connecticut correspondent. One of these must have been imagined by Poe. There is also at least one other coding error, which Poe didn't italicize.

in Latin: *Suaviter in modo, fortiter in re.* Placing the alphabet beneath this phrase in a letter-for-letter manner,

```
SUAVITERINMODOFORTITER I NRE
ABCDEFGHIJ KLMNOPQRSTUVWXYZ
```

we see that, even knowing the key, the reader has to decide whether the character

O in the message stands for L, N, or P
I in the message stands for E, I, S, or W     etc.

Poe notes that although his initial boast was not said *suaviter in modo*, his pursuit of the problem was at least done *fortiter in re*. It seems more probable, however, that the solution should be taken *cum grano salis*.

Although Poe's concern that readers might suspect him of "inditing ciphers to himself" seems justified, the circulation of *Graham's Magazine* went from almost nothing to 25,000 subscribers in 1841. The success was probably at least partially due to the column "Secret Writing," which occupied the editorial page from July on (with excessive enciphering of silly sibilants in randomly chosen multiple-substitution codes). Yardley (1931, p. 20) comments that in his initial quest for information on cryptography he searched through the letters of Edgar Allan Poe for some outline of scientific treatment of the subject. All he found were "vague boasts of skill—nothing more . . . Poe [was] merely floundering around in the dark and did not understand the great underlying principles." Yet, Poe was clearly smart enough to realize that the principles must exist; he just did not have time for the details. During the 16-month period in which he served as editor (at a salary of $800 per year), Poe published in *Graham's Magazine* four of his "Tales," several poems, numerous articles on literary criticism, and many book reviews in addition to the article and column on "Secret Writing" (not to mention an occasional article in *The Saturday Evening Post*).

---

**4.18
PROBLEM 27**

Write a program that codes characters according to "*suaviter in modo*, etc." and try it out on the English message "translation" of Poe's hard cipher 2. See how many coding errors you can find (the discussion of some subroutines in the following section may help; see Fig. 4-15).

**4.18
RESEARCH
PROBLEM**

A decoding matrix for Poe's hard cipher 2 (see Fig. 4-15) may be written:

| Character: | A | D | E | F | I | M | N | O | R | S | T | U | V |
|---|---|---|---|---|---|---|---|---|---|---|---|---|---|
| Meaning | C | M | G | O | E | K | J | L | H | A | F | B | D |
|  |  | U | I |  | X | N | Q |  | R |  |  |  |
|  |  | Z | S |  |  | P | V |  | T |  |  |  |
|  |  |  | W |  |  |  | Y |  |  |  |  |  |

For example, there are 20,736 $(= 3 \cdot 1 \cdot 3 \cdot 4 \cdot 4 \cdot 3 \cdot 4 \cdot 4 \cdot 1 \cdot 1 \cdot 3)$ possible "solutions" for the first word in the message OFOIIOIIASO. In principle, one could write a program to maximize the products of pair-correlation matrix elements for the different choices, one word at a time (i.e., starting and ending with a space symbol). Investigate the possibility of carrying out this type of procedure using the correlation matrix for English in Fig. 4-6.

---

If Poe contributed anything to cryptography it was surely in the invention of the "literary crypt" (Poe, 1841). We shall define such things to be single-substitution ciphers in which the space between words is preserved (although not necessarily by the space symbol).

**4.19
Program To Solve Literary Crypts**

Obviously what Poe would have liked is a program where you enter the cipher, type RUN, and the computer prints out one correct solution in a reasonably short time. Reading between the lines of his initial challenge, he probably would also have liked to be able to do this when the source language was "French, Italian, Spanish, German, Latin, or Greek (or any dialects of these languages)."

Accomplishing the above objective is not entirely trivial, even with a long text. Because of the statistical uncertainties involved, it becomes especially tricky when the message is limited to just a few hundred characters. However, the second part of the objective is not as hard as the first. That is, as long as you know *what* language is involved, the approach is the same. The programmer does not have to know Japanese to write a program to decipher substitution cryptograms in Japanese. All he has to know is (1) that the source language *is* Japanese; (2) the *standard* correlation matrix for Japanese; and (3) that he has a long-enough enciphered message in Japanese to give adequate statistical accuracy.[25] When your program completes deciphering the cryptogram, you ask one of your Japanese friends to translate it into English. (One, of course, has to make obvious modifications in dimension statements.) As a matter of fact, one should really narrow the specification of the source language even further. For example, best results really require the "standard" correlation matrix for the language as used by the author of the message. For example, a correlation matrix based on "The Gold Bug" will not do as well as a correlation matrix based on Shakespeare's own writing in deciphering a cryptogram from *Hamlet*. Ironically, a correlation matrix based on *Hamlet* also seems to do better at deciphering cryptograms in contemporary English than does one based on "The Gold Bug."

Before designing a program to solve substitution ciphers automatically, it will be helpful to construct several subroutines of a purely manipulative nature. These subroutines are required just to do the bookkeeping for us, and can also be very easily incorporated in an interactive program that lets the operator solve ciphers by guesswork.

For the purpose of illustration, we shall limit ourselves to a 28-character substitution code and our original 28-character list. We shall assume that the character-printing subroutine discussed earlier in the chapter is still available at line 5ØØ. It is helpful to keep its properties summarized in a few REM statements at the start of the subroutine:

```
5ØØ   REM SUB TO PRINT A, B, C,.. X, Y, Z, , ' , –
5Ø1   REM WHEN X = 1,2,3, . . . . . . . 28,29
5Ø3   REM Q9 COUNTS COLUMNS, "PRINTS" AFTER SPACE WHEN Q9 > 6Ø
5Ø4   LET Q9 = Q9 + 1
  .
  .
  .
```

(the rest of the subroutine can take anywhere from 7 to 84 lines, depending on the level of string commands available; see the previous discussion).

Next we need a data array, $D(N)$, in which to store the NØ characters in the original cipher. The cipher could be entered from the keyboard using string commands or specially written CALL statements to machine-language subroutines; it could be READ from disc or tape files or merely from standard DATA statements within the program. In the latter case, we are free to specify the cipher in our 1–28 alphabet (fixed code) right from the start. (See, for

---

[25] The last requirement is, of course, the real difficulty in deciphering most cryptograms. As noted in Section 4.17, one needs messages of much greater than 10,000-character length to do this problem satisfactorily in Japanese.

example, the DATA statement containing the first portion of Hamlet's soliloquy used in the discussion of bit compression.) We shall adopt the latter
method here to avoid overly restricting the program to specific computing
equipment or compilers. If the array is suitably dimensioned, a single statement

MAT READ D

can be used to enter the initial cipher data.

We shall solve the cipher by defining a substitution code array, $X(I)$, which
operates on the original cipher data array, $D(N)$, to provide a decoded array
$C(N)$ in which

$$C(N) = X(D(N)) \tag{52}$$

for each of the $N\emptyset$ terms in the cipher. Thus we shall leave the original cipher
data array untouched and repeatedly alter the current code array, $X(I)$, so as
to provide best deciphering possible in the array $C(N)$.

Although each code is made up from the same set of 28 integers, it is
important to realize that there are actually three codes to worry about in the
present problem:

1.  The original fixed code on which subroutine $5\emptyset\emptyset$ works: namely, 1, 2, . . . ,
    28 corresponds to the letters A, B, C, etc.
2.  The current code in $X(I)$—which ultimately will be used to transform the
    cipher array into the deciphered array, $C(N)$, which can then be printed by
    subroutine $5\emptyset\emptyset$.
3.  The inverse code to $X(I)$.

We shall merely compute the "inverse code" as we need it rather than
introduce still another array in the problem. The distinctions between these
codes will become clearer as we proceed.

We shall assume that the current substitution code stored in array $X(I)$ is
confined to the domain of integers 1–28. (Later we shall introduce the integer
29 to stand for the hyphen—in some instances to indicate message array
elements that have not been identified.)

It is useful to have a subroutine that prints a table to identify the "current"
code, $X(I)$. Although the table may be most easily printed vertically, through
statements of the type

```
FOR I = 1 TO 28
LET X = X(I)
GOSUB 5ØØ
PRINT I
NEXT I
```

that approach wastes entirely too much paper. (Alternatively, if you are using a
CRT terminal, the list runs off the screen too fast.)

A more useful subroutine can be written to print the current code in a
horizontal format of the type

CURRENT CODE IN X(I):

| 1 | 2 | 3 | 4 | 5 | 6 | 7 | 8 | 9 | 1Ø |
|---|---|---|---|---|---|---|---|---|----|
| V | N | I | U | W | F | G | X | C | R |

| 11 | 12 | 13 | 14 | 15 | 16 | 17 | 18 | 19 | 2Ø |
|----|----|----|----|----|----|----|----|----|----|
| Y | L | ' | K | Q | T | O | J | H | P |

| 21 | 22 | 23 | 24 | 25 | 26 | 27 | 28 |
|----|----|----|----|----|----|----|----|
| | D | E | S | M | Z | A | B |

Here it is implied that if $D(1) = 1$ and if we enter subroutine $5\emptyset\emptyset$ with a
value of $X$ defined by

$$X = C(1) = X(D(1))$$

the terminal will print out the letter V, corresponding to the number $X = 22$ in the fixed code.

Producing tabular output of the above type can be something of a struggle in BASIC. The problem is the stringent limitation on column format that results when numbers are printed through a command of the type

```
PRINT K;
```

Even if $K$ is only a two-digit integer, the compiler leaves room for a six-digit number. (The problem can be easily overcome through addition of suitable machine-language subroutines CALLable from BASIC.)

Staunch FORTRAN users will gloat at this point. However, the inconvenience is a small price to pay for the other advantages of BASIC. We shall probably have completely deciphered our cryptogram long before the typical FORTRAN batch-process user has managed to debug the first section of his program.

The following subroutine provides the desired horizontal format for printing the code array.

```
700   REM SUB TO PRINT CODE
701   PRINT
702   PRINT "CURRENT CODE IN X(I):"
703   FOR I = 1 TO 3
704   FOR J = 1 TO 2
706   FOR K = (I−1)*10+1 TO (I−1)*10+10
708   IF K>28 THEN 724
710   PRINT TAB(6*(K−(I−1)*10)−5);
711   IF J#1 THEN 718
712   PRINT K;
713   PRINT " ";
714   GOTO 722
718   LET X = X(K)
719   PRINT " ";
720   GOSUB 500
722   NEXT K
724   PRINT
726   NEXT J
728   PRINT
730   NEXT I
732   PRINT
734   RETURN
```

(Some versions of BASIC handle the format in the PRINT K; statement differently from the Hewlett-Packard BASIC assumed above and will require appropriate modification of this subroutine.)

---

**4.19**
**PROBLEM 28**
Figure out how the above subroutine (700) works. Try it out, using a code generated by letting $X(I) = I$ for $I = 1$–28. This check will test both subroutines 700 and 500.

---

At the start of the program we shall let $X(I)$ initially equal the fixed code:

```
20   FOR I = 1 TO 28
22   LET X(I) = I
23   NEXT I
```

We then enter the cipher data in array $D(N)$ and start out with array $C(N)$ equal to $D(N)$. We shall also introduce an array $E(N)$ with the same dimensions to keep track of identified terms in the cipher. We shall use the

165

convention that when the Nth element in the cipher is unidentified, $E(N) = 29$; when the Nth element later becomes identified, we shall let $E(N) = C(N) =$ the identified value. If we make a point of storing the number of terms ($N\emptyset$) in the cipher in the data statement, these first few operations are accomplished by commands of the type

```
25   READ NØ
26   FOR N = 1 TO NØ
28   READ D(N)
3Ø   LET C(N) = D(N)
35   LET E(N) = 29
4Ø   NEXT N
```

Next we need a subroutine to print the current version of the cipher stored in $C(N)$. For example,

```
850   REM SUB PRINT CURRENT C(N)
855   LET Q9 = Ø
860   FOR N = 1 TO NØ
864   REM LET X = E(N) HERE TO DISPLAY E(N)
865   LET X = C(N)
87Ø   GOSUB 5ØØ
875   NEXT N
880   PRINT
885   PRINT
890   RETURN
```

($Q9 = \emptyset$ initializes the column counter in subroutine $5\emptyset\emptyset$.) A statement of the type

```
GOSUB 85Ø
```

after line $4\emptyset$ permits displaying the initial cipher. For example, it might take the form

PQU'WUQJUBQPUPQU'WUPS PUTXUPSWUFDWXPTQBUISWPSWJUAPTXUBQ'CWJUT
BUPSWUZTBEUPQUXDKKWJUPSWUXCTBYXU BEU JJQIXUQKUQDPJ YWQDXUKQJ
PDBWUQJUPQUP OWU JZXU Y TBXPU UXW UQKUPJQD'CWXU
BEU'VUQGGQXTBYUWBEUPSWZ                                        (53)

An immediate display of the current code using subroutine $7\emptyset\emptyset$ gives

CURRENT CODE IN X(I):

| 1 | 2 | 3 | 4 | 5 | 6 | 7 | 8 | 9 | 1Ø |
|---|---|---|---|---|---|---|---|---|----|
| A | B | C | D | E | F | G | H | I | J |

| 11 | 12 | 13 | 14 | 15 | 16 | 17 | 18 | 19 | 2Ø |
|----|----|----|----|----|----|----|----|----|----|
| K | L | M | N | O | P | Q | R | S | T |

| 21 | 22 | 23 | 24 | 25 | 26 | 27 | 28 |
|----|----|----|----|----|----|----|----|
| U | V | W | X | Y | Z | | |

and would facilitate a solution through guesswork. For example, if we thought the first letter of the cipher should be a T instead of a P, we would want to exchange the sixteenth and twentieth terms of the code array, $X(I)$, and then recode the cipher $C(N) = X(D(N))$ in terms of the new code.

Consequently it is useful to have a subroutine that interchanges any two members ($I\emptyset, J\emptyset$) of the code array and then recodes the cipher.

```
75Ø   REM SUBINTERCHANGES TWO CHARACTERS IØ,JØ
751   PRINT "IØ,JØ TO BE INTERCHANGED"
752   INPUT IØ,JØ
```

```
753   PRINT "MORE? (NO = Ø)"
754   INPUT X9
755   REM ENTER SUB HERE IF YOU KNOW IØ,JØ
756   LET N1 = X(IØ)
757   LET N2 = X(JØ)
758   LET X(IØ) = N2
759   LET X(JØ) = N1
760   IF X9 = Ø THEN 769
765   GOTO 75Ø
768   LET X9 = Ø
769   PRINT
77Ø   REM SUB FOR RECODING CIPHER
771   REM E(N) STORES IDENTIFIED ELEMENTS OF CIPHER ARRAY
775   FOR N = 1 TO NØ
78Ø   LET C(N) = X(D(N))
782   IF C(N)#IØ THEN 785
784   LET E(N) = IØ
785   NEXT N
795   RETURN
```

As written above, the input parameter *X9* permits returning to the start of the subroutine for additional interchange operations before going on to the more time-consuming operation of recoding the entire cipher. This process adds to the efficiency of the guesswork approach as long as you do not exchange the same code element more than once before recoding the cipher. Note that lines 782 and 784 keep track of identified elements, assuming that your guess for the true identity of *IØ* was correct. Later we shall enter this subroutine at line 755, after having computed most probable values for *IØ* and *JØ*.

A set of statements such as

```
4ØØ   GOSUB 7ØØ
4Ø5   GOSUB 75Ø
41Ø   GOSUB 85Ø
42Ø   GO TO 4ØØ
```

then provides a simple reiterative method for solving the cipher through guesswork by the operator. If you happen to have what Yardley referred to as "cipher brains," the program can be pretty effective. At least all of the dull, tedious bookkeeping is taken care of automatically.

---

**4.19
PROBLEM 29**

Write a simple interactive program of the above type and try it out on cipher (53) above. (The main point is to make sure the subroutines are working properly and to emphasize the desirability of having the computer make some pretty reliable, most-probable guesses at the start.) (*Note:* If you have the CHANGE statement or equivalent CALL statement available, the cipher can be read in directly from the keyboard. Otherwise, use the initial current-code printout to help prepare the DATA statements.)

**4.19
PROBLEM 30**

Write a subroutine that permits use of the RND(*X*) function in BASIC to generate a random-substitution code for making up single-substitution ciphers. Note that one can improve on the results provided by RND(*X*) alone by following it up with a trip through subroutines 75Ø and 85Ø.

---

Before attempting to write a more general program, it is worth taking a closer look at the statistical problem involved with a specific case. Consider the third act of *Hamlet*, which contains something over 35,200 characters. The frequency table based on the dialogue from Act III is shown rearranged in

Table 6. Noting that the expected fluctuation in a random count $N$ is roughly $\approx \sqrt{N}$, it is evident that we cannot do very much with single-character frequencies alone. From Table 6, we could determine the space between letters and the letter E, but that's about as far as we could go. The letters O and T are statistically indistinguishable from the frequency table. Going farther down the list, we see that we could not distinguish among the group S, H, N, I, and so on. Yet, intriguingly, there are fairly definite statistical boundaries around many of the less probable characters.

**4.19: Table 6** Frequency Table — Dialogue from Act III of *Hamlet* (35,224 Characters)

| Character | Occurrence | Uncertainty |
|-----------|------------|-------------|
| Space | 6934 | 83 |
| E | 3277 | 57 |
| O | 2578 | 51 |
| T | 2557 | 51 |
| A | 2043 | 45 |
| S | 1856 | 43 |
| H | 1773 | 42 |
| N | 1741 | 42 |
| I | 1736 | 42 |
| R | 1593 | 40 |
| L | 1238 | 35 |
| D | 1099 | 33 |
| U | 1014 | 32 |
| M | 889 | 30 |
| Y | 783 | 28 |
| W | 716 | 27 |
| F | 629 | 25 |
| C | 584 | 24 |
| G | 478 | 22 |
| etc. | | |

*Note:* The statistical boundaries are indicated by dashed lines.

Ordering the elements in the $28 \times 28$ correlation matrix for Act III provides some more insight (see Table 7). Here the total number of counts per element is much smaller (i.e., down by about a factor of 28 on the average), and we can only draw five definite statistical boundaries near the top of the list. Worse, we can only identify the first three matrix elements unambiguously, even with a text containing as many as 35,200 characters.

One could, of course, arrive at a solution to a cipher by systematically permuting the identification of the more probable characters, using the larger terms in Tables 6 and 7 as a guide. One then depends on recognizing the

# 4.19: Table 7 Correlation Matrix, $M(I, J)$, from Act III of *Hamlet* (35,224 Characters)

| $M(I, J)$ | Uncertainty | I | J | |
|-----------|-------------|-----|-----|---------|
| 1283 | 36 | 5 | 27 | E, space |
| 962 | 31 | 27 | 20 | space, T |
| 878 | 30 | 20 | 8 | T, H |
| 805 | 28 | 20 | 27 | |
| 786 | 28 | 19 | 27 | |
| 664 | 26 | 4 | 27 | |
| 630 | 25 | 8 | 5 | H, E |
| 627 | 25 | 27 | 1 | |
| 494 | 22 | 15 | 21 | |
| 489 | 22 | 27 | 13 | |
| 481 | 22 | 27 | 23 | |
| 479 | 22 | 27 | 19 | |
| 475 | 22 | 25 | 27 | |
| 462 | 21 | 27 | 9 | |
| 450 | 21 | 27 | 8 | |
| 447 | 21 | 18 | 27 | |
| 420 | 20 | 1 | 14 | |
| 416 | 20 | 15 | 27 | |
| 408 | 20 | 14 | 27 | |
| 383 | 20 | 5 | 18 | E, R |
| 349 | 19 | 9 | 14 | |
| 329 | 18 | 27 | 2 | |
| 328 | 18 | 14 | 4 | |
| 314 | 18 | 1 | 20 | |
| 311 | 18 | 18 | 5 | |
| 305 | 17 | 15 | 18 | |

*Note:* The statistical boundaries are indicated by dashed lines. The most probable digram decoding path is shown by circles and solid lines.

correct solution as it goes by. Recognition might be by eye, or perhaps by computing some quantity characteristic of the language.

Yardley did it by eye. In fact, there is a striking parallel between Yardley's method of solution in Military Intelligence Department MI-8 and Bob Newhart's monkey inspectors. In each case an army of typists (about 50 in the Yardley effort) was hammering away while an inspector roamed about to see if a message had yet come through. Yardley had, of course, organized a systematic permutation of the cryptograms on the basis of digram and trigram tables, as well as single-letter frequencies. To be sure, he also worked on much harder things than single-substitution ciphers, and he helped to catch lots of spies. Nevertheless, systematic permutation is pretty boring, even when you have a computer to do the monkey work. We would, therefore, like to formulate a procedure for determining a most probable solution to the cipher—one that may not necessarily be perfect with short messages but will at least give us a good start in the right direction.

It is pretty clear that the *only* thing we can get out of Table 6 with much reliability is the space between words. The conclusion is especially true with short messages. For example, a frequency table based on the first few lines of

| | |
|---|---|
| **English** | |
| *Hamlet* (Act III) | THERDOUSINGALYMP' |
| "The Gold Bug" | THERANDISOUPLYF'BJ |
| **German** | |
| Wiese | DERANGSTICHUMOLBJ |
| **French** | |
| Baudelaire | DESITANOURMPL'HYG |
| **Italian** | |
| Landolfi | CHERANOLITUSP |
| **Spanish** | |
| Cervantes | DENTOSURALICH |
| **Portuguese** | |
| Coutinho | ESTICAORMPLUNDJ |

*Note:* In all these languages, the "space" between words is the most frequent character, with the possible exception of German (e can be more frequent than the space when umlauts are not used).

Hamlet's soliloquy runs

space, T, O, E, A, . . .

Here E is *fourth* on the list and Legrand's approach would not even have gotten off the ground.

In order to get any further, we have to examine the correlation matrix more carefully and to notice that there is a basic statistical asymmetry to its structure. This asymmetry probably has to do with the fact that languages are written in the forward and not the backward direction. Whatever the basic cause, the common European languages contain most probable digram decoding paths in the forward direction through the correlation matrix, which seem to be remarkably well defined even in fairly short messages. For example, consider entering the matrix in Table 7 with the symbol representing the space between words firmly established. If you look for letter pairs near the top of the table of the form $(I, 27)$, you see that there are several candidates of comparable importance. That is, lots of words in English end with E, T, S, and D. Clearly, with a really long sample, you could expect to identify the letter E that way—but that's about all.

In contrast, if you look for pairs of the type $(27, I)$, there is only one that is conspicuously near the top; the pair $(27, 20)$ stands well isolated from the next most probable case. Equivalently, more words in English start with T than with any other letter, and the next most probable starting letter (A) is pretty far down the list. A still more surprising thing is that if you identify T = 20 and ask for the most probable value of

$$M(20, J) \qquad \text{where } J \neq 20 \text{ or } 27$$

the answer is, $J = 8$. That is, the letter H follows T far more probably than anything else other than the space between words (already identified). This behavior continues a considerable way down the matrix. One can determine a most probable decoding digram[26] path, which runs space, THERDOUSINGALYMP' in *Hamlet*. These paths differ somewhat between authors writing in the same language, and of course they differ substantially from one language to the next (see Table 8). These digram paths seem almost

[26] The term "digram" is used in cryptography to denote probable pair sequences. The concept of a most-probable decoding digram path computed from the correlation matrix as shown in Table 7 appears to be original with this manuscript.

to spell out representative words in the languages; and as previously discussed, one can identify the language from the digram path itself. The sixth or seventh entry on the path tends to vary significantly with the author and with the historical period. Of course, if you have a long sample of writing by the suspected author of the cipher, you can compute a path from his or her correlation matrix directly.

---

**4.19**
**PROBLEM 31**     Write a program to compute Tables 6 and 7, starting with the correlation matrix (Fig. 4-6). Draw in the statistical boundaries with the hyphen, assuming that they occur between elements $N_1$ and $N_2$ such that $N_1 - N_2 > SQR(N_1 + N_2)$.

---

We shall make use of these observations to develop a program to determine a most probable solution to short cryptograms. Although the technique should work equally well (or badly, depending on your point of view) with most languages, we shall specifically illustrate its operation by application to the cipher (53) on p. 166. Because we have reason to suspect that the original message was something uttered in the third Act of *Hamlet*, we shall store the *Hamlet* correlation matrix early in our program.

```
8  MAT READ A
9  MAT B = A
```

The second matrix ($B$) is required for a later second-order computation. If you do not have room in your computer for all these matrices, it is worth advertising in advance that we shall obtain a partial decoding of the cipher before we really need matrix $B$.

Before we can implement our discovery in a program to decipher cryptograms, it is necessary to compute the most probable digram decoding path for the individual language of concern. Because the space is the most common character in nearly all languages, we shall compute the decoding path which starts with the space symbol. We shall store the values obtained for the decoding digram path in the array $P(K)$ and use subroutine $5\emptyset\emptyset$ to type out the letter equivalents as we find them. We assume that the correlation matrix for the language was stored in the array $A(I, J)$ at the start of the program. In what follows we shall also count the terms located with the variable $L\emptyset$. The procedure is simply to find the successive series of connected maxima in the correlation matrix under conditions where we continuously add the new terms to the array $P(K)$ and choose maxima $A(I, J\emptyset)$ which have values of $J\emptyset$ that are not yet stored in $P(K)$.

```
5Ø  PRINT "COMPUTE BEST DECODING DIGRAM PATH, P(I), FOR LANGUAGE:"
52  PRINT
54  LET LØ = Ø
56  MAT P = ZER
58  LET JØ = 27
6Ø  LET X = JØ
62  GOSUB 5ØØ
64  FOR I = 1 TO 28
66  LET A(I,JØ) = Ø
68  NEXT I
7Ø  LET M = Ø
72  FOR J = 1 TO 28
74  IF M > A(X,J) THEN 86
76  FOR K = 1 TO LØ
78  IF X = P(K) THEN 86
8Ø  NEXT K
82  LET M = A(X,J)
```

```
84   LET J0 = J
86   NEXT J
88   IF M = 0 THEN 95
90   LET L0 = L0 + 1
92   LET P(L0) = X
94   GOTO 60
95   PRINT
```

The maxima are found in the usual way on lines 70 through 86. The specific one found has index $J0$ as a result of line 84. Lines 64–68 set the elements containing $J0$ to zero so we avoid finding them all over again on the next trip through the program. The maxima are counted on line 90 and we get out of the loop on line 88, when there are no more maxima to be found.

After printing the original cipher (53), our program results in the following output:

COMPUTE BEST DECODING DIGRAM PATH, P(I), FOR LANGUAGE:
   THERDOUSINGALYMP'

(based on the *Hamlet* correlation matrix).

We leave this section of the program with another print statement and three initialization statements for the next section.

```
96   PRINT
97   MAT A = B
98   LET L0 = 0
99   MAT L = ZER
```

Both matrices $A$ and $B$ were initially set equal to the correlation matrix for the language. Matrix $A$ was substantially altered during lines 50 through 94, and we now wish to restore it to its original value (line 97). (This could also be accomplished with a RESTORE command and MAT READ A.) In the next sections we shall use the parameter $L0$ to count the number of identified characters, and we shall store those identified characters in the array $L(I)$, initialized by line 99.

First we need to find the space symbol used in our cryptogram. We accomplish that objective merely by computing the most frequently occurring character in the cipher. Of course, the standard literary crypt usually provides this information for you ahead of time. Because it really is the easiest thing to compute, we shall go ahead and locate it anyway. That objective is accomplished in the following few lines:

```
100   PRINT L0 + 1;"COMPUTE 'SPACE':"
101   REM FIND SPACE SYMBOL FROM CHARACTER FREQUENCIES
105   LET M = 0
110   MAT F = ZER
115   FOR N = 1 TO N0
120   LET J = C(N)
125   LET F(J) = F(J) + 1
130   IF M > F(J) THEN 145
135   LET M = F(J)
140   LET J0 = J
145   NEXT N
150   LET I1 = I0 = P(1)
155   LET Q1 = 1
159   LET P0 = 0
```

Line 100 prints what we plan to do as step number 1. We both compute the total distribution of characters in $F(J)$ and do a running computation of its maximum value and maximum location ($J0$) at the same time. This is an obvious type of time-saver which we shall try to use whenever practical.

After passing line 159, we have located the symbol ($J0$), used to disguise the space character; we have stored the value that it should have, $P(1)$, in $I\emptyset$; and we have also noted that the fixed code value for this symbol ($I1$) is also equal to $P(1) = 27$ in the present case. (As we begin interchanging more and more characters, $I1$ will not necessarily be equal to $I\emptyset$.) Having identified these quantities, we print them out, exchange $I\emptyset$ and $J\emptyset$, recode the cipher, print the recoded cipher, and update the matrices $A(I, J)$ and $B(J, K)$ (in a manner that we shall presently discuss) through the harmless-looking statement

```
160   GOSUB 945
```

Line $16\emptyset$ enters at the middle of a fairly long subroutine ($9\emptyset\emptyset$), which is discussed below in greater detail. Line $16\emptyset$ results in

```
1  COMPUTE 'SPACE':
FREQ. = 38      I0 = 27      J0 = 21      I1 = 27      P0 = 0
```

PQ 'W QJ BQP PQ 'W PSUP TX PSW FDWXPTQB ISWPSWJ APTX BQ'CWJ TB PSW
ZTBE PQ XDKKWJ PSW XCTBYX UBE UJJQIX QK QDPJUYWQDX KQJPDBW QJ PQ   (54)
PUOW UJZX UYUTBXP U XWU QK PJQD'CWX UBE 'V QGGQXTBY WBE PSWZ

and we have broken up the cipher (53) into words. Note that the space symbol occurred 38 times and that the author of the cipher had cleverly concealed it from us by avoiding its use at the beginning and end of the message!

Next we want to follow the most probable digram decoding path, $P(I)$, starting with the space-symbol identification:

```
162   REM USE MOST PROBABLE  DIGRAM PATH, P(I)
165   PRINT L0+1;"COMPUTE '";
168   LET P0 = P(L0)
170   LET X = I1 = P(L0+1)
176   GOSUB 500
180   PRINT "':"
190   GOSUB 900
191   IF M = 0 THEN 199
197   GOTO 165
199   PRINT
```

The above section of the program is used over and over until we exhaust the statistical accuracy of the message ($M = \emptyset$ at line 191). In each case the computer first prints which character it is going to locate (lines 165–180), stores the identity of the character being sought in the fixed code in variable $I1$ (line $17\emptyset$), and then does all the work in subroutine $9\emptyset\emptyset$. Note that $P\emptyset$ (line 168) is the previous character identified. Subroutine $9\emptyset\emptyset$ does the things summarized in the following REM statements:

```
900   REM SUB TO FIND J0 = J FOR MAX F(J) = M(I0,J)
901   REM ENTER SUB WITH VALUE OF I1 (FIXED CODE)
902   REM SUB COMPUTES I0 AND J0 FROM DIGRAM PATH IN CURRENT CODE
903   REM P0 IS THE VALUE OF I0 FROM PREVIOUS TIME SUB.ENTERED
```

It computes values of the $P\emptyset$ row of the correlation matrix for the cipher array $C(N)$ and performs a running computation of the location $J\emptyset$ for which $M(P\emptyset, J\emptyset)$ is a maximum. Because we only need to compute one row at a time (and in fact will run out of statistical accuracy after a few rows), there is no point in either computing the entire correlation matrix based on the cipher, or in squandering the computer core necessary to store it all. We can use the same array $F(J)$ with which we previously found the space identity. After the initial statements,

```
904   LET M = Q9 = 0
906   MAT F = ZER
```

(where we have again reset the column counter $Q9$ for subroutine $5\emptyset\emptyset$), we

next store the $P\emptyset$ row of the matrix computed from $C(N)$ in $F(J)$, using the
following statements:

```
908  LET I = C(1)
914  FOR N = 2 TO NØ
916  LET J = C(N)
918  IF I≠PØ THEN 932
919  REM AVOID CASES WHERE 2ND TERM ALREADY KNOWN
920  FOR K = 1 TO LØ
921  IF J = L(K) THEN 932
922  IF X(J) = L(K) THEN 932
923  NEXT K
924  LET F(J) = F(J) + 1
926  IF M > F(J) THEN 932
928  LET M = F(J)
930  LET JØ = J
932  LET I = J
933  NEXT N
```

A running computation of the maximum value of $F(J)$ and its location, $J\emptyset$, is done on lines 928 and 93$\emptyset$. The loop from 92$\emptyset$ through 923 eliminates examining values of $J$ that have been identified previously. Line 918 makes sure that we only compute the $P\emptyset$ row of the matrix in $F(J)$. $F(J)$ thus literally corresponds to the number of times the $J$th character followed the $I = P\emptyset$th character throughout the presently decoded version of the cipher stored in $C(N)$. Line 93$\emptyset$ stores the running value $J\emptyset$ for the maximum location during the loop on $N$. Consequently, $J\emptyset$ contains the location of the maximum after completion of line 933.

In principle, we should really check the statistical meaningfulness of $M$ by computing the value $M1$ of the next-highest maximum for different $J\emptyset$. The latter would be easy to accomplish by adding the statement LET $M1 = M$ as line 927. One could then require that $M$ be an integer greater than $M1 + \sqrt{M + M1}$. However, the typical literary crypt is much too short to permit using such a stringent statistical requirement. A reasonable compromise is to stop computing successive maxima when the statistical uncertainty on $M$ is $\approx 1$. We can accomplish that objective with the statements

```
934  REM STOP FOLLOWING DIGRAM PATH WHEN M TOO SMALL
935  IF INT(SQR(M) + .5) > 1 THEN 938
936  LET M = Ø
937  RETURN
```

In practice line 935 is equivalent to the statement

```
935  IF M > 2 THEN 938
```

That is, we shall make the computer return from the subroutine when the criterion on line 935 is not satisfied, and indicate this fact to the main program by setting $M = 0$ on line 936. The conditional statement on line 191 of the main program then goes on to the next stage when $M = 0$.

If the statistical criterion is met on line 935, we then compute the value of $I\emptyset$ in the current code corresponding to $I1$ in the fixed code, define a new $P\emptyset$ ("previous value of $I\emptyset$"), print the numerical values computed, exchange $I\emptyset$ and $J\emptyset$ in the current code, recode the cipher, and print the recoded version of the cipher.

```
938  REM FIND VALUE OF IØ CORRESPONDING TO I1 IN FIXED CODE
939  FOR I = 1 TO 28
940  IF I1 = X(I) THEN 942
941  NEXT I
942  LET IØ = I
```

```
944  LET P∅ = I∅
945  PRINT "FREQ. = ";M, "I∅ = "; I∅, "J∅ = "; J∅, "I1 = "; I1, "P∅ = "; P∅
946  PRINT
947  REM EXCHANGE I∅, J∅ AND PRINT CIPHER
948  GOSUB 755
949  GOSUB 85∅
```

We then update the matrices $A(I, J)$ and $B(J, K)$, which will be needed for a later second-order correction. (The process is very similar to that used in the previous discussion of bit compression–expansion techniques.) In particular, we want to set elements of $A$ and $B$ equal to zero whose columns and rows, respectively, are designated by the identified character, $I1$, in the fixed code. Thus

```
95∅  REM UPDATE A(I,J) AND B(J,K) FOR 2ND-ORDER CORRECTION
952  REM A(I,J) = B(J,I) = ∅ WHEN J = I1; OTHERWISE A(I,J) = B(I,J) = M(I,J)
953  REM ENTER AT 955 FOR 2ND-ORDER CORRECTION
955  FOR I = 1 TO 28
96∅  LET A(I, I1) = B(I1,I) = ∅
965  NEXT I
```

Finally, we want to update the list of known characters stored in array $L(L\emptyset)$ and increment the total number, $L\emptyset$, computed.

```
97∅  REM COUNT KNOWN LETTERS IN L∅
975  LET L∅ = L∅ + 1
985  PRINT
99∅  LET L(L∅) = I1
995  RETURN
```

We then introduce a routine initialization statement of the type

```
7 LET Q9 = P∅ = X9 = ∅
```

and the first part of the program is ready to run.

After the first trip through subroutine $9\emptyset\emptyset$, the computer has printed

```
2  COMPUTE 'T':
FREQ. = 1∅      I∅ = 20      J∅ = 16      I1 = 20      P∅ = 20
TQ 'W QJ BQT TQ 'W TSUT PX TSW FDWXTPQB ISWTSWJ ATPX BQ'CWJ PB TSW
ZPBE TQ XDKKWJ TSW XCPBYX UBE UJJQIX QK QDTJUYWQDX KQJTDBW QJ TQ    (55)
TUOW UJZX UYUPBXT U XWU QK TJQD'CWX UBE 'V QGGQXPBY WBE TSWZ
```

That is, it has identified the letter T from the maximum number of times (10) that a character followed the space symbol. The program keeps going through the loop until the statistical rejection criterion on line 191 diverts the program to line 199.

With the present cipher (53), the rejection criterion is inoperative until after the fifth step, at which point the computer has printed

```
5  COMPUTE 'R':
FREQ. = 3      I∅ = 18      J∅ = I∅      I1 = 18      P∅ = 18
TQ 'E QR BQT TQ 'E THUT PX THE FDEXTPQB IHETHER ATPX BQ'CER PB THE
ZPBW TQ XDKKER THE XCPBYX UBW URRQIX QK QDTRUYEQDX KQRTDBE QR TQ    (56)
TUOE URZX UYUPBXT U XEU QK TRQD'CEX UBW 'V QGGQXPBY EBW THEZ
```

At this point, the program has identified the space, T, H, E, and R; and we are forced to go to another method of attack. Note that the last identification was made using a letter-pair frequency of 3 (for the pair ER) and the statistical accuracy is getting to be very marginal indeed.

It is worthwhile at this point to have a look at what we have stored in the array $E(N)$. Here $E(N) = 29$, except where $C(N)$ is regarded as identified. Because subroutine $5\emptyset\emptyset$ has been constructed to print "–" when $X = 29$, we

175

obtain the following output after the fifth step:

```
T- -E -R --T T- -E TH-T -- THE --E-T--- -HETHER -T-- ----ER -- THE
---- T- ----ER THE ------ --- -RR--- -- --TR--E--- --RT--E -R T-
T--E -R-- ------T - -E- -- TR----E- --- -- -------- E-- THE-
```
(57)

when line 865 of subroutine 850 is modified to read

865   LET X = E(N)

---

| | |
|---|---|
| **4.19**<br>**PROBLEM 32** | Draw a flowchart of the program through line 199 (the start of the second-order corrector). |
| **4.19**<br>**PROBLEM 33** | Write a program that follows the most probable digram decoding path for *Hamlet* and then jumps to a guesswork loop (such as that discussed above, starting on line 400) after exhausting the statistical accuracy. Try it out on the cryptogram above or The Gold Bug cipher (at the end of this section). (*Note:* Once you have computed the most probable digram path for the particular language, it would be best stored in an array rather than recomputed each time.) |

---

The next section of the program (second-order corrector) requires a fair amount of computer core. It will be necessary to start the program with initial dimension statements of the type

**4.20**
**Second-Order Crypt Corrector**

```
2   DIM A(28,28),B(28,28),K(28,28)
3   DIM C(192),D(192),E(192)
4   DIM F(28),X(28),L(28),P(28)
```

The arrays in line 3 have arbitrarily been dimensioned equal to the length of the cipher under discussion. The real space consumers are the matrices $A$, $B$, and $K$. $K$ could be pruned somewhat in practice (to perhaps $28 \times 10$). The space needed is readily available on most large computers; however, it will be hard to do the program on the average minicomputer.

Our next approach is to compute a most probable second-order identification for the remaining characters. That is, we want to pick sequences of the type

$$E(N-1),29,E(N+1) \tag{58}$$

in which an unknown character is surrounded by two known characters. For each such set of sequences throughout the cipher we want to compute a most probable value of $J$ such that the quantity

$$F = A(E(N-1),J)*B(J,E(N+1)) \tag{59}$$

is a maximum. Further, we want to do this in such a way as to bypass previously identified terms. In addition, we must store correlated pairs of the identity of the most probable characters in the fixed $I1 = J$ code and their corresponding values in the current code, $J0 = C(N)$, with which they should be interchanged. We shall store those correlated pairs in the matrix $K(I, C(N))$.

The first part of this problem is handled by the following statements:

```
200   PRINT "REACHED STATISTICAL LIMIT. 2ND-ORDER CORRECTION NEXT"
201   PRINT
202   LET M0 = 0
203   MAT K = ZER(28,28)
204   FOR N = 2 TO N0 - 1
205   REM UNIDENTIFIED TERMS HAVE E(N) = 29; FIND SEQ. E(N-1),29,E(N+1)
```

```
206   IF E(N) #29 THEN 290
207   IF E(N−1) = 29 THEN 290
208   IF E(N+1) = 29 THEN 290
209   REM EXCLUDE C(N) ALREADY ON IDENTIFIED LIST, L(I)
210   FOR I = 1 TO L0
212   IF X(C(N)) = L(I) THEN 290
214   NEXT I
220   LET M = 0
230   REM CHOOSE I = J FOR MAXIMUM (M) VALUE OF F (SEE BELOW)
235   FOR J = 1 TO 28
240   LET F = A(E(N−1),J)*B(J,E(N+1))
245   IF M > F THEN 260
250   LET M = F
255   LET I = J
260   NEXT J
265   IF M = 0 THEN 290
269   REM COUNT AND FIND MAX (M0) OF CORR.PAIRS I,C(N) IN K(I,C(N))
270   LET K(I,C(N)) = K(I,C(N)) + 1
275   IF M0 > K(I,C(N)) THEN 290
277   LET M0 = K(I,C(N))
280   LET I1 = I
285   LET J0 = C(N)
290   NEXT N
294   REM END HERE IF CAN'T FIND MAXIMUM, M0
295   IF M0 = 0 THEN 400
```

A running computation of the number of correlated pairs is done on line 270, and the coordinates for the running maximum are stored on lines 280 and 285.

If we reach line 295 with $M0 = 0$, it means that the maximum is indeterminate. Hence the conditional statement at line 295 takes the program to line 400 for a final bit of guesswork on the cipher.[27]

If a nonzero value for $M0$ is found by line 295, we now have the values of $I1$ (in the fixed code) for the identity of the new character and the value of $J0$ in the current code with which that character is to be exchanged. We next have to compute the value of $I0$ in the current code corresponding to $I1$ in the fixed code. The latter is accomplished by lines 300–315 in the following steps:

```
299   REM NEED I0 = INVERSE CODE FOR I1
300   FOR I = 1 TO 28
305   IF I1 = X[I] THEN 315
310   NEXT I
315   LET I0 = I
```

After that, we print out the numerical values obtained and use subroutines 755, 850, and 955 to exchange $I0$ and $J0$, recode the cipher, print the current cipher, and update matrices $A$ and $B$ and the array $L$.

```
316   REM NOW KNOW I1,I0,J0
317   PRINT L0+1;"COMPUTE '";
318   LET X = I1
319   GOSUB 500
320   PRINT "':"
322   PRINT "FREQ. = ";M0,"I0 = ";I0,"J0 = ";J0,"I1 = ";I1
324   REM EXCHANGE I0,J0 IN CODE ARRAY X(I) AND RECODE CIPHER
325   GOSUB 755
```

---

[27] The second-order correction is approximately equivalent to finding the value of $J$, for the maximum third-order correlation matrix element $M(I, J, K)$ in which $I$ and $K$ are fixed. If you have a third-order correlation matrix available, it would be best used in the program section starting on line 200 (as opposed to tacking it on at line 400). One could then go on to estimate still-higher corrections from the third-order matrix.

```
329  REM PRINT CIPHER AND RECORD NEW CORRECTIONS
330  PRINT
335  GOSUB 850
340  GOSUB 955
344  REM REITERATE UNTIL M0 = 0 ON LINE 295
345  GOTO 202
```

We then reiterate to line 202 until no further second-order correction is determinate.

With the present cipher (53), the second-order corrector deduces the right values for three more characters (O, S, and U) and finally hits the indeterminate state after the thirteenth computation (during which it thought it was identifying the letter A). At that point the program yielded

```
13  COMPUTE 'A':
FREQ. = 1      I0 = 1      J0 = 22      I1 = 1
```

```
TO ME OR YOT TO ME THDT PS THE FUESTPOY CHETHER VTPS YOMIER PY THE
ZPYW TO SUNNER THE SIPYBS DYW DRROCS ON OUTRDBEOUS NORTUYE OR TO   (60)
TDQE DRZS DBDPYST D SED ON TROUMIES DYW MA OGGOSPYB EYW THEZ
```

and gave up. It may not seem like much; however, the program has successfully identified the following characters:

$$\text{space, T, H, E, R, O, S, U}$$

Further note that it is trying to make decisions at the end where only *one* case has occurred within the cipher. Obviously, it would do much better with a significantly longer message.

Doubtless there will be a skeptical reader who will toss the result aside with the comment: "Well, after all, you used a correlation matrix for Act III of *Hamlet* in the first place. No wonder the program worked so well." It is therefore of interest to see what would have happened if we fed in somebody else's correlation matrix.

The following result was reached after 15 steps using a correlation matrix based on "The Gold Bug":

```
15  COMPUTE 'A':
FREQ. = 1      I0 = 1      J0 = 1      I1 = 1
```

```
TO ME OR IOT TO ME THVT PS THE FUESTPOI CHETHER ATPS IOMBER PI THE
ZPIW TO SUNNER THE SBPIDS VIW VRROCS ON OUTRVDEOUS NORTUIE OR TO   (61)
TVQE VRZS VDVPIST V SEV ON TROUMBES VIW MY OGGOSPID EIW THEZ
```

Compare statements (60) and (61).

Although it took longer to get there (see Table 9), the program eventually arrived at exactly the same set of correctly identified characters. Some of the other symbols are identified differently, and the program pursued a riskier path. "The Gold Bug" program started making mistakes on the seventh and eighth steps but got S correct on the ninth and U correct on the twelfth.

**4.20: Table 9**  Results in Deciphering 192 Characters of Hamlet's Soliloquy (Shakespeare vs. Poe): Summary of "Identified" Letters

| Step: | 1 | 2 | 3 | 4 | 5 | 6 | 7 | 8 | 9 | 10 | 11 | 12 | 13 | 14 | 15 |
|---|---|---|---|---|---|---|---|---|---|---|---|---|---|---|---|
| *Hamlet* matrix | space | T | H | E | R | O | S | N*[a] | Y* | M* | I* | U | A* | — | — |
| "Gold Bug" matrix | space | T | H | E | R | O | N* | I* | S | M* | B* | U | D* | Y* | A* |

[a] Erroneous identifications are marked *. In each case, the program started making mistakes when the particular pair frequency computed from the cipher got down to 2. However, the same set of eight correctly identified code symbols was found in each case.

What else could we have done to improve the accuracy of the final result? The answer seems to be: not much with only second-order correlations to work with. For example, after exhausting the statistical accuracy in the message during the second-order correction process, we might have introduced a section that computed most-probable identical-letter pairs. There are two words in the final cipher,

SUNNER    and    OGGOSPYB    (or OGGOSPID)

which contain different unidentified doubled letters, and one might argue that we could benefit by consulting a double-letter frequency table. However, these doubled pairs each occur only once. The word SUNNER might thus be most probably interpreted as SULLER, with SUFFER and SUPPER occurring much farther down the list. A human being with knowledge of words in English would probably rule out the first choice; but he might also think that Hamlet was inviting someone named ZPYW to dinner. The only real way to handle these sequences within the present type of computer program is use higher order correlation matrices from the start. However, the present program is complicated enough for our purposes and already occupies more core than is really desirable. Further, it has gotten us to a point where a few quick exchanges of characters will permit us to narrow in rapidly on the correct answer through interactive guesswork and application of our personal knowledge of higher-order correlations.

---

**4.20
PROBLEM 34**

Draw a flowchart for the second-order corrector starting on line 200.

**4.20
PROBLEM 35**

Write a program to compute a frequency table of doubled letters from a pair-correlation matrix based on Act III of *Hamlet* (Fig. 4-6).

**4.20
PROBLEM 36**

Solve one of the following historically interesting single-substitution ciphers:

    1. The original "Gold Bug" cipher did not exhibit representative statistical properties of English, except for the first four characters in the most-probable decoding digram path. Resetting the message from the 1895 edition of the complete works of Poe with standard characters yields

```
BEYNNUEYCBXXETFE'SWEPTXSNGAXESNX'WCETFE'SWEUWQTCAXEXWB'EKNJ'VENFWEUWYJWW
XEBFUE'STJ'WWFEZTFD'WXEFNJ'SWBX'EBFUEPVEFNJ'SEZBTFEPJBFRSEXWQWF'SECTZPEW
BX'EXTUWEXSNN'EKJNZE'SWECWK'EWVWENKE'SWEUWB'SAXESWBUEBEPWWECTFWEKJNZE'SW
E'JWWE'SJNDYSE'SWEXSN'EKTK'VEKWW'END'
```

where we have also used characters to represent the space symbol and apostrophe. After computing the sequence, space THE, you can probably unscramble the rest. However, you have to resort to fairly high order correlations in the guesswork: for example, by identifying such words such as

TH--TEE-

This single-substitution cipher is the only one of its length tried by the author in which the second-order corrector did absolutely no good whatsoever. The problem seems in part to be that the cipher was artificially loaded up with E's—so much so that the rest of the statistics suffered.

    2. The following cipher is based on the first published version of *Hamlet*†:

```
BE OF EX KEB BE OF 'R BVFXFUN BVF PEAKB BE HAF BE NMFFP AN BV'B 'MM
'R 'MM KE BE NMFFP BE HXF'Q 'R Q'XXR BVFXF AB CEFN TEX AK BV'B HXF'Q
ET HF'BV LVFK LF 'L'ZF 'KH OEXKF OFTEXF 'K FGFXM'NBAKC DSHCF TXEQ
LVFKYF KE P'NNFKCFX FGFX XFBSXKFH
```

† This pirated edition is known as *The First Quarto* (see Hubler, 1963).

3. Rumor has it that the following type of cryptogram appeared as an advertisement in a scientific journal in recent years:

IF I'M GLAZZAUTI I'MFLAWI A BUTI IF OFLY U DIFEAUT PFYEUTS I'UI BAZZ
GM YURM FO I'FWM WYULI WPAMTIAWIW WDP' UW SFDLWMZQ B'F BUTI IΓ W'ULM
PFEAFDWZS AT I'M ELFOAIW WIFE I'M MNEZFAIUIAFT FO FDL DTDWDUZ YATRW
UTR IIFAT YM OUYFDW TFGMZ BATTML

It was supposedly followed by the solitary reply:

MA MOW BALWC JYBBWT MOUBS FAD NWTF ID'O EAT MOW AEEWT LDM Y UI NWTF
OUGGF JYMO IF GTWVWBM PAL UBABFIADV

The ad is long enough to exhibit many of the statistical properties of Shakespearean English. Note that the second cryptogram is very much harder than the first, owing to its extremely short length. It therefore would not be surprising to learn that the author of the ad had a great deal of trouble reading the reply.

Do you think a company of this type would be a success? *Note:* If you don't like any of the above ciphers, pick one out of *Saturday Review/World* instead.

---

Poe had a penchant for describing the primary objectives in cryptography as if he had developed a powerful, general method to carry them out. For example, in a later version of his famous paper on secret writing, Poe states:

## 4.21
### Is a Decipherable Message Present?[28]

"Out of perhaps one hundred ciphers altogether received, there was only one which we did not immediately succeed in resolving. This one we *demonstrated* to be . . . a jargon of random characters having no meaning whatsoever."

Poe revealed neither the "fake" cryptogram nor the method of demonstration. If nothing else, he had seized upon a very good idea. When faced with something as perplexing as the Balzac cipher or the Voynich Manuscript, it would be very nice to know ahead of time that there *is* a message present. Otherwise, there is a danger that one might spend several decades trying to decipher the "message" in a railroad timetable or in a list of tonnages of naval vessels.

There are two primary questions that we can ask:

1. Do the statistical properties of the coded message differ in a meaningful way from those of a randomly selected string of characters?
2. Do the statistical properties of the coded message agree with those for text in the proposed source language within the statistical uncertainty?

If the answer to the first question is "no," the message is undecipherable for all practical purposes and we might as well not waste our time on it. This would not necessarily mean that no message is there. One can always transmit a message coded in a purely random key. However, unless you have a duplicate copy of the random key, you will not be able to decipher it. (At least, if you do "decipher" a message, you should be extremely skeptical of its meaning.) If the answer to the second question is "yes," it is reasonable to go ahead with a systematic unscrambling process according to the various coding methods that seem most probable. (Just which method is usually a guess.)

It is possible to formulate the above questions in terms of the entropy per character of the coded text. That is, one may make an objective computation of the quantities $h_0$, $h_1$, $h_2$, . . . defined earlier. If you know the character set, a

---

[28] The remaining sections of this chapter rely on the concept of entropy per character in various statistical orders developed in Section 4.13.

direct comparison with $h_0$ for a random string is meaningful. In many instances one simply does *not* know the entire character set. However, the values for $h_1$, $h_2$, $h_3$, ... in most languages are relatively independent of the exact number of characters in the set for long sections of text.

It is useful to investigate the dependence of $h_0$, $h_1$, $h_2$, ... on the number ($N$) of characters in the string in the purely random case. As can be seen from the basic definitions of these quantities,

$$\lim_{N \to \infty} h_m = h_0 \qquad (62)$$

for a perfectly random string. However, the speed with which $h_m \to h_0$ with increasing lengths of text falls off with increasing $m$.

This effect can be demonstrated very easily by using the random-number generator to produce a long string of numbers. For example, the following statements permit computing a $28 \times 28$ correlation matrix for a string $N$ characters long chosen randomly from a 28-character set.

```
1500   REM SUB TO COMPUTE M(I,J) FROM RANDOM CHARACTERS
1505   LET I = 28
1510   MAT M = ZER(28,28)
1515   FOR N0 = 1 TO N
1520   LET J = 1 + INT(RND(1)*27 + .5)
1525   LET M(I,J) = M(I,J) + 1
1530   LET I = J
1535   NEXT N
1540   RETURN
```

Use of our previously described programs to compute $h_0$, $h_1$, and $h_2$ from the correlation matrix results in the values shown in Table 10. Note that randomly selected character strings with $N \approx 10{,}000$ are required before $h_2 \approx h_1$ within $\approx 1$ percent; whereas $h_1 \approx h_0$ within 1 percent for $N \approx 500$. One, of course, will get slight differences each time you rerun the program from a new table of random numbers. Ultimately, the convergence of the quantities in Table 10 with increasing $N$ will be a measure of the randomness of the RND($X$) function itself.

**4.21: Table 10**  Speed with Which $h_2 \to h_1 \to h_0 = \log_2 28 = 4.80735$ for a String of $N$ Characters Chosen Randomly, by Use of RND($X$), from a Set of 28 Characters

|  | N | | | | | | |
|---|---|---|---|---|---|---|---|
|  | 100 | 200 | 500 | 1000 | 2000 | 5000 | 10,000 |
| $h_0/h_1$ | $1.04_3$ | $1.01_7$ | $1.00_9$ | $1.00_7$ | $1.00_4$ | $1.00_4$ | $1.00_3$ |
| $h_1/h_2$ | 2.46 | 1.81 | 1.31 | 1.14 | 1.05 | 1.02 | 1.01 |

**4.21
PROBLEM 37**  Use the RND($X$) function to generate a random key that can be added to messages in a standard ASCII character set. (Such messages could, of course, be deciphered easily by someone else with access to the same BASIC compiler, if it were known where the message started in the random-number table.) Transmit Hamlet's soliloquy (or some other text in English) using this key and compute $h_1$, $h_2$, and $h_1/h_2$ for the result. Compare the values with those for Shakespearean English.

**4.21
PROBLEM 38**  Write a program that computes $h_0$, $h_1$, and $h_2$ for the first several hundred digits in $\pi$ (see Fig. 4-16).

```
1415926535  8979323846  2643383279  5028841971  6939937510  5820974944  5923078164  0628620899  8628034825  3421170679
8214808651  3282306647  0938446095  5058223172  5359408128  4811174502  8410270193  8521105559  6446229489  5493038196
4428810975  6659334461  2847564823  3786783165  2712019091  4564856692  3460348610  4543266482  1339360726  0249141273
7245870066  0631558817  4881520920  9628292540  9171536436  7892590360  0113305305  4882046652  1384146951  9415116094
3305727036  5759591953  0921861173  8193261179  3105118548  0744623799  6274956735  1885752724  8912279381  8301194912
9833673362  4406566430  8602139494  6395224737  1907021798  6094370277  0539217176  2931767523  8467481846  7669405132
0005681271  4526356082  7785771342  7577896091  7363717872  1468440901  2249534301  4654958537  1050792279  6892589235
4201995611  2129021960  8640344181  5981362977  4771309960  5187072113  4999999837  2978049951  0597317328  1609631859
5024459455  3469083026  4252230825  3344685035  2619311881  7101000313  7838752886  5875332083  8142061717  7669147303
5982534904  2875546873  1159562863  8823537875  9375195778  1857780532  1712268066  1300192787  6611195909  2164201989

3809525720  1065485863  2788659361  5338182796  8230301952  0353018529  6899577362  2599413891  2497217752  8347913151
5574857242  4541506959  5082953311  6861727855  8890750983  8175463746  4939319255  0604009277  0167113900  9848824012
8583616035  6370766010  4710181942  9555961989  4676783744  9448255379  7747268471  0404753464  6208046684  2590694912
9331367702  8989152104  7521620569  6602405803  8150193511  2533824300  3558764024  7496473263  9141992726  0426992279
6782354781  6360093417  2164121992  4586315030  2861829745  5570674983  8505494588  5869269956  9092721079  7509302955
3211653449  8720275596  0236480665  4991198818  3479775356  6369807426  0425522625  5181841757  4672890977  7727938000
8164706001  6145249192  1732172147  7235014144  1973568548  1613611573  5255213347  5741849468  4385233239  0739414333
4547762416  8625189835  6948556209  9219222184  2725502542  5688767179  0494601653  4668049886  2723279178  6085784383
8279679766  8145410095  3883786360  9506800642  2512520511  7392984896  0841284886  2694560424  1965285022  2106611863
0674426287  2039194945  0471237137  8696095636  4371917287  4677646575  7396241389  0865832645  9958133904  7802759009

9465764078  9512694683  9835259570  9825822620  5224894077  2671947826  8482601476  9909026401  3639443745  5305068203
4962524517  4939965143  1429809190  6592509372  2169646151  5709858387  4105978859  5977297549  8930161753  9284681382
6868386894  2774155991  8559252459  5395943104  9972524680  8459872736  4469584865  3836736222  6260991246  0805124388
4390451244  1365497627  8079771569  1435997700  1296160894  4169486855  5848406353  4220722258  2848864815  8456028506
0168427394  5226746767  8895252138  5225499546  6672782398  6456596116  3548862305  6010150330  8617928680  1742495853
1507606947  9451096596  0940252288  7971089314  5669136867  2287489405  7564014270  4775551323  9208747609  3746234364
9009714909  6759852613  6554978189  3129784821  6829989487  2265880485  2314429524  4775551323  7964145152  5902799344
5428584447  9526586782  1051141354  7357395231  1342716610  2135969536  2314429524  8493718711  0145765403  8067491927
0374200731  0578539062  1983874478  0847848968  3321445713  8687519435  0643021845  3191048481  0053706146  8067491927
8191197939  9520614196  6342875444  0643741123  7181921799  9839101591  9561814675  1426912397  4894090718  6492319614

5679452080  9514655022  5231603881  9301420937  6213785595  6638937787  0830390697  9207734672  2182562599  6615014215
0306803844  7734549202  6054146659  5201497442  2850732518  6660021324  3408819071  0486331734  6496514539  0579626856
1005508106  5913440171  2749470420  4052571459  1028970641  4011097120  6280439039  7595156771  5770042033  7869936007
2305587631  7635942187  3125147120  5832228718  2618612586  7321572083  4148488291  6447060957  5270695722  0917567116
7229109816  9091528017  3506712748  5832281613  3520935396  5725121083  5791513698  8209144421  0067510334  6711031412
6711136990  8658516398  3150197016  5151168517  1437657618  3515565088  4999999859  9823873455  2833163550  7647918535
8923261854  8963213293  3089857064  2046752590  7091548141  6549859461  6371802709  8199430992  4489575711  2828905923
2332609729  9712084433  5732654893  8239119325  9746366730  5836041428  1388303203  8249037589  8524374417  0293127656
1809377344  4030707469  2112019130  2033038019  7621101100  4492932151  6084244485  9637669838  9522868478  3123552658
2131449576  8572624334  4189303968  6426243410  7732269780  2807318915  4411010446  8232527162  0105265227  2111660396

6557130925  4711055785  3763466820  6531098965  2691862056  4769312570  5863566201  8558100729  3606598764  8611791045
3348850346  1136576867  5324944166  8039626579  7871185560  8455296541  2665408530  6143444318  5867697514  5661406800
7002378776  5913440171  2749470420  5622305389  9456131407  1127000407  8154732266  6143444318  4645880797  2708266830
6343285878  5698305235  8089330657  5740697954  7163775254  2021149557  6158140025  0126228594  1302164715  5097925923
0990796547  3761255176  7829666454  7791745011  2996148903  0463994713  0463994713  2962107340  4375189573  5961925901
9389713111  7904297828  5647503203  1986915140  2870808599  0480109412  1472213179  4764777262  2414254854  5403321571
8530614228  8137585043  0632175518  2979866223  7172159160  7716692547  4873898665  4494450114  6540628433  6639379003
9762689621  1463853067  3609657120  9180763832  7166416274  8888007869  2560290228  4721040317  2118608204  1900042296
6171196377  9213375751  1495950156  6049708822  9674276364  9472306538  0367515906  7350235072  2118608204  8354056704  0386743513
6222247715  8915049530  9844889333  0963408780  7805419341  7805419341  4437744418  4263129860  8099888687  4132604721
```

**Fig. 4-16.** The first few digits in a computation of $\pi$ done by Shanks and Wrench (1962) using the formula $\pi = 24 \tan^{-1}\frac{1}{8} + 8 \tan^{-1}\frac{1}{57} + 4 \tan^{-1}\frac{1}{239}$ through 100,625 decimal places (333,075 bits).

The fluctuations in $h_1$ and $h_2$ expected from statistical effects due to the finite length of a character string from a particular text can be estimated readily in the following manner. As a rough approximation, we note that the average uncertainty is $\approx \sqrt{N}$ in a counting experiment where one obtains $N$ counts on the average. Hence for each matrix element $M(I, J)$ which represents the number of times the $J$th character followed the $I$th in the set throughout the entire string of $N$ characters, we can expect a fluctuation of $\approx \pm \sqrt{M(I, J)}$. These fluctuations in the individual matrix elements obviously will not add up in phase throughout the entire matrix. In fact, they will tend to add up to $\approx \sqrt{N}$, where

$$N = \sum_{I,J} M(I, J) \qquad (63)$$

Hence by redefining the correlation matrix through the subroutine

```
REM SUB TO COMPUTE SPREAD IN M(I,J)
FOR I = 1 TO 28
FOR J = 1 TO 28
LET X = SQR(M(I,J))
LET M(I,J) = M(I,J) + 2*(RND(1) − .5)*X
NEXT J
NEXT I
RETURN
```

we can recompute representative values of $h_1$ and $h_2$ that arise from the statistical fluctuations. It is worth printing out the new sum over all the elements in the altered matrix to verify that it differs from the original $N$ by $\approx \sqrt{N}$.

---

| | |
|---|---|
| **4.21**<br>**PROBLEM 39** | Write a program that computes $h_1$ and $h_2$ from the original correlation matrix and then estimates the error in $h_1$ and $h_2$. Try it out on the $28 \times 28$ correlation matrix from Act III of *Hamlet* (Fig. 4-6). |
| **4.21**<br>**PROBLEM 40** | Compute the correlation matrix for an $N$-character string chosen randomly by use of $RND(X)$ from a 28-character alphabet. Try it out for the value $N = 424$ in the Waberski cipher (see Fig. 4-18). Compute $h_1$ and $h_2$ from this matrix, together with an estimate of the spread in values. |

---

Now we are ready to have a look at the famous Balzac cipher. In 1829, Honoré de Balzac introduced a cipher of some 3660 characters in length in the middle of his handbook on marriage, *La Physiologie du Marriage* (see Fig. 4-17). Stimulated by the admonition from Balzac himself that one ought to reread the principal passages several times to really understand the sense of the text, readers of this book for the next decade attempted in vain to decipher the cryptogram. It was thought that Balzac had provided tantalizing clues, such as "end" at the end and "sin!" in the middle. However, the text of the cipher differs from one edition to the next and one suspects that Balzac left instructions to the printer after the line "L'auteur pense que la Bruyère s'est trompé. En effet" that a monkey should be allowed to choose the type for the next two pages. (Cynics will note that Balzac was paid by the word.) Obviously, Balzac was just having a practical joke at the reader's expense. However, it is of interest to compute the values of $h_1$ and $h_2$ for this cipher and compare them with values expected from French, or any other western European language. Although a large character set has been used, the more exotic (upside-down) symbols occur very rarely (at least in the 1870 edition of the cipher shown in Fig. 4-17). As previously noted, if we include all the most-probable characters

L'auteur pense que la Bruyère s'est trompé. En effet, ennarsns
fiiNfidgdc·:',jptqvgvtmffo.dt-aoto;todfda:dhoiOo₁dasadècssmeirders
qvt'odht.tditoadgdaodtgtdotahtodceoed'tètoegodèvo'deàadsdieaiasab
dB:oaovfiPsèfiB,a.'oqbma0;to;afvatmtdodèi'diafitbdmvoh;1oèothdt
oBdoodtbtfitflidoad'go:daoqtè-adto;omacsàooshoflt',doqtdpotoqtdo
-fdt;di'dètost;itdot;'dàosièasdo';'vBlf.llfsohPaosfiè.dcèètofid.tdodias
fiohdflh-.sadomfi;oeoq;d-ditsoaLfdsso,vda.o₁s-ètta'èo todoqotd-gèo
ɔbdtotdtdoqd;to1dhdhvpbcdtt'odqdhq.dhogaàodtqarttncasccavsvis
fldodh tædà'dttLfi'qo1ddtdfg.otbtto;qtdod;t casfliasscsà vsdovscstsaa
dototbacaidgbxlq,tdtogɔttd.oedtmtsrdèm:ldP'd'odod'aèocotaLt'assas
q's;fittqt;doqsdodffss₁t:t-l.dtatdotsatbcqæd-tod.tdè-ohèh go;odàsns
at-oàᶠfto'vetPdcɔise'sdotno'.aosrs-₁,è'.id;èvcet;.desdte-thmæbdLoin
bNffiodbq'mto'qodè.to9-:o:d-doqtdqoddhooo4oqtdadthd;ada.terata
ePaïdototoèè'-tt'a-'tèdtoeaobtototaqdffghdov'otèo'doe-'.bddgodhos
moh;e1dodoaet-:ooPde;odtobddsdeg»o1eqffliogièooftdot..àotLodddr
oa-doodl d'od,dtododgfbodc'oddoo'ddhffilfddLodfflitdtqdtè'od'oootg
ffigffattqo1-tbddg'cqddobo:ddt't-doflhdèod;odo'oeomomoPdabadcm
dg'·otd-qɔ-'docioeot»d.doi'b'og'hPcffiimctda;om;ootpdqoohoamsc
td'oèdo'tgdtoodtotottfdffiodffi;ddoχ₁ttd.vooopdtododàmbgo,tgddeae
dcttt.-ooɪg;tqc.oarciodd;;omqtd'pohodtttæLfi:-d₁dvdt..hoLdhifiede

utmcbdeé-cecf;hg.rtauxmevn ietoarqf ctuvtxirnmcbc-'h:fi.ratnimæ
dv,1fidgéoætdodtPadoLgqod-gvot;ffob àdtrsidhddqcot'tdodoldada o
xéz-entmicsostaqraep;gdhfi;rtamluxcny tiznimdce-éɪq.ad,tuxvmcbz
ɔbo;otobodtoqo-tædd.o.fftt.foo,bPttdm:do'dsoèdsáaqoedesracfi:fiod
mbxzlemciutvdfuflcàùyrrqoia,q.fi;hecbccè-idmoidzbyvlmigqio'tupr
dédoPtot»ao moP.tohPt;sfottocvoàdPqdfficdN vdo'odqoe otodtffoed
lutica.rqfgsicdmcb-éwinantuifi:khθidmtxoq:,g.qarbzxàmidesoratm
to'dofliqdocovidtqtoidotooæ1odtoadhtoqdoqoaogadodaèo;ffiatsedob-
rvybzé-dcfee;qointxᵉèmq tubno praid nmûqarlocinlmbzyxfn1itqmu
doèdo'dtot.vo.'cod;to'dgototovdoado.:dèt-vtdtot;odott1.ovd'dho'tdé
vtrodqzyxtmidofapr.fi,h;9aodivytbcdéc-mqinopeiébxtublcdcfqgoran
eveàsdthocv;.otsed-mdædotdotdvqdtdo'ædtotoèfdobfitd:.dOiao.od,d
Ld(dmɑedey cbmutiantosdeg;ffi.qoipr,figdfcnlybzuiqnfTbfd-ébmcn
tPotb-o'oct8ffo-èoboffiotddosobotdᶦoDo'dfi:odhcd'dèvd;'otffidcdt.do
ecymgzih.aoqimbvtnxd-ps.ri,atcb,fi;ecindoyluuuvmd-écèEflᵐsin!rao
qgdahdgoɪadoᵒocqh-è9èqpbᵈd-ttv1odqom8:ododdootèdotcodtiffotèvt
mxutd-éçᵉH'ém-eToq;ffih9fdcSmtuyinzdufq.raxvLmlcberinbuavrq
y;vo.mqyytéivq.gqtsqé1qègqqgitaia.yé;qé.gi;qémgoPy(dytmtdigqb
æicbéyiqtmqoécbgiva-æg'éd1bmæo'tététioéto.éqocia.m-ébyæié1it;i
yimqvtqtgébvttmryvt;vyamimxtqtqioi-o.écéémaicdétqitæntcbgqmiy
gyyb-r.tqxméyg.itgmtræt'ncqrdaq,,æiqyrtgtbaryæq,'xæy'gtoyrₐiæ
gaéaéytmé,xaBth èc'qvffbeg-»ésq,aàæthmibqriési;OEy.iq-èh»,,gdæ
Flaurnt igsbO'èceebà,qCs1,rs»ràsoqm h(q'q,méqCséfffsffah.mefz
ɪ.Biseie,BfèfᶦpBca' otlffhét zt-c(C;éCfftoyotPofR,æte.sciPizèdotoèdo
gɪz.ofYzBie,Pyso,dtoeaécésæosèho-tboyeBzà(PhCqzcj'nàhasfmdèfeff
æcabmd,steftfmPzszgts;oqaéP èeo æ,,n,xæh nhÆRehyCe.ei,iɪsàbq
éfRrhɪofob qfja..émysei th ffèffsf-R rive,xh xrdtcezyPecffstsjRtqza
yd.xs.reCèfz'imbirgæeqàqbsrgdirièecffefeqé,é.ensDsCfmffche,eeyeé
biqsh',vreevr'æeqéé;otbritr,évqzCéuuRà.yze-xeesæ.ém,mrxvbég,gx
ɪ,y.é.eyfzj'r1àgti,ré,ètxto.x.et.dyaac;tatrxegcqysty,trqye's(bmsdigq
qètcycia,ej-tcxvé;oivqe-y ycngteroeqqtæqéti cuutdtqteéᵗ'c,Pg.s';agm
ag'bætairnitirmatiooitéyt.itviotiætgffgmt.tirsnddégtéctefeédém',tyéy
meéqsxeyscrtgtféf-étiq;,qcqt;yo-eè'céénéit1t-agcaectobt.iet.sgbcfæɪ
y.yg.éi,1a.ca c'gtvécntozoigté.itàqirdcb.séèm,tdtffairtedvsytotyo.ɔa
ɪ,qétbbsavtfatr-s'icrotq-qdérstv1trdreè,y;t'qmsy;ia'ro'esgngéotesiyd
ɔy-ébg'éiatrtéitcd-tdtigt,ito.bétév'qiuɪ,itq-xthirtéi-isie.q.sieot'todio
gyvtzdt;aortrtyi.odt.gtsostd'ia.ès'éirtéé,d;r1totaéiod''qtisvti,tgtày'ro
ᵒvièiff,tdfig'vqosas.gs étàdadta,tæ-c'iiad.qégeg èdcmlzxt uvai1for.q
meeaeefilcb»û ᵒendceuveegxvt orq;hfeiemntilzbcPùiSdctadrpqoiend

**Fig. 4-17.** The cipher from Balzac's *La Physiologie du Marriage* (edited by Alexandre Houssiaux, Paris, 1870), pp. 563, 564.

within our set, the actual values computed for the entropy per character are fairly independent of the total number in the set. If we do not distinguish between upper and lower case, inverted characters, or accent marks, there are still the following 37 characters (including the space symbol):

Section 4.21
Is a Decipherable Message
Present?

ABCDEFGHIJKLMNOPQRSTUVWXYZ '.:;–(2489

Use of the above set to compute $h_1$ and $h_2$ yields the values in Table 11. Although it is pointless to assign any real meaning to values of $h_0$ in this problem, it is clear that the statistical properties of the Balzac cipher are very much closer to those for a purely random character distribution than to the normal properties of French writing of the period. Note that you do not have to know French to reach that conclusion. The only really surprising thing about the cipher is that the monkey that set the type managed to do so well in simulating a completely random distribution.

---

**4.21**
**PROBLEM 41**
Compute $h_1$, $h_2$, and $h_1/h_2$ for some 20-line section of the Balzac cipher and compare with the results in Table 11 (see Fig. 4-17).

---

**4.21: Table 11**  Entropy per Character in Balzac Cipher

| Input | $h_1$ | $h_2$ | $h_1/h_2$ |
|---|---|---|---|
| 3656-character RND($X$) cipher (28-letter alphabet) | 4.79 | 4.65 | 1.03 |
| 3656-character Balzac cipher (37-letter alphabet) | $4.45 \pm 0.01$ | $4.11 \pm 0.04$ | $1.08 \pm 0.01$ |
| 5572-character French text[a] (28-letter alphabet) | $4.00 \pm 0.01$ | $3.14 \pm 0.01$ | $1.27 \pm 0.01$ |

[a] Baudelaire.

Lothar Witzke (*alias* Pablo Waberski) was the only German spy sentenced to death in the United States during World War I. His conviction was primarily the result of work in Yardley's department, MI-8, in deciphering the cryptogram shown in Fig. 4-18. The cryptogram was a multiple-transposition cipher that involved considerable reshuffling of the order of the original letters, but without the use of letter-substitution codes. (A detailed analysis of the cipher is given in Yardley, 1931, Chapter 7.) The really interesting thing about this

```
SEOFNATUPK      ASIHEIHBBN      UERSDAUSNN
LRSEGGIESN      NKLEZNSIMN      EHNESHMPPB
ASUEASRIHT      HTEURMVNSM      EAINCOUASI
INSNRNVEGD      ESNBTNNRCN      DTDRZBEMUK
KOLSELZDNN      AUEBFKBPSA      TASECISDGT
IHUKTNAEIE      TIEBAEUERA      THNOIEAEEN
HSDAEAIAKN      ETHNNNEECD      CKDKONESDU
ESZADEHPEA      BBILSESOOE      ETNOUZKDML
NEUIIURMRN      ZWHNEEGVCR      EODHICSIAC
NIUSNRDNSO      DRGSURRIEC      EGRCSUASSP
EATGRSHEHO      ETRUSEELCA      UMTPAATLEE
CICXRNPRGA      AWSUTEMAIR      NASNUTEDEA
ERRREOHEIM      EAHKTMUHDT      COKDTGCEIO
EEFIGHIHRE      LITFIUEUNL      EELSERUNMA
ZNAI
```

**Fig. 4-18.** Pablo Waberski was condemned to be hanged as a German spy during World War I because of evidence in the above transposition cipher. (See Yardley, 1931, Chapter 7.) Waberski was suspected of setting off the "Black Tom" explosion in New York Harbor.

cipher is the extreme degree to which the statistical properties of German are preserved in the final message. First, one can determine that the source language is indeed German from the total occurrence frequencies of the letters involved. Second, in spite of the considerable (systematic) scrambling of the letter order, the value for $h_2$ obtained from the cipher is just about the same as that from normal German.

After dividing the unscrambed message into German words, Yardley's group concluded that the original message was (Yardley, p. 168):

AN DIE KAISERLICHEN KONSULAR BEHOERDEN IN DER REPUBLIC MEXIKO PUNKT STRENGGEHEIM AUSRUFUNGSZEICHEN DER INHABER DIESES IST EIN REICHSANGEHOERIGER DER UNTER DEM NAMEN PABLO WABERSKI ALS RUSSE REIST PUNKT ER IS DEUTSCHER GEHEIMAGENT PUNKT ABSATZ ICH BITTE IHM AUF ANSUCHEN SCHUTZ UND BEISTAND ZU GEWAEHREN KOMMA IHM AUCH AUF VERLANGEN BIS ZU EIN TAUSEND PESOS ORO NACIONAL VORZUSCHIESSEN UND SEINE CODE TELEGRAMME AN DIESE GESANDTSCHAFT ALS KONSULARAMTLICHE DEPESCHEN ABZUSENDEN PUNKT VON ECKARDT

The Pablo Waberski cipher does raise a basic philosophical question: Should a person (other than the cryptographer who generated the code) really be condemned on the basis of a multiple-transposition cipher? The point here is that the method of solution is based on any systematic rearrangement that produces a "message." The cryptanalyst is also allowed to put in spaces and throw out null characters. As long as the periods of rearrangement are short, the result is fairly convincing. However, in a certain sense, an anagram could be regarded as a transposition cipher with very long periods. (The first period in the Pablo Waberski cipher was 108 characters out of 424 and was determined by looking for CH letter pairs.) Because of the $N!$ effect, there is a possibility that one might end up being condemned for possessing a laundry list in the wrong language. Such a list would exhibit the normal first- and second-order statistics of the source language, and if a damning message were extracted from the list, it would be very hard to explain away during time of war. It may perhaps have been worries of this type that led President Wilson to commute the death sentence. Instead of being hanged by a 424-character string (as implied in the Yardley account),[29] Waberski was released from prison in 1923.

---

**4.21**
**PROBLEM 42**

(a) Compute the total character frequencies in the Waberski cipher (Fig. 4-18).

(b) Compute expressions of the type

$$S = \sum_{I=1}^{26} F_x(I)F_y(I)$$

where $F_x(I)$ represents the total normalized character frequencies of the unknown language of the cipher and $F_y(I)$ represents the normalized character frequencies of the various known languages in Table 4. By determining which known language $y$ yields the maximum value of $S$, deduce the source language of the Waberski cipher (Fig. 4-18). Use the normalization of Eq. (16C) and exclude the space symbol and apostrophe.

**4.21**
**PROBLEM 43**

Compute the first- and second-order entropy ($h_1$ and $h_2$) per character for the Waberski cipher and compare the values with those for German in Table 5.

In 1912, Wilfred M. Voynich acquired a 232-page (i.e., 116 folio numbers) manuscript that had been stored in the Jesuit College of Mondragone in Frascati, Italy. This volume of strange drawings and secret "scientific" writing (which now resides in the Beinecke Rare Book and Manuscript Library at Yale University under the name MS 408) has aptly been described as the "most mysterious manuscript in the World." More than half the book contains colored drawings of wierd, nonexistent plants; the rest is divided comparably between strange astrology charts, a "physiology" section, a herbarium, and a section at the end which merely contains drawings of pointed stars in the margins. The drawings were evidently done first and the secret writing filled in around them (see Fig. 4-19). The drawings may just be a "cover up," or merely represent numbers. No one has yet been able to produce an unambiguous deciphering of the manuscript,[30] although expert cryptanalysts such as Herbert Yardley, John Manly, and William Friedman have worked on it. The source language has variously been assumed to be Latin, Elizabethan English, and old German, and may possibly even be Spanish. No one has been able to identify all members of the character set as belonging to standard languages. Useful articles regarding the historical background of the manuscript have been written by Oneil (1944), Friedman (1962), and Tiltman (1967).

Voynich believed that he had traced the authorship to the thirteenth-century English philosopher and monk, Roger Bacon, and it has been described (e.g., by Pratt, 1939) as one of the oldest known examples of cipher writing that has survived until the present time. The earliest firm date for the manuscript is that on a letter by Joannes Marcus Marci (Rector at the University of Prague) written in 1666, which stated that the manuscript had been purchased for 600 gold ducats by Emperor Rudolph II of Bohemia (1552–1612) and that Rudolph believed the manuscript to be the work of Roger Bacon. The manuscript had evidently been signed at one point by Jacobus de Tepenecz (died 1622), director of Rudolph's botanical gardens. (Rudolph is better known to scientists for his court astrologer, Johannes Kepler.)

It is suspected that the most probable salesman of the manuscript to Rudolph was an Englishman named Dr. John Dee (see Fig. 4-20), who spent a little more than two years at Rudolph's court, ending early in 1586. Dee was a strange and remarkable man. He gave popular lectures to packed audiences on

---

[29] There are other discrepancies in Yardley's book. According to Yardley (1931, Chap. 7), he and his department unscrambled the Waberski cipher in one all-night stand after receiving the message from Colonel Van Deman early in February 1918, and Van Deman was understandably surprised to get the translation of this "most amazing document" early the following day. According to Kahn (1967, p. 354), the Waberski cipher did not get to "MI-8 until spring and then it kicked around a few more months while several men there tried and failed to solve it." A Chaucerian scholar named John Manly eventually solved it in a three-day marathon with one other member of the department. Kahn (p. 362) also quotes a later conversation between Manly and Yardley regarding the exaggerations in *The American Black Chamber*. Yardley admitted to Manly: "If I didn't dramatize [the material]...in some manner, the reader would go to sleep."

[30] For unconvincing solutions, see Newbold (1928), Feely (1943), and Strong (1945), or the summary of this material in Kahn (1967). The works by Newbold and Feely especially indicate the dangers of an ambiguous decoding method coupled with a vivid imagination regarding the picture content. Newbold had Roger Bacon inventing the microscope, telescope, discovering the Andromeda nebula, and so on, in the thirteenth century. Feely came up with some colorful, but nearly senseless translations describing the drawings on the right side of Folio 78 (which he felt depicted the female reproductive system). Brumbaugh (1974) has recently published a partial key based on the last leaf of the text and used it to decipher several words in the herbarium section. However, this key still contains a threefold ambiguity, and the average word in the manuscript still has several hundred possible letter sequences (presumed to be in Latin).

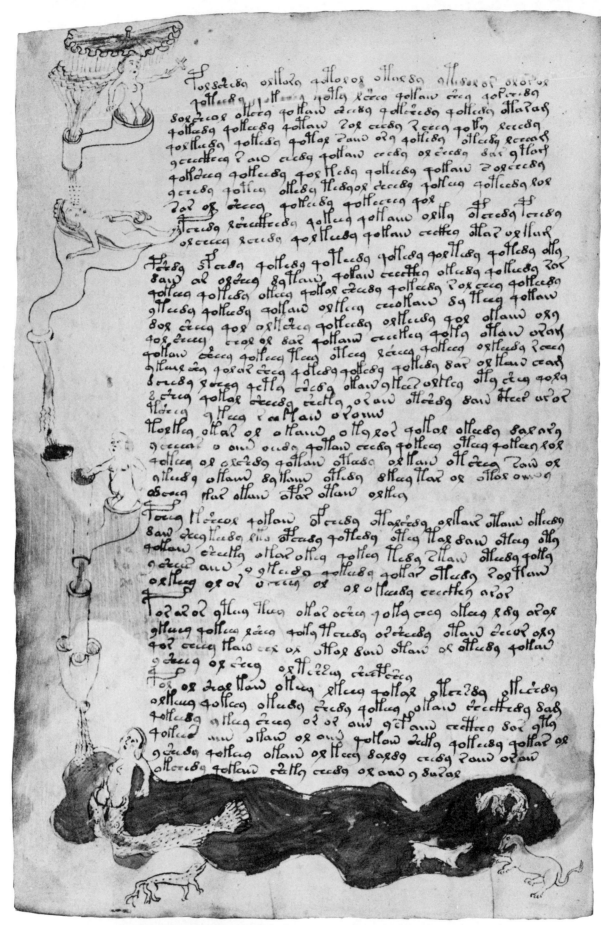

**Fig. 4-19.** Folio 80 from the Voynich manuscript. (Reproduced by permission of the Beinecke Rare Book and Manuscript Library at Yale University.)

**Fig. 4-19.** (Cont'd)

189

**Fig. 4-20.** Dr. John Dee (1527–1608). (Reproduced by permission of the As-
molean Museum, Oxford.)

Euclidean geometry, taught navigation to Francis Drake's officers, and fixed up
the Julian Calendar at Queen Elizabeth's request. He has variously been
described as one of the original "applied scientists"; a Hermetic philosopher; a
court astrologer, geographer, necromancer, and espionage agent for Queen
Elizabeth I; and Shakespeare's model for the character Prospero in *The
Tempest*. The popular belief that Dee was a sorcerer resulted in his home and
library being ransacked after he had left for Prague late in 1583. His history
has been so obscured by occultists and historical novelists that it is hard to
separate fact from fiction. If anyone in Elizabethan England had access to a
Roger Bacon cipher manuscript, Dee is among the most probable. He had the
largest library of his time in England—some 4000 works, perhaps one fourth of
them handwritten manuscripts (see the discussion and references in French,
1972). Dee was known to have other works by Roger Bacon and was also in
the habit of copying manuscripts on secret writing by hand. He was also
familiar with many languages. He had a fanatical interest in early English
history, the King Arthur legend, and British domination of the World. It seems
clear that Dee at least *wanted* to play the role of "Merlin" to Queen Elizabeth.

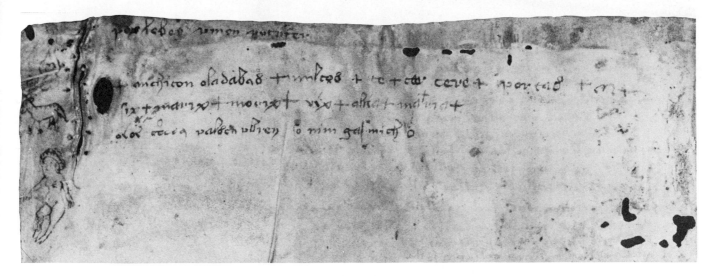

**Fig. 4-21.** "Key" to the Voynich manuscript, appearing on the rear side of the last page. (Reproduced by permission of the Beinecke Rare Book and Manuscript Library at Yale University.)

One author (Deacon, 1968) has him as the organizer of a gigantic espionage system and argues that Dee's "spiritual diaries" were really ciphers related to spying. It would be comforting to an appraisal of Dee's rationality if the occult activities were just a big cover-up. However, it is much easier to visualize the use of John Dee's "Great Seal" to encipher secret messages than it is to imagine the minutes of Dee's "first angelic conference" as an espionage document. Nevertheless, Dee's close association with so many important political figures in Elizabethan England is intriguing and suggests that Dee may have played some role, with the help of Rudolph II, in aligning the northern Protestant factions against Spain and the Pope on Queen Elizabeth's behalf during the encounter with the Spanish Armada (1588).[31]

Thus the Voynich Manuscript might actually have been written by Roger Bacon; it might have been copied from a Bacon manuscript by Dee; it might have been forged by Dee to hoodwink Rudolph II (who was fond of alchemy and the occult); it might even have been some sort of espionage document. If Dee wrote it, there is a chance that the source language was English. It is also possible that it is the work of a lunatic or prankster.

Many experts believe the "key" to the manuscript is contained within an inscription on the last page (see Fig. 4-21). This page has been badly treated by time and is extremely hard even to copy by hand the same way twice in succession. The line that is usually quoted starts off

+michiton oladabas+ . . .

after a large hole in the manuscript. In fact, Newbold (1928) started out boldly by declaring the hole to be the letter A, which after dropping several "null characters" gave him the Latin sentence

A mihi dabas multos portas

meaning

Thou wast giving me many gates

This, in turn, was interpreted to mean a cipher with many keys. From there on,

[31] See the various documents from the British Museum and from Dee's diaries reproduced by French (1972).

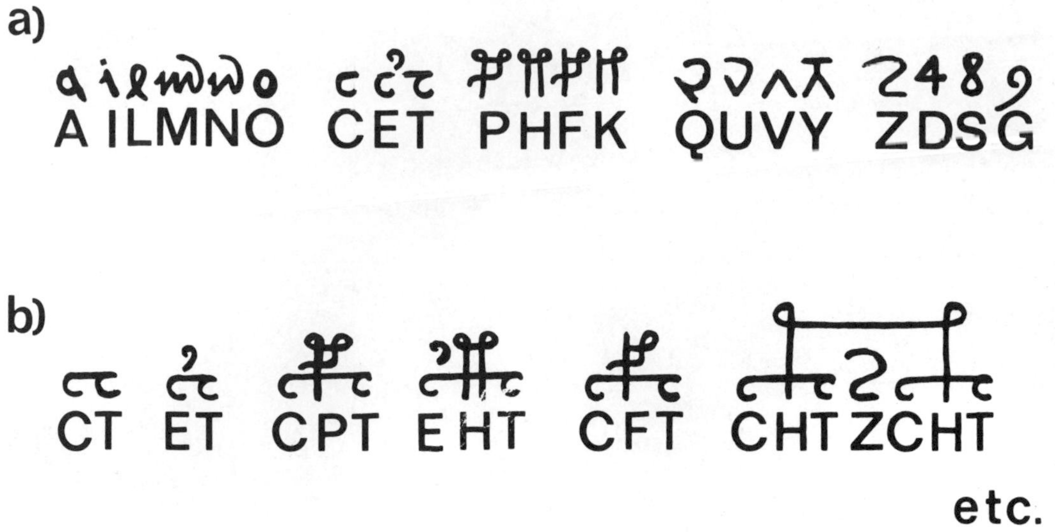

a)

**A ILMNO  CET  PHFK  QUVY  ZDSG**

b)

**CT  ET  CPT  EHT  CFT  CHTZCHT**

etc.

**Fig. 4-22.** (a) Top row: more important members of the character set within the Voynich manuscript. Bottom row: one way to achieve an unambiguous transcription of the manuscript character set into standard teletype characters.

(b) Top row: representative sequences of symbols in the manuscript. Bottom row: method of transcribing these complex symbols into standard teletype characters. In this approach, the long horizontal bar over the c characters is associated with the second c (labeled T). Other authors have treated these groups as separate characters. Although that assumption has justification, it does build in a statistical bias at the start. There are lots of other highly correlated sequences (e.g., AM, AN, QA, QC) which should be similarly treated for consistency.

Newbold was off to the text with no holds barred. On the other hand, Brumbaugh (1974) believes that OLADA deciphers as RODGD and hence that CON OLADABA is a simple anagram for Rodger Bacon.

However, one might equally well argue that the message on the back cover is at least partly in German (for example, from the appearance of words such as *so* and *mich* throughout the message). Also, the large number of plus signs may just mean that it is a statement in some medieval FORTRAN—an interpretation not unlike Brumbaugh's. It is also far from obvious that this inscription was written by the same hand that did the text; others (e.g., Tepenecz) might have been responsible. There is at least one other place within the manuscript (top of Folio 17 at the right) where a brief, similar inscription occurs. The language of the source is further obscured by the fact that several months of the year (March, April, May, October, and November) are clearly recognizable on the astrology charts and appear to be in Spanish! The words may, of course, be a decoy.[32]

Before we can analyze the statistical properties of the Voynich manuscript, it is necessary to adopt a convention which permits getting the character set onto a computer. It is also desirable to accomplish that objective without distorting the statistical distribution of the text right from the start.

A labeling of the character set which permits unambiguous reconstruction of the text, that is reasonably easy to remember and that keeps the correlation matrix to a modest size is shown in Fig. 4-22. (The reader is, of course, quite welcome to adopt any other convention which accomplishes the same objectives.)

One should not worry too much about any literal identification of all these characters. One can fill in most of the strange ones by selecting occasional

[32] Rudolph II was educated in Spain and the various royal families involved in England, Bohemia and Spain were thoroughly intermingled.

symbols in the Cyrillic, Glagolitic, and Ethiopian alphabets, along with two or three Chinese ideographs. However, it seems more plausible that most of the "strange" ones were merely invented by the author of the Voynich Manuscript through variations on common Greek and Latin characters.

The symbols labeled A, I, L, M, N, and O in Fig. 4-22 are straightforward to interpret apart from the normal difficulty in reading lowercase handwritten letters. There are four distinct species of tall, wiggly P- or Π-shaped characters which are similar to characters found in early Bulgarian Glagolitsa (see, Diringer, 1953; p. 476). The one labeled P in Fig. 4-22 often starts paragraphs. The one labeled H is similar to characters used for that letter in the Glagolitic alphabet. The others in Fig. 4-22 were filled in mnemonically.

At least three species of lowercase c are required. Note that c occurs frequently when followed by many other symbols. However, the apostrophe appears only to follow c throughout the entire manuscript. Hence c' has been identified as a separate character, labeled E in Fig. 4-22. (John Dee frequently wrote lower case e's in that manner in his personal correspondence.) We need at least one more species of c (e.g., that having a horizontal bar on top and labeled T in Fig. 4-22a) for unambiguous reconstruction of sequences of the type shown in Fig. 4-22b. These character sequences appear frequently throughout the Voynich Manuscript. Here, we shall associate the long horizontal bar through the sequence as being attached to the final character (labeled T in Fig. 4-22).

The characters labeled Q, U, Z, S, and G at least correspond to some script versions of those letters. The one labeled Y may be a Chinese ideograph (e.g., No. 11 in Fenn, 1971); however, it looks more like a variation on the one labeled V in Fig. 4-22.

The last four symbols in Fig. 4-22 may be the numbers 2, 4, 8, and 9. However, script versions of these characters are found as letters within many early alphabets in the Mediterranean area. For example, the character 4 is regarded as the letter P in Ethiopian and as R in Sindjiru, Moabite, and Phoenician (e.g., see Giles, 1926 or Diringer, 1953). The letter D was chosen here merely because it is the fourth letter in the English alphabet and had not been used for another symbol. It is also desirable to use symbols within the normal ASCII code for the alphabet to keep the correlation matrices within reasonable dimensions.

As the reader may show by doing the problems listed below, the statistical properties of the Voynich Manuscript are quite remarkable. The writing exhibits fantastically low values of the entropy per character over that found in any normal text written in any of the possible source languages (see Table 5). The values of $h_1$ are comparable to those encountered earlier in this chapter with tables of numbers. Yet the ratio $h_1/h_2$ is much more representative of European languages than of a table of numbers alone.

**4.22: Table 12**  Values of $h_n$ Computed from the First 10 Pages of the Voynich Manuscript Using the Convention in Fig. 4-22

|  | $h_1$ | $h_2$ | $h_3$ |
|---|---|---|---|
| Bits/character | 3.66 | 2.22 | 1.86 |

The values in Table 12 are displaced by about one order from normal writing in any western European language. That is, it appears that

$$(h_n)_{\text{Voynich}} \approx (h_{n+1})_{\text{European language}}$$

where a very rough approximation is implied. (No one has done an accurate computation of $h_4$ in any language.) A basic mystery in this writing rests in the fact that most *recoverable* coding procedures tend to make the entropy per character go up. (It is the second law at work again.) If the entropy per character in a recoverable cipher goes *down*, it means that you are putting some of the message in the key. For example, in the extreme type of cipher discussed by Poe (1841), consisting of

iiiiiiii

it is evident that *all* the message is in the key. The cipher just tells you when and how much of the key to read.

The only example of coded English text considered within the present chapter that has comparable statistical properties to those in Table 12 is in Poe's multiple-substitution cipher 2 based on *Suaviter in modo, fortiter in re* (the hard one from an "anonymous reader in Stonington, Conn."; see Fig. 4-15 and the associated discussion in Section 4.18). This is, in fact, precisely the same sort of ambiguous code that Brumbaugh (1974) believes he has pieced together from the inscription on the last leaf of the manuscript. The fact that the entropy per character is so low (Table 12) does indeed give some support to Brumbaugh's conclusions. If a complete first key could be put together, it would be possible in principle to write a computer program that used a pair-correlation matrix in the source language to determine most probable letter sequences on a word-by-word basis (see the discussion in the Research Problem in Section 4.18). However, Brumbaugh's comment that the plain text seems to be written "in an artificial pseudo-Latin . . . [with]phonetic but unprecedented mis-spellings . . ." is rather disquieting to anyone tempted to embark on such a project. There is one further disturbing question: Why would anyone have worked so hard to generate such an elaborate manuscript using a cipher that he himself would have found virtually impossible to decode?

As a final comment on this problem, it is worth mentioning that there actually are languages in some parts of the world that do have values of the entropy per character as low as those listed in Table 12. Although there is no reason to suspect that any of the Polynesian languages were known to Roger Bacon (or other principal characters in the plot), it is interesting to note that a language such as Hawaiian has very comparable values of $h_1$, $h_2$, and $h_3$ to those computed from the Voynich Manuscript (see Table 13). If the source text for this manuscript had actually been written in a language such as Hawaiian, a simple single-substitution code would give results similar to those in Table 12.

**4.22: Table 13**  Values of $h_n$ Computed from a 15,000-Character Sample of Hawaiian[a]

|  | $h_1$ | $h_2$ | $h_3$ |
|---|---|---|---|
| Bits/character | $3.20_5$ | 2.454 | 1.982 |

[a] Hawaiian requires 12 letters plus the space symbol ($h_0 = 3.700$). The source text was from a book entitled *No Ke Kalaiaina* published prior to 1878 and found in the Yale Library under catalog number Fyh-H317-1. (No author or publisher is listed.) The oldest available sample of printed text was chosen to minimize the effects of pollution by other languages. The 12-letter alphabet was introduced by missionaries in the mid-1800s for syllabic spelling (e.g., see Andrews, 1865). The author is indebted to Thaddeus P. Dryja for preparing the ASCII coded tape of the source text used in the computation and for tracking down the Hawaiian references. (It has been estimated that only about 100 people still use this language in daily communication.)

| **4.22**<br>**PROBLEM 44** | Compute the frequency distribution of characters in the sample of the Voynich Manuscript shown in Fig. 4-19. Print out a character-frequency table. |
|---|---|

<table>
<tr>
<td>4.22<br>PROBLEM 45</td>
<td>Compute $h_1$, $h_2$, and $h_1/h_2$ for the text in Fig. 4-19 and compute an estimate on the statistical spread in those values.</td>
</tr>
</table>

**4.22**
**PROBLEM 46**

A character sequence (using the labels in Fig. 4-22) of the type

$$POQGCTKZPOQGCTZPOQGCTSGCKG$$

is written in the left margin of Folio 50 of the Voynich Manuscript. Assuming that this sequence is used in the manner of the key phrase, "*suaviter in modo, fortiter in re*" of Poe's hard cipher 2 (see Fig. 4-15 and related discussion),

  1. Generate a long string of text using the second order monkey program and code these characters in the above manner;

  2. Compute $h_1$, $h_2$, and $h_1/h_2$ for the coded "text" and compare with values computed directly for the Voynich Manuscript.

**4.22**
**RESEARCH**
**PROBLEM**

Design a program to translate the Voynich Manuscript assuming a decoding matrix with three-level ambiguity of the type proposed by Brumbaugh and a second-order pair-correlation matrix computed from Latin. Before actually carrying out the program, it would be desirable to check Brumbaugh's specific suggestions by computing $h_1$, $h_2$, $h_3$ for a simulated Voynich Manuscript obtained by applying the Brumbaugh coding method to the text produced by a third-order monkey typing in Medieval Latin. (If the numbers don't agree reasonably well with ones extracted from the Voynich Manuscript using the same character set convention, there would be no point in attempting the translation.)

**4.22**
**RESEARCH**
**PROBLEM**

It is thought that the Malayo-Polynesian languages diffused eastward from Madagascar with little influence from European, or even oriental, languages. See if you can trace the path of development by computing $h_n$ for the different languages involved.

# REFERENCES

ANDREWS, LORRIN (1865). *A Dictionary of the Hawaiian Language*. Printed by Henry M. Whitney, Honolulu.

ASH, ROBERT (1967). *Information Theory*. New York: John Wiley & Sons, Inc.

BAILEY, R. W. (1968). *An Annotated Bibliography of Statistical Stylistics*. Ann Arbor, Mich.: University of Michigan, Department of Slavic Languages and Literatures.

BALZAC, HONORÉ DE (1870). *La Physiologie du marriage* in *La Comédie humaine*, Vol. 16; part 3 of *Etudes philosophiques et études analytiques*, edited by A. Houssiaux, Paris, pp. 563, 564.

BAUDELAIRE, C. (1869). *Les Paradis artificiels*. In *Oeuvres Complete de Charles Baudelaire*, Vol. 4; *Petits poëmes en prose*, Paris: Michel Lévy frères.

BENNETT, W. R., SR., AND J. R. DAVEY (1965) *Data Transmission*. New York: McGraw-Hill Book Company.

BRUMBAUGH, R. S. (1974). "Botany and the Voynich 'Roger Bacon' manuscript Once More." *Speculum*, Vol. 49 (July), pp. 546–548.

BUDGE, SIR E. A. W. (1904). *The Decree of Canopus*, Vol. III (from Vol. XIX of *Books on Egypt and Chaldaea*). London: Oxford University Press.

BUDGE, SIR E. A. W. (1929). *The Rosetta Stone in the British Museum.* London: The Religious Tract Society.

COHEN, ANTONIE (1971). *The Phonemes of English.* The Netherlands, Martinus Mijhoff.

COUTINHO, AFRANIO (1969). *A Literatura No Brasil* Rio de Janeiro: Editorial Sul Americana S.A.

CRAIG, W. J. (ed.) (1966). *The Oxford Shakespeare.* London: Oxford University Press. (Reprinting of the 1905 edition.)

DEACON, RICHARD (1968) *John Dee: Scientist, Astrologer and Secret Agent to Elizabeth I.* London: F. Muller Co.

DEWEY, F. H. (1918). *Caesar's Commentaries on the Gallic War,* Books I–VII (original Latin text with an interlinear translation). New York: The Translation Publishing Co. (More recent printings of the same text are available.)

DEWEY, GODFREY (1923). *Relativ Frequency of English Speech Sounds.* Cambridge, Mass.: Harvard University Press. (If you read this book, you will never be able to spell again!)

DIRINGER, DAVID (1953). *The Alphabet—A Key to the History of Mankind,* New York, Philosophical Library Inc. (A more recent two-volume edition is available.)

DOLEŽEL, LUBOMÍR, AND R. W. BAILEY, eds. (1969). *Statistics and Style.* New York: American Elsevier Publishing Co.

DUDLEY, HOMER (1939). "Remaking Speech." *J. Acoustical Soc. America,* Vol. 2.

DUDLEY, HOMER (1940). "The Carrier Nature of Speech." *Bell System Tech. J.,* Vol. 19, pp. 495–515.

EDDINGTON, SIR A. S. (1927). *The Nature of the Physical World.* The Gifford Lectures, Cambridge.

EDDINGTON, SIR A. S. (1935). *New Pathways in Science.* The Messenger Lectures, Cambridge.

EINSTEIN, ALFRED (1945). *Mozart, His Character, His Work.* New York: Oxford University Press.

FARAGO, LADASLAS (1967). *The Broken Seal.* New York: Random House, Inc.

FEELY, J. M. (1943). *Roger Bacon's Cypher—The Right Key Found.* Rochester, N.Y.

FENN, C. H. (1971). *The Five Thousand Dictionary.* Cambridge, Mass.: Harvard University Press.

FIRTH, J. R. (1934–1951). *Papers in Linguistics 1934–1951.* New York: Oxford University Press, 1969.

FRENCH, P. J. (1972). *John Dee—The World of an Elizabethan Magus.* London: Routledge & Kegan Paul Ltd.

FRIEDMAN, E. S. (1962). "The Most Mysterious Manuscript: Still an Enigma." *The Washington Post,* Aug. 15, p. 5.

FUCKS, WILHELM (1962). "Mathematical Analysis of Formal Structure of Music." *IRE Trans. Information Theory,* Vol. IT-8, pp. S225–S228.

FUCKS, WILHELM (1968). *Nachtalen Regeln der Kunst.* Stuttgart: Deutsche Verlag Anstalt.

GALLAGER, R. G. (1968). *Information Theory and Reliable Communication.* New York: John Wiley & Sons, Inc.

GIBBS, J. W., THE ELDER. (1857). *Philological Studies with English Illustrations.* New Haven, Conn.: Durrie and Peck.

GILES, PETER (1926). "Alphabet." *The Encyclopedia Britannica*, Vol. 1, 13th ed. London, pp. 723–732.

HALLO, W. W. (1974). "The First Half of History." *Yale Alumni Magazine*, Vol. 37, No. 8, pp. 13–17.

HARTLEY, R. V. L. (1928). "Transmission of Information." *Bell System Tech. J.*, Vol. 7, p. 535.

HEMINGWAY, ERNEST (1929). *A Farewell to Arms*, New York: C. Scribner Sons.

HOLTON, GERALD (1973). *Thematic Origins of Scientific Thought—Kepler to Einstein.* Cambridge, Mass.: Harvard University Press.

HOPPER, V. F. (1970). *Chaucer's Canterbury Tales, An Interlinear Translation.* Woodbury, N.Y.: Barron's Educational Series.

HUBLER, EDWARD, ed. (1963). *William Shakespeare—The Tragedy of Hamlet, Prince of Denmark.* New York: New American Library Signet Classic.

HUFFMAN, D. A. (1952). "A Method for the Construction of Minimum Redundancy Codes." *Proc. IRE*, Vol. 40, pp. 1098–1101.

KAHN, DAVID (1967). *The Codebreakers.* New York: Macmillan Publishing Co., Inc.

KANG, G. S. (1974). "Application of Lanier Prediction Encoding to a Narrowband Voice Digitizer." *Naval Research Laboratory Report*, Washington, D.C.

LANDOLFI, TOMMASO (1961). *Racconti.* Florence: Valecchi Edition.

LINCOLN, H. B., ed. (1970). *The Computer and Music.* Ithaca, N.Y.: Cornell University Press.

MALONEY, RUSSELL (1945). *It is Still Maloney.* New York: The Dial Press, Inc.

MANLY, J. M. (1931). "Roger Bacon and the Voynich MS." *Speculum*, Vol. 6 (July), p. 345.

MARR, DAVID (1969). "A Theory of Cerebellar Cortex." *J. Physiol.*, Vol. 202, p. 437.

MARSHACK, ALEXANDER (1972). *The Roots of Civilization.* New York: McGraw-Hill Book Company.

MOLES, A. (1956). "Informationstheorie der Musik." *Nachrichtentechnische Zeitschrift,* (NTF) Vol. 3.

NEWBOLD, W. R. (1928). *The Cipher of Roger Bacon.* Philadelphia: University of Pennsylvania Press. (This volume, based on notes, was published two years after Newbold's death by a well-meaning friend.)

NEWHART, BOB (1960). "An Infinite Number of Monkeys." Warner Bros. Recording 1393, Side 2.

NYQUIST, HARRY (1924). "Certain Factors Affecting Telegraph Speed." *Bell System Tech. J.*, Vol. 3, p. 324.

ONEIL, HUGH (1944). "Botanical Observations in the Voynich Manuscript." *Speculum,* Vol. 19, p. 126.

PIERCE, J. R. (1961). *Symbols, Signals and Noise.* New York: Harper & Row, Inc.

POE, E. A. (1841). "Review of Sketches of Conspicuous Living Characters of France." *Graham's Magazine*, Vol. 18 (April), p. 203.

POE, E. A. (1841). "A Few Words on Secret Writing." *Graham's Magazine*, Vol. 19 (July), pp. 33–38.

POE, E. A. (1843). "The Gold Bug," $100 prize story in *The Dollar* [a year] *Newspaper* of Philadelphia, June.

POE, E. A. (1895). *The Works of Edgar Allan Poe in Eight Volumes.* Philadelphia: J. B. Lippincott Company.

PRATT, FLETCHER (1939). *Secret and Urgent.* Indianapolis, Ind.: The Bobbs-Merrill Company, Inc.

SCHOLES, P. A. (1950). *The Oxford Companion to Music.* London: Oxford University Press.

SHAKESPEARE, WILLIAM. Complete Works. See Craig (1966).

SHANKU, D., AND J.W. WRENCH, JR. (1962). "Calculation of $\pi$ to 100,000 Decimals." *Math. Computation,* Vol. 16, p. 76. (The value of $\pi$ occupies a 20-page table.)

SHANNON, C. E. (1948). "A Mathematical Theory of Communication." *Bell System Tech. J.,* Vol. 27, pp. 379–423, 623–656.

SHANNON, C. E. (1949). "Communication Theory of Secrecy Systems." *Bell System Tech. J.,* Vol. 28 (October), pp. 656–715.

SHANNON, C. E. (1951). "Prediction and Entropy of Printed English." *Bell System Tech. J.,* Vol. 30, pp. 50–64.

STRONG, L. C. (1945). "Anthony Ascham, the Author of the Voynich Manuscript", *Science,* new series, CI (June 15, 1945), pp. 608–609.

THACH, W. T. (1972). "Cerebellar Output: Properties, Synthesis, and Uses." *Brain Res.,* Vol. 40, p. 89.

TILLOTSTON, ARCHBISHOP JOHN (1719). *Maxims and Discourses—Moral and Divine,* London: J. Tonson, at Shakespear's Head, over-against Katherine Street in the Strand.

TILTMAN, J. H. (1967). "The Voynich Manuscript—The Most Mysterious Manuscript in the World." Private publication within the Beineke Collection for MS 408, based on a paper delivered to the Baltimore Bibliophiles in 1967.

VONNEGUT, KURT, JR. (1950). "Epicac." First published in *Collier's Magazine:* see also *Welcome to the Monkey House.* New York: Dell Publishing Company, Inc., 1970, pp. 277–284.

WIEGER, L. (1965). *Chinese Characters,* (translation by L. Davrout), Dover Publications, New York.

WIESE, BENNO VON (1962). *Das Deutsche Drama.* Dusseldorf: August Bogel Verlag.

WRIGHT, E. V. (1939). *Gadsby* (A Story of Over 50,000 Words Without Using the Letter E). Los Angeles: Wetzel Publishing Co. (Available on interlibrary loan from the Library of Congress under reference number PZ3 W93176 Gad.)

YARDLEY, H. O. (1931). *The American Black Chamber.* Indianapolis, Ind.: The Bobbs-Merrill Company, Inc.

ZIMANSKY, C. A. (1970). "Editor's Note: William F. Friedman and the Voynich Manuscript." *Philolog. Quart.,* Vol. 49, p. 433.

# Appendix

# Summary of common BASIC commands and programming statements*

(entered from terminal and followed by carriage return)   **SYSTEM**

RUN               Computer starts to run program              **COMMANDS**

STOP              Computer stops running program

LIST              Computer lists program on terminal

SCRATCH           Computer erases program

(individual systems have various specialized commands such as

REN               renumber lines in steps of 1∅

REN 2, 1∅, 2∅∅, 3∅∅   renumber lines in steps of 2 from line 1∅ through 2∅∅ and start result as line 3∅∅

LIST 2∅∅, 25∅     list the lines from 2∅∅ to 25∅.

DEL 2∅∅, 3∅∅      delete lines 2∅∅ through 3∅∅, etc.

plus other specialized commands for reading (PTAPE) and punching (PLIST) programs on tape, reading and writing files on discs, and more powerful editing operations)

(Escape key usually permits telling computer to ignore characters typed prior to carriage return).

READY             computer is ready to accept program statements or RUN   **COMPUTER**
                  in BASIC.      *10, 11*                                 **REPLIES**

?                 computer is waiting for input data plus a carriage return
                  from terminal    *6, 13*

(error diagnostic messages that are self-explanatory or follow a simple convention provided by the computer service)

(entered after the line number, from the terminal and followed by a carriage   **COMMON**
return; statements are cancelled by typing line number and carriage return).    **BASIC**

REM               Remark, ignored by the computer when program runs;            **PROGRAM**
                  useful to remind one of purpose of program or                 **STATEMENTS**
                  segment     *21, 23, 26, 109, 163, 177*

* Page references supplied for representative use or explanatory comment.

199

## Variable Defining Statements

| | | |
|---|---|---|
| LET X=3.45E−6 | New value of $X = 3.45 \times 10^{-6}$ | *19, 24* |
| LET X=... (function of variables *A, B, C*,...). | New value of the variable at the left ($X$) is given in terms of the old values for the variables on the right. ("LET" may be omitted with some versions of BASIC) | *13, 17* |
| LET X=X+1 | New value of $X$ equals old value plus one. | *13* |
| LET A(I)− | defines Ith element of array *A*. I must be integer such that $1 \leq I \leq 10$ unless specific dimension statements added | *27, 28, 54, 70, 71, 164* |
| LET M(I, J)=... | defines *I, J* element of matrix *M*. *I, J* must be integers such that $1 \leq I, J \leq 10$ unless specific dimension statements added | *54, 57, 82, 83, 149* |

## Arithmetic Statements

| | | |
|---|---|---|
| LET X=A+B | $X = A + B$ | *11, 20* |
| LET X=A−B | $X = A - B$ | *11, 20* |
| LET X=A*B | $X = A \times B$ | *11, 20, 51, 176* |
| LET X=A/B | $X = A \div B$ | *11, 20* |
| LET X=A↑B | $X = A^B$ | *11, 38, 40, 46, 54, 70, 71, 87* |

## Statements in the Function Format Built into BASIC

| | | |
|---|---|---|
| LET X=SQR(A) | $X = \sqrt{A}$ | *12, 87, 174* |
| LET X=SIN(X) | $X = \mathrm{Sin}(X)$ | *12, 43, 44, 80, 81, 83, 96* |
| LET X=COS(X) | $X = \mathrm{Cos}(X)$ | *12, 43, 44, 80, 81, 83, 96* |
| LET X=TAN(X) | $X = \mathrm{Tan}(X)$ ⎰ X in radians | *12* |
| LET X=ATN(Y) | $X = \arctan(Y)$   $(-\pi/2 \leq X \leq +\pi/2$ for ATN case) | *12* |
| LET Y=EXP(X) | $Y = \exp(X)$ or $e^X$ | *12, 42, 43, 83, 90* |
| LET Y=LOG(X) | $Y = \log_e(X)$ | *12, 70, 71, 137* |
| LET Y=ABS(X) | $Y = |X|$ | *12, 37* |
| LET Y=INT(X) | $Y =$ first integer less than or equal to $X$. | *19, 29, 70, 71, 75, 83, 89, 99, 152* |
| LET Y=SGN(X) | $Y = +1$ if $X > 0$; $Y = 0$ if $X = 0$; and $Y = -1$ if $X < 0$. | *48* |
| LET Y=RND(X) | $Y =$ pseudo random number between 0 and 1 ($X$ must be defined but its value does not affect $Y$). | *37, 81, 99, 110–112, 117, 121, 181, 183* |

## Functions Defined Within the Program [labelled FNA($X$), FNB($X$),...FNZ($X$)]

| | | |
|---|---|---|
| LET Y=FNA(X) | Let $Y =$ value of previously defined function FNA($X$) for argument $X$. | *26, 27, 92, 109, 174, 175* |
| DEF FNA(X)=1+X*X | Defines function FNA($X$) to be $1 + X^2$ | *25, 40, 47, 48, 71, 84* |
| DEF FNA(X, Y) LET FNA=... ... FNEND | Format for multiple line function statements (not available on all BASIC compilers) | *25* |

## Data-Related Statements

| | | |
|---|---|---|
| INPUT A, B, C | Computer returns? for each requested variable and waits for operator to enter numerical values from keyboard (followed by carriage return) for *A*, *B*, and *C*. | *6, 13, 20, 21* |
| READ D, E, F | Read values for *D, E, F* sequentially from DATA statements | *14* |
| DATA 1.2,4,−1.2E−6,3.56 | Data to be assigned (row-wise) in READ statements. | *14, 16, 23, 118, 147* |
| RESTORE | The next READ statement starts reading entries (row-wise) from the first DATA statement. | *14, 172* |

## Print Statements

| | | |
|---|---|---|
| PRINT X | Print numerical value of *X*. | *6, 11, 15* |
| PRINT "X" | Print the character *X*. | *15, 20, 21* |
| PRINT X,Y,Z | Print numerical values of *X, Y, Z* in coarse spacing. | *15* |
| PRINT X;Y;Z | Print numerical values of *X, Y, Z* in close spacing. | *15, 177* |
| PRINT "X", "Y", "Z" | Print the characters *X, Y, Z* in coarse spacing. | |
| PRINT "X"; "Y"; "Z" | Print the characters XYZ in adjacent spacing. | *15, 75* |
| PRINT | Activate carriage return and advance roller. | *15* |
| PRINT TAB(X);"*" | Print character * on the $(X+1)^{\mathrm{th}}$ column. | *16, 76, 77, 82, 89, 165* |

## String Statements (Not available on some computers)

| | | |
|---|---|---|
| PRINT CHR$(I); | Prints character corresponding to ASCII code for integer, *I*, in closely-packed form. (Prints A...Z when $I = 65,...,90$). | *31, 32, 84, 99, 109* |
| INPUT A$ | Input string variable from keyboard | *33* |
| LET V$="ABCD" | Defines *V$* to be the string ABCD. | *31, 32* |
| CHANGE V$ TO V | Stores ASCII integers for characters in string in array *V(I)*; Here $V(1) = 65$, $V(2) = 66$, $V(3) = 67$, $V(4) = 68$ and $V(0) = 4 =$ length. | *32, 33, 146* |

## Conditional Statements

| | | |
|---|---|---|
| IF A=B THEN 75 | If A=B, then go to line 75 | *16* |
| IF A>B THEN 75 | If A>B, then go to line 75 | *16, 17, 24, 77, 78, 109* |
| IF A>=B THEN 75 | If A≥B, then go to line 75 (The order >= is important). | *16, 79, 153* |
| IF A<B THEN 75 | If A<B, then go to line 75 | *16, 24, 30, 160* |
| IF A<=B THEN 75 | If A≤B, then go to line 75 (The order <= is important). | *16* |
| IF A#B THEN 75<br>IF A<>B THEN 75 | If A≠B, then go to line 75 | *16, 77 (see also note on "super BASIC". 78)* |

## Additional Statements Used in Loops and Branch Points

| | | |
|---|---|---|
| GOTO 75 | computer jumps to line 75 when program is running. (normally used with one of the conditional statements above if GOTO results in a loop) | *16* |
| FOR I=2 TO 11 STEP .5<br>...<br>NEXT I | Sets up loop starting with I=2 and running in increments of 0.5 until I>11. If "STEP .5" is omitted, positive unit steps would be assumed. Start, stop and step size may be computed. Loops may be nested (within limits characteristic of the computer) so long as they do not cross. | *17, 18, 36, 80, 81* |
| 10 GOSUB 100 | At line 10 computer jumps to subroutine starting on line 100 and continues to the first RETURN statement. It then returns to first program line after 10. GOSUB statements may be nested (within limits characteristic of the computer). | *26, 27, 92, 93, 109, 110, 118, 167, 175* |
| RETURN | denotes end of subroutine. Computer leaves subroutine when first RETURN statement encountered. There can be any number of RETURN statements, so long as they are not encountered before a GOSUB statement. | |
| END | Normal end statement for program. (Can only be one and must be last line number.) | |
| STOP | Program jumps to END statement (can be any number). | |

## Matrix Statements and Dimension Statements* (MAT operations are not available on some computers)

| | | |
|---|---|---|
| DIM X(15),M(12,30) | Dimension column array X with 15 elements (treated same as matrix with 15 rows and 1 column), dimension matrix M with 12 rows and 30 columns. (Dimension statements are not required unless more than 10 rows and columns are used.) | *27, 52, 57, 58, 60, 83, 117, 120, 176* |
| MAT M=ZER | All elements in matrix M are set equal to zero. (Dimensions must have been explicitly given.) | *52* |
| MAT M=ZER(11,12) | All elements in M are set to zero and matrix is redimensioned to 11 rows and 12 columns.* | *53, 55, 60, 149* |
| MAT M=CON | All elements in M are set to one. (Dimensions must have been explicitly given.) | *52, 85, 119* |
| MAT M=CON(9,11) | All elements in M are set to one and matrix is redimensioned to 9 rows and 11 columns.* | *53* |
| MAT M=IDN | All diagonal elements set to one, off-diagonal elements set to zero. (M must be square and explicitly dimensioned) M becomes the identity matrix. | *52, 60* |
| MAT M=IDN(11,11) | M is set equal to an 11×11 identity matrix.* | *53* |
| MAT READ M | Read all elements of M row-wise from DATA statements. (Dimensions of M must have been specified.) | *52, 58, 117* |
| MAT PRINT M | Print all elements row-wise on separate lines. | *52* |
| MAT PRINT M, | Print all elements row-wise with coarse spacing. | *52* |
| MAT PRINT M; | Print all elements row-wise with close spacing. | *52, 54* |
| MAT B=A | B is set equal to A element-by-element. (The dimensions of B and A must be the same and have been specified.) | *56* |
| MAT C=A+B | C is set equal to A+B, element-by-element. (The dimensions of A, B, C must be the same and have been specified.) | *56* |
| MAT C=A−B | C is set equal to A−B, element-by-element. (The dimensions of A, B, C must be the same and have been specified.) | *56* |
| MAT C=(K)*A | C is set equal to A after multiplying each element by the same scalar constant K. (Dimensions of A and C must be the same and specified.) | *55, 85* |
| MAT C=A*B | C is set equal to the matrix product, A*B, element by element. (Dimensions must have been specified, consistent with matrix multiplication.) | *56–58, 60, 119* |
| MAT C=TRN(A) | C is set equal to the transpose of A. (Dimensions must have been specified, consistent with the matrix operation.) | *55, 58* |
| MAT C=INV(A) | C is set equal to the inverse matrix of A. (Dimensions of both must be the same, square and specified.) | *59, 60, 63* |

*Note:* the redimensioning statements cannot result in greater dimensions than those contained in the initial DIM statements (or in absence of the latter, 10 rows and 10 columns).

# Index